A Word for Nature

– A Word for –
Nature

Four Pioneering Environmental Advocates, 1845–1913

ROBERT L. DORMAN

The University of North Carolina Press

Chapel Hill and London

© 1998 The University of North Carolina Press

All rights reserved

Designed by April Leidig-Higgins

Set in Quadraat by Tseng Information Systems, Inc.

Manufactured in the United States of America

The paper in this book meets the guidelines for permanence
and durability of the Committee on Production Guidelines for
Book Longevity of the Council on Library Resources.

Library of Congress Cataloging-in-Publication Data

Dorman, Robert L.

A word for nature: four pioneering environmental

advocates, 1845–1913 / by Robert L. Dorman.

p. cm.   Includes bibliographical references and index.

ISBN 0-8078-2396-1 (cloth: alk. paper)

ISBN 0-8078-4699-6 (pbk.: alk. paper)

1. Environmentalists — United States — Biography.

2. Environmentalism — United States — History — 19th century.

I. Title.

GE55.D67   1998   97-23896

333.72'092'2 — dc21   CIP

[B]

Excerpts from *Man and Nature* by George Perkins Marsh,
edited by David Lowenthal. Copyright © 1965 by the President
and Fellows of Harvard College. Reprinted by permission
of Harvard University Press.

02 01 00 99 98   5 4 3 2 1

For Sarah

Contents

Illustrations

Preface

ON JULY 4, 1845, Henry David Thoreau began his two-year sojourn on the shore of Walden Pond, an obscure intellectual exploring alone the value and meanings of nature. Seven decades later, on December 6, 1913, the U.S. Senate passed a bill approving construction of a dam and reservoir at Hetch Hetchy Valley inside Yosemite National Park, a decision reached after ten years of organized opposition and nationwide public controversy. The two events are justifiably famous in the history of American conservation, but they provide the chronological frame of this study for more reasons than mere convention. Walden and Hetch Hetchy symbolize the evolution of environmental concern in America from its nineteenth-century origins as the subject of artistic and scholarly discourse to its early-twentieth-century emergence as an issue of national public policy. To understand why the ideas of a few came in time to influence the opinions of the many is one important focus of this book.

The years marking Walden and Hetch Hetchy have also been chosen as a framework for the very reason that they do represent the conventional history, even the mythology, of American conservation. Their prominence in the popular memory of present-day environmentalists signifies a tradition at work, a common body of seminal events, basic assumptions, classic texts, sacred places, villainous figures, and reverenced heroes shared from generation to generation. Needless to say, this tradition has been elaborated, disputed, redefined, and extended from one era to the next. But over the past century and a half, certain individuals have retained their positions at its core. They are among its founders, those who in the nineteenth century asked some of the original definitive questions and provided long influential answers, cited and debated endlessly by their twentieth-century heirs. These early founders, George Perkins Marsh, Henry David Thoreau, John Muir, and John Wesley Powell, are the main subjects of this study. Yet others also made substantial contributions to the larger corpus of environmental thought and culture during the 1800s, some of whom—especially women writers and advocates—have only recently begun to receive the recognition that they deserve. Susan Fenimore Cooper, Mary Treat, and other significant but lesser-known women and men have therefore been woven into the context of this book to indicate more fully the richness and diversity of the tradition of American environmental advocacy.

In confining myself to four major progenitors of this tradition, I should note that they had successors of equal stature—Gifford Pinchot, Aldo Leopold, and Rachel Carson, to name three. But these were essentially twentieth-century figures, in my view, whereas Marsh, Thoreau, Muir, and Powell were men of the nineteenth century. Their ideas and careers were defined by older intellectual and cultural currents (evangelicalism, Romanticism, and agrarian-republicanism, for example) that made the transition to the twentieth century only piecemeal, if at all. They were inspired and constrained by a political culture that was greatly more suspicious and doubtful of governmental authority than the era of welfare-state liberalism that was to come after them, just dawning in the final years of Muir's life. The purpose of this book is to trace the origins as well as the lasting impact of their ideas, and to do so we must place them in the world of the nineteenth century, its faiths and ambitions, its tragedies and achievements. For even as they bequeathed ideas to an unfolding tradition linking them to the future, each of these men was an individual living in a discrete time and place. While they were "ahead of their time," each was also in large measure representative of their respective periods. Social, economic, political, and cultural contexts converged in their lives, as did the intellectual discourses within which they wrote. Biographical portraits are the best means to synthesize these many elements into a satisfactorily complex yet readable interpretation, written in light of the author's understanding of the larger trends and forces shaping nineteenth-century America.

To depict environmental thought and politics during the period 1845–1913, I will be relying on some other conventions of traditional accounts besides the benchmarks of Walden and Hetch Hetchy. *Conservation* is here defined as that set of ideas, practices, and policies which seek to bring human activities into greater harmony with physical nature. Historians distinguish the two major tendencies of conservation (particularly as it developed into a movement at the turn of the century) in terms of *utilitarian* goals and *moral-aesthetic* values. Utilitarian conservationists regarded nature as a limited but renewable supply of resources for human economic use, requiring careful management and planning within those limits to promote sustainable economic growth and prevent waste, depletion, and disaster. In contrast, aesthetic conservationists—or *preservationists*—wanted a pristine nature protected from intensive economic exploitation and preserved for a more symbiotic purpose, recreation. To apply these terms to the four subjects of this study is somewhat anachronistic, since the words "conservation" and "preservationism" were rarely employed until after 1900. But the labels remain useful and clarifying, especially in those episodes such as the Hetch Hetchy controversy when the utilitarian and preservationist wings of the early conservation movement fell into conflict. The reader should keep in mind that the utilitarian and moral-aesthetic valuations set on nature really represented positions on a spectrum of belief, not irreconcilable differences. Both the utilitarian school and the moral-aesthetic school were interested in human *use* of nature; the debate centered on the type and extent of that use. Many staunch utilitarian conservationists (like John Wesley Powell) were also avid outdoorsmen. Most preservationists (including John Muir), despite their commitment to saving scenic areas, certainly supported the prudent and sustainable exploitation of resources. A careful reading of the ideas of our four early advocates will tend to blur any too strict distinctions between them in terms of the utilitarian and moral-aesthetic categories. Generally speaking, Marsh and Powell may be considered precursors of utilitarian conservation, Thoreau and Muir, of preservationism. But in a deeper sense all four were engaged in understanding and reconfiguring the human-nature relationship according to both rational and moral constructs. Scientific knowledge of the natural world was important to each of them, for example, and each was guided by what he considered to be a compelling ethical or religious imperative.[1]

In writing of the full sweep of the tradition of environmental advocacy, I have occasionally chosen to use the word "environmentalism" in a broader sense than it is usually within conventional accounts. Environmentalism most often refers to the post–World War II phase of American environmental history, specifically to the modern movement that arose in the 1960s and 1970s on behalf of such issues as pollution abatement and the control of toxic substances. But it is also possible to define environmentalism in a historically cumulative sense, as encompassing all of the different movements of environmental concern that have manifested themselves since the mid-nineteenth century. Although wilderness preservation and resource conservation received the most public attention at the turn of the century, they have not since ceased to be important environmental issues; nor have urban and regional planning, which enjoyed a heyday in the first half of the twentieth century, particularly in the early 1900s and again in the 1930s. The postwar emphasis on environmental protection may be seen as the latest stage in an ever-expanding awareness of the damage that humans may do to the natural world and to themselves in their interdependence with nature. I sometimes define the word "environmentalism" in a broader sense because the tradition has itself broadened.

This advent of environmental concern in the national awareness is typically presented as a shift in fundamental ethical assumptions, and here again the conventional terminology of environmental historiography and journalism is helpful and will be invoked in this book. *Anthropocentric* (or human-centered) ethical values are said to govern the human-nature relationship whenever human interests are held as the foremost and paramount good. Anthropocentrism is founded on the belief that human beings are both superior to and qualitatively different from the natural world because of human self-consciousness, intelligence, and divine favor. *Biocentrism*, on the other hand, involves a recognition and respect for the interests (and "rights") of nature in itself, as distinct from any and all human wants and desires. Biocentric doctrines posit human interdependence with nature and conceive of humanity as merely one of many species whose interests deserve ethical consideration. Strictly speaking, all conceptions of nature are anthropocentric to some degree because all are the products of human consciousness, reflective of the values and meanings that the human mind projects onto a neutral reality. Nevertheless, the historical emergence of environmental concern in American culture may be described as a gradual shift in ethical emphasis away from anthropocentrism (nature serves humanity) and toward biocentrism (human beings and nature are interdependent)—a transformation that can be attributed in considerable measure to the work of Marsh, Thoreau, Muir, Powell, and their successors in the tradition of environmental advocacy.

The organization of this book falls roughly into two parts, corresponding to the first two generations of environmental advocates. Chapters 1 and 2 will examine the intellectual projects of Marsh and Thoreau, who embarked on pathbreaking efforts to find answers to some fundamental questions: respectively, what is the relationship between nature and humankind, and more fundamentally still, what is nature itself? Chapter 1 explores the antebellum setting in which both men lived and worked, particularly with reference to the industrializing landscape of New England, their common home. The story then proceeds to the making of Marsh's classic *Man and Nature* (1864), the formative text of utilitarian conservation and (arguably) environmental consciousness in general. Chapter 2 delves more deeply into the cultural and intellectual context of the antebellum period, and Thoreau is followed on his Concord-based odyssey to comprehend the "wild" in nature and its consequences for his life, his personal politics, and his concept of wilderness preservation. The second generation led by Muir and Powell is taken up in Chapters 3 and 4, and in contrast to the individual, primarily literary efforts of their predecessors, we see them engaged in campaigns to institutionalize preservationism and utilitarian conservation culturally and politically on a national stage. Muir in Chapter 3 is shown to have found a form of divine revelation in wild nature, and on its behalf he proselytized (through popular articles and the Sierra Club) to help create the nation's first national parks and monuments. In Chapter 4, an account of John Wesley Powell's heroic descent through the Colorado River's canyonlands becomes the point of departure for understanding the work of his U.S. Geological Survey and the trial balloons of regional planning proposals that he attempted to launch. Finally, in a brief epilogue, I discuss some of the implications of the ideas of Marsh, Thoreau, Muir, and Powell for the current and future direction of environmental thought and politics. These men still have much to say to us, and as we continue to debate their ideas the tradition of environmental advocacy will remain a vibrant and on-going intellectual enterprise.

A NUMBER OF people have given this book and its author their support, advice, and expertise. I wish to express my gratitude to John L. Thomas, Lewis Bateman, Donald J. Pisani, Richard Lowitt, Paul Gilje, James T. Patterson, and Robert E. Cook. The history departments at the University of Oklahoma, Brown University, and the University of New Mexico all helped to make this book possible. My parents, Jack and Sybil Dorman, and my grandmother, Alta Dorman, were very helpful and supportive, especially in the earliest stages of writing. Discussions with my wife, Sarah, improved the book's argument, as did her skills as an editor. This book is dedicated to her.

A Word for Nature

I wish to speak a word for Nature. . . .

Henry David Thoreau, "Walking, or The Wild" (1851)

CHAPTER ONE

George Perkins Marsh

Man . . . is to be regarded as essentially a destructive power.

Man and Nature

George Perkins Marsh
(Courtesy of the Prints and Photographs Division, Library of Congress)

IT WAS IN 1797 that Charles Marsh first constructed the bridge which would be washed away time and again by floods during the boyhood of his son, George. Three years later, in the summer before George's birth, a forest fire ravaged the slopes of the mountain where sat the Marsh family home, destroying most of whatever trees remained after generations of cuttings had already been burned in the stoves of the farmers and villagers below. Young George came to know that bare mountainside intimately—Mt. Tom was its homely name—and the thrice-doomed bridge he crossed daily to attend the little village school at Woodstock. His father was also obliged to descend to the bridge and walk over it, creaking above the waters of the Ottauquechee River, in order to reach his law offices in town. Charles Marsh was a prominent man of affairs, the U.S. attorney for Vermont, an erstwhile member of Congress and the state Council of Censors, and an investor in turnpikes, sawmills, and the farmlands of his estate. Some called him an aristocrat; his son's biographer describes him as a "brilliant and sardonic tyrant."[1] He was a Federalist in his politics and he believed in Calvin's God; his family was indoctrinated accordingly. It was said of such people that they were made of stern stuff, that they bore misfortune well. Three times in a decade the bridge was carried off, and three times the elder Marsh rebuilt it. Perhaps in those floods he saw a test of faith, or perhaps he did not want his turnpike blocked.

George Perkins Marsh was born in the opening year of the nineteenth century, and thus he could never be his father's son. During his eighty-one years Marsh lived a life that was multifarious even by the standards of a frontier country. His vocations were lawyer, manufacturer, gentleman farmer, speculator, newspaper editor, road builder, lumber dealer, state bureaucrat, congressman, and ambassador. His avocation was genteel scholar, on subjects ranging from Scandinavian languages to camels. In 1864, he published the book for which he is principally remembered, *Man and Nature*, a work that has been called "the fountainhead of the conservation movement."[2] Marsh was a contemporary with the more famous progenitor of American environmentalism, Henry David Thoreau, whom he was born twenty years before and was to outlive by another twenty. This bracketing of their lives is symbolic of a prefatory truth about both of these New Englanders, who never met:

Marsh, a man of affairs like his father, participated fully in the economic, political, and cultural life of the antebellum era, while Thoreau, as a member of the Romantic reaction against much of what that era had to offer, held himself apart from it, living more marginally and obscurely. Our signature image of Thoreau is of him standing on the shore of Walden Pond, listening to trains pass in the distance. Marsh, however, was an investor in railroads, and eventually he became government regulator of them as well.

To comprehend the transcendental and solitary Thoreau one must therefore first understand the worldly Marsh and the affairs in which he was involved, the affairs of an industrializing nation, and how these disintegrated the pious provincial society into which both men were born. Yet to appreciate completely Marsh's evolution toward his own dissent from the expansionary praxis of his compatriots—*Man and Nature*—one must also come to grips with the intellectual revolution of which Thoreau was an idiosyncratic representative. Marsh's wife once called him "the last of the Puritans," and in their broadest sense her words are apt not only for her husband but also for Thoreau.[3] As social critics both men were agents in the ongoing dissolution of the received culture of their colonial forebears, a culture still influencing the attitudes and beliefs of their own time. As moralists not entirely free of the values and styles of that culture, they sermonized to their contemporaries on nature's behalf in a manner akin to the old Puritan clerics, though with chapter and verse taken from fresher faiths—science, history, poetry, philosophy. But even as they saw out the last of an older way of life and of an older way of thinking, Marsh and Thoreau were ultimately to take their place among the first of a new tradition, the tradition of American environmental advocacy.

THAT TWO OF the founders of this tradition were fellow New Englanders was no coincidence. By 1800, New England was one of the longest settled and most densely populated of the country's regions, and in the first half of the nineteenth century it became the national crucible of a commercial and industrial revolution that was to transform America. Both Marsh and Thoreau bore witness to the effects of this revolution on society and landscape alike: Marsh in eastern and northern Vermont, where he spent most of his youth and early adulthood trying to launch a successful career, and Thoreau in eastern Massachusetts and northern Maine, his lifelong residence at Concord serving as base for excursions to rivers, seashores, mountains, and woods from Cape Cod to Moosehead Lake. Marsh, in fact, did far more than take note of the dynamic new economy. After graduation from Dartmouth in 1820, he started out in his father's footsteps, establishing a law firm at Burlington and, over the next thirty years, becoming involved in a wide array of business ventures. It was an appropriate career path and one that an entire generation of well-to-do younger sons was pursuing. A commerce-friendly law profession and an entrepreneurial ethos were two of the chief historical bequests of Charles Marsh's own post-Revolutionary generation, a legacy that was in time to foster a middle-class society. Already in 1800 the world of Marsh's father was a quiescent one, as republican political values and free market liberalism eroded communal ties and unsettled the old farm and village life of two centuries past. Free individualism was the tendency of the age (for white adult males, at least), and the economic transformation was an important motive force behind it, leveling and atomizing the intimate hierarchy of superiors and dependents that constituted traditional social structure. Out of its remnants a new society of small-propertied nuclear households was taking shape, headed by fathers bestowed with the rights of ownership and citizenship. Traditionalist and informal economic transactions were gradually replaced with modern and formal ones—handshakes with contracts, barter with cash, self-sufficiency with credit, subsistence with speculation, squatter's rights with land titles, craft secrets with patents, family-owned concerns with joint-stock corporations. By these means the legal and political institutions of the antebellum republic not only facilitated the transfer and acquisition of private property, they also protected and sanctified it. Individual opportunity, personal mobility toward ownership, and technological advance were to be central articles of a bedrock belief in progress by midcentury, for Northern Americans in general and New Englanders in particular, as many became consumed with the task of industrial and commercial growth.[4]

George Perkins Marsh was one of a regionful, a nationful, of such men-on-the-make. Besides his law practice and his investments in railroad stock, Marsh tried his hand at real estate speculation, a bank partnership, lumber sales, sheep farming, road construction, newspaper publishing, a woolens mill, a marble quarry, and precision surveying instruments. The range of his various money-making schemes might have been unusual, but the enterprising and opportunistic motives behind them, the sense of boundlessness, he shared with countless other antebellum entrepreneurs. Uncoordinated and unplanned, their individual ventures built piecemeal the rudiments of a national economy, most important of all, the beginnings of a nationwide transportation system. Thoreau, for example, traveled as much down man-made canals as he did natural streams over the course of his *Week on the Concord and Merrimack Rivers* (1849). The Merrimack was among the most heavily used rivers in America by midcentury. There was scarcely a ten-mile stretch along its course that men like Marsh had not dammed for power or diverted into canals. The Lawrence Dam on the Merrimack, completed in the year before Thoreau's *Week* was published, was then the largest in the world, nearly one-third of a mile of granite blocks. And nationally, the scores of dams, the hundreds of miles of canals, and the thousands of miles of roads constructed during the antebellum era were just an overture to the more transformative advent of the railways. None had existed as late as the 1820s, but by the 1850s the United States encompassed more miles of track than that of the rest of the world combined.[5]

The national transportation network that was slowly emerging from this decentralized hodgepodge of "internal improvements" linked hinterlands to market towns and market towns to urban ports. Yet the new system could scarcely keep up with a population that was continually streaming westward, clearing virgin forests and spreading a grid of fields well past the Mississippi River by 1860. It was an era of unprecedented *movement*, "geographical mobility," in the jargon of latter-day demographers, "manifest destiny," in the jingoistic rhetoric of contemporary stump politicians. They exhorted Americans to fill out the map to the Pacific coast—native tribes and Mexicans notwithstanding—and Americans did so, impelled by ideology and ambition. While the nation's population grew dramatically in the decades before the Civil War, from 5 million to 31 million, the center of population shifted west of the Appalachians for the first time, representing the aggregate migration of millions of opportunity-seekers into the vast interior of the continent.[6]

Marsh, who decried this "life of incessant flitting," was no frontiersman. Instead, he confined his own business ventures to his native Vermont, and this element of his biography serves to underscore another crucial dimension of the era's economic transformation, a dimension that New Englanders spearheaded: the creation of the "American system" of manufacturing. Rather than focusing their interest solely on internal improvements or agricultural expansion, entrepreneurs in the New England states took advantage of the region's plentiful river resources to carry out America's first intensive industrial development. Waterpower, derived from fast-flowing voluminous streams like the Merrimack dropping down the real and artificial falls of a hilly topography, was the key to New England's predominance, and so was the much-vaunted Yankee ingenuity, responsible for a disproportionate number of the nation's patents. Small-scale workshops with only a few employees were the production norm until the 1850s, but increasingly in certain industries (such as textiles, shoemaking, and arms manufacture) they were displaced by large mills and factories that lined the riverbanks of former country towns suddenly become cities with soot and slums. People were moving not only westward but cityward: the antebellum years as a whole witnessed the highest rate of urbanization in American history. Lowell, Massachusetts, which pioneered the new factory system, was the classic example, exploding in population from 1,500 in 1820 to more than 33,000 by 1850.[7]

Among all regions New England's economic modernization proceeded earliest and fastest, resulting in the most urbanized population, the most intricate rail network, and the greatest concentration of industry. And surely all of these factors must be considered to explain why New England became the birthplace of American environmentalism. Still, it would be a mistake to differentiate developments in New England too sharply from those in the rest of the country. New York, Ohio, and other Northern states were following much the same trends, and the "agrarian" South's land-hungry cotton economy was predicated on machinery, especially Whitney's gin and the water-driven looms of Lowell and Manchester. Moreover, regardless of region, all sectors of the new economy required capital and credit, for construction costs, physical plant, land acquisition, and speculation purposes. The flow of money was facilitated by other innovations of the antebellum economic revolution, particularly state banks and national stock markets. But as the country's economy became through these institutions more market-oriented, interconnected, systemic—and more dynamic —it also became more subject to the busts that went with the unprecedented booms that many were experiencing. During Marsh's business career, nationwide depressions hit in 1819–23, 1837–43, and 1857.

One local and personal vantage on these broader trends of antebellum commercialization, industrialization, and urbanization appears in Susan Fenimore Cooper's 1850 book, *Rural Hours*. A significant contribution to the early corpus of environmental writing in itself (predating the major works of Marsh and Thoreau), *Rural Hours* provides an account of national change as it came to bear on the rural environs of Cooper's home in upstate New York. The sheer pace of change was most impressive to Cooper, as it was to many of her contemporaries. "[W]henever we pause to recall what has been done in this secluded valley during the lifetime of one generation," she wrote, "we must needs be struck with new astonishment." The area had been mostly a "silent wilderness" where the "red man" was the "lord of the land" until the time of the Revolution. Thereafter, "the white man came to plant a home on this spot, and it was then the great change began; the axe and the saw, the forge and the wheel, were busy from dawn to dusk." Cooperstown and its neighborhood, she noted, had already taken on the "aspect of an old country," transformed into a landscape of "broad and fertile farms" and "well beaten roads." The forest had "fallen in all the valleys," while the hills were "becoming more bare every day," as residents strove to turn "timber into banknotes with all possible speed." Cooper perceived the acquisitive spirit in the bustling village as well. She thought it odd that "in a little town of some 1400 souls there should be three jewelers and watchmakers" along with "seven taverns" and "half a dozen 'stores' on quite a large scale," all filled with "a thousand things required by civilized man in the long list of his wants." The village "eating-houses" and the urban excess that they represented evoked a more pointed observation from Cooper, a pious spinster and devoted homebody: "[T]heir number is quite humiliating; it looks as though we must needs be a very gormandizing people."[8]

As Cooper implied, the economic expansion necessary to fulfill the "wants" of this "gormandizing people" had substantial environmental effects, both in her region and throughout the country. Dyes and waste products from the new factories polluted rivers and streams. Wildlife and fisheries were depleted as they were fished or hunted out and their habitats were destroyed. Above all, the forests most visibly registered the consequences of the antebellum economic transformation. Sawmills dotted the landscape everywhere. Wood was utilized for building purposes, and it remained the principal source of heat and fuel for most Americans throughout the period. Huge amounts of wood were needed to construct railroads — an estimated 2,500 wooden ties per mile. Steamboats burned several hundred cords of timber on each round-trip, altogether consuming hundreds of thousands of cords annually on the nation's riverways. The railing-style fences used by farmers required thousands of wooden rails to encircle even a modest field, and there were more than three million miles of such fencing around the country by 1850. In addition, broad areas of land were cleared by frontier farmers as well as those engaged in more modern, mechanized production that demanded extra pastureland for draft animals. The consequence of this unlimited wood consumption was startling. During the 1850s alone, deforestation in America amounted to some 40 million acres, one-third of the total that had occurred over the previous two centuries.[9]

These profound changes, perhaps most profound in New England, left their mark on the places that Marsh and Thoreau called home. The Woodstock that Marsh grew up in during the early 1800s was already a mill town serving a substantial agricultural district. Grain, flour, timber, flaxseed oil, dairy containers, maple syrup, and wool were only some of the products processed by Ottauquechee waterpower and shipped out to Boston and Connecticut via turnpikes. Later, in the 1830s, Marsh was to construct one of the largest woolens mills in the Burlington area, where he lived and practiced law. After two centuries of this increasingly intensive development, Vermont and the rest of New England showed some scars. In 1620, the region had been as much as 95 percent forested. By 1850, Vermont had only 45 percent forest cover, and in Thoreau's Massachusetts the forested area was at 40 percent and falling. Concord itself was not exactly the idyllic small-town retreat as it is often depicted. By the time young Thoreau returned home from college in the mid-1830s, Concord too had its sawmills, gristmills, and cotton mills, along with warehouses, two new banks, two large factories (lead pipe and shoes), and a wide array of small manufacturers (clocks, pencils, bricks, hats, and others), all in due course connected by train and canal to the ports and stores of Boston.[10]

As a part-time teacher and full-time loner, Thoreau could stand back from this hubbub with some equanimity and criticality. Disdainful of the harried enterprisers scurrying around New England, he wrote a stinging and oft-quoted epigram about their "quiet desperation"—and in Marsh's case, the observation was very probably apt. At heart a "gentle and timid" soul (according to his biographer), Marsh was not cut out for business. Virtually every scheme he launched, every angle, every gambit, every sure thing he attempted turned to proverbial dross. The woolens mill was undermined by the late 1830s depression and a series of unfavorable tariff policies; the Vermont Central Railroad, in which he was a stockholder, went belly-up in the early 1850s; the marble quarry venture of the mid-1850s ("Everybody is running marble mad," he wrote hopefully) was never viable. To exacerbate matters, Marsh loathed his work as a lawyer. His worries over money were perpetual, and finally in the 1850s, he fell into outright bankruptcy.[11]

IF MARSH'S private dealings of these years were thus something of a shambles, his more successful public life as a congressman, diplomat, and scholar afforded him some solace and, ultimately, both figurative and literal escape. His New England background and ill-starred business career are important to explaining his political orientation, and his politics—Whig Party politics—are essential to understanding the origins of the conservationist arguments that he was to put forward in *Man and Nature*.

Not surprisingly, as in so many areas of his life, Marsh came to his ideological leanings through his strong-willed father. First and foremost, he inherited from his father's conservative Federalism two tendencies: an abiding concern for social stability, and an unwavering belief in leadership by the enlightened, educated few. Charles Marsh had been of an older, classical school of political thought that enshrined in timeless principle the rule of wise disinterested elites as the only means to social harmony, because such a rule was reflective of the divinely ordained, hierarchical nature of society itself. By the time the elder Marsh was elected to public office in the early 1810s, these ideals—shared by many Federalists—were being challenged and undermined. His unheeded proposal to the Vermont Council of Censors that senators be elected only by a propertied franchise of the respectable, to serve as a check against the "hasty, inconsiderate, violent rabble" of the popular Assembly, went directly and futilely counter to the democratizing tendencies of the age. Thwarted, he vested his atavistic beliefs in the promise of a more up-to-date didactic institution, the private moral reform organization. A devout Congregationalist, Marsh's father became an officer of the American Bible Society, the American Education Society, and the American Society for the Promotion of Temperance, among others. The primary end of these associations was to provide moral instruction on a nationwide scale to create order and cohesion, especially among pioneer rowdies and isolated farm towns out on the ever-expanding western edge of Christendom, lest righteous values disperse into a frontier vacuum of self-interest and vulgarity.[12]

George Perkins Marsh carried many of these assumptions and prejudices with him into the Whig Party of the 1830s and 1840s, and he had them with him still in some form when he wrote Man and Nature. Marsh was, by one account, "every inch a whig," and the Whigs were preeminently a party of men like himself—striving, upstanding, native-born middle- and upper-class entrepreneurs, advocates of economic progress and industrial development. They were in addition the party of Protestant moral reform, upholding personal piety and social order as chief national goals. Whiggery thus combined a relatively modern set of beliefs regarding industrial capitalism and governmental activism with a more conservative and traditionalist emphasis on social conformity and hierarchy, an ideological mix not without contradiction, to be sure. The greater and greater degrees of mobility and individualism made possible by the new expansive economy inevitably caused the traditional politics and society of deference to be less and less viable, virtually obsolete, by midcentury. The "gentlemen of property and standing" who were dominant within the Whig Party based their "standing" increasingly on their "property" rather than high birth, property that represented not patrimony but mobility, a rise through natural talent. Education too became a badge of gentility and a prerequisite for leadership. Just as a rational mind was needed to discipline personal passions, so too rational men were needed to govern the behavior of the irrational, emotive masses.[13]

For all of its paternalism, this Whig conception of society, divided into betters and common folk, was yet quite unlike the frozen ranks of Charles Marsh's twilit traditionalism. Family ties, the duties of citizenship, membership in church and private associations, the reciprocity of market networks—these overlapping bonds constituted the (white adult male) individual self and connected him organically with society, according to the Whig worldview. His dependents—wife, children, servants, apprentices, or slaves—participated in the social organism in more limited degrees, their ability to act as "individuals" much more constricted. Yet inevitably, the culturewide celebration of individualistic self-perfection and mobility worked as a solvent on the old-fashioned hierarchical and organicist residues still informing Whig beliefs. Spiritual redemption and perfection within a this-worldly context of temptation and sin were possible only through individual free will. The opportunity to better oneself toward respectable middle-class status had to be broadly available if society itself were to progress. The glaring disjunction between these ideals and the "peculiar institution" of slavery or women's continued subordination led to reform movements that challenged the very bases of the antebellum social order.

For Whigs like Marsh, however, the ethos of self-improvement implied a process of self-cultivation and self-control, which must result not in conflict and discord but in greater social discipline and harmony. Personal development and upward mobility had to take form as "the harmonizing of Desire and Duty, not through the blotting out of the latter, but through the chastening, renovating, and purifying of the former," one Whig reformer wrote. The party's emphasis on reform issues like education and temperance was in obvious accord with these assumptions, and they were also extended rhetorically to include economic behavior. Whigs equated material progress and moral progress very literally. Individual striving and ambition, if turned in constructive directions, contributed to the greater social good. Conversely, a prosperous, growing economy provided a setting in which individual faculties and talents could be realized, where self-improvement could occur. As Marsh himself wrote in 1848, the "great branches of productive industry," agriculture and the "mechanic arts," were the "means and instruments of civilization and social progress." The mechanic arts, he declared, were "eminently democratic in their tendency" because they "popularize knowledge . . . cheapen and diffuse the comforts and elegancies as well as the necessaries of life," and "they demand and develope intelligence in those who pursue them." Similarly, Marsh praised the agricultural practices of the farmer who maintained "the order of his dwelling and his courtyard" and extended it to "his stables, his barns, his granaries, and his fields"; such farmers knew the manifold "blessings of a comfortable and well-ordered home." The Whigs fancied themselves the party of these solid citizens, townsmen and yeomen, pillars of the community, whose labors and wealth added "physical and financial strength to the commonwealth, and . . . general benefit to society." [14]

Material and moral progress could not be found in the big cities of the republic, Marsh and the Whigs were certain. "Every foreign heresy or folly in religion and in government finds a congenial soil in the corrupted mass of outlandish renegades and adventurers, and denaturalized Americans, that composes so large a proportion of our largest towns," Marsh once noted of the electoral strongholds of the Democrats. He and many other New England Whigs also did not believe that progress might stem from mere frontier expansion, which in their opinion spread the wasteful habits of poor subsistence farmers, incited the greed of imperialists and speculators, and dissipated the nation's energies. There was, Marsh concluded, "little to admire . . . and little to entice in the rude domestic arrangements, the coarse fare, and the coarser manners of the Western squatter." Instead, as Whig leader Daniel Webster argued, "the mighty agents which are working out our greatness are time, industry, and the arts. Our augmentation is by growth, not by acquisition; by internal development, not by external accession."

Henry C. Carey, the preeminent Whig economic theorist, defined the good society as one "abounding in villages and towns," where "the farmer and the artisan . . . take their places by each other's side" and live in harmonious, profitable, and productive "association." The more closely America approached this social ideal, Carey believed, "the more will man be enabled to control and direct the various [natural] forces provided for his use; and the more rapidly will he pass from being a creature of necessity towards attaining his true position, that of a being of power." [15] The Whigs' utopia was this intensively developed, small-town political economy revolving around home, church, school, and meeting hall and balancing commercial farms and workshop manufactures, a world that was innovative yet stable, prosperous yet pious, where "Duty" and "Desire" were reconciled. It looked a lot like an idealized New England, and it embodied the elusive calm, settled life that Marsh pursued unsuccessfully for thirty years.

In some ways this Whig utopia was a domestic idyll writ large, a middle-class world that was tended, nurturing, and bountiful, overseen by upright breadwinning fathers and virtuous bread-making mothers. The irony was that, despite the Whig rhetorical faith in balancing "Duty" and "Desire," entrepreneurial striving often was reckless: witness Marsh's own bumbling parade of ventures. In seeking to master natural forces and wrest from them a respectable livelihood, Carey's "being of power" too frequently overmastered them, laying waste to the antebellum environment. To make matters worse, the period's strict gender codes countenanced the supremacy of the paternal over the maternal and relegated women's domestic sphere—presumably the seat of moral discipline—to the margins of society both economically and environmentally. As the larger natural realm beyond married women's separate sphere was rationalized by men to serve science, commerce, and industry, women's work shifted from traditional production (home manufactures, for example) toward a more narrow and exclusive focus on reproductive labor (housekeeping, child rearing). In the public world of men, nature had become commodified; the regime of the market could be extended infinitely throughout a limitless nature, just as the grid of fields was spreading across the wilderness continent. In the private world of middle-class women, where nature was confined to yards and gardens surrounding the home, other valuations might be set on it, indeed, must be, for social stability, to provide succor and relief from the harsh demands of the market: moral and aesthetic valuations.[16]

This fundamental antebellum shift in attitudes toward nature and gender, reflective of the industrial-capitalist revolution as a whole, necessitated Marsh's project of intellectual guidance toward a conservation ethic. But there were any number of cultural obstacles in his path, evident especially from the perspective of the women's sphere. Susan Fenimore Cooper and her book *Rural Hours* are once again instructive. As a woman who lived in the shadow of her famous father's household, Cooper idealized the hardy farmwives of her neighborhood who still clung to the disappearing traditional folkways of women's work. "How pleasant things look about a farm-house!" she wrote. "[I]t seems natural to like a farm, or a garden, beyond most workshops." On a visit to one particular farm, Cooper observed that "the food of the family, as well as their clothing, was almost wholly the produce of their own farm; they dealt but little with either grocer or butcher." Standing in one corner of the farmhouse parlor was a "great spinning wheel," she saw with admiration; "all the yarn for stockings, for flannels, for the cloth worn by the men, for the colored woolen dresses of the women . . . was spun in the house by our hostess, or her grand-daughter." Yet Cooper seemed well aware that this folk-agrarian way of life was ending, that the urban world of commerce and industry was ever encroaching. "The wives and daughters of our farmers are very often notable, frugal women — perhaps one may say that they are usually so until they go from home." Village girls, in contrast, were "often wildly extravagant" and "restless following the fashions." The very same "wants" had driven the farmer to "turn his timber into banknotes," deforesting the countryside. But as Cooper objected, "independently of their market price in dollars and cents, the trees have other values; . . . they have their importance in an intellectual and in a moral sense." Significantly, however, she was acknowledging a nature that was now bifurcated between the sphere of "dollars and cents" and the sphere of the "moral" and "intellectual." [17]

These perceptions of Cooper's and those of growing numbers of educated women and men in the antebellum period were expressions of the sensibility of Romanticism (see Chapter 2). Of course, not every woman with leisure was a writer like Cooper, but in their more conventional domestic round, many were able to participate in Romantic "nature appreciation" through reading and other hobbies, such as botany. A "sentimental flower literature," which combined moral lessons, pleasing illustrations, uplifting verse, and a smattering of science, met with their enthusiastic response. *Flora's Interpreters* (1832) by Sarah Hale was one popular example of the genre, as was *The Lady's Book of Flowers and Poetry* (1848) by Lucy Hooper. Yet, although these books seemed to reinforce gender assumptions regarding nature, confining lady readers to their parlors and gardens, other works subtly challenged the bifurcation that Cooper lamented. Almira Phelps's *Familiar Lectures in Botany* (1829), while suggesting the value of nature study for women's roles as mothers, also encouraged its readers to gain a scientific understanding of their surrounding countryside and to go farther afield, to the "banks of winding brooks, on the borders of precipices, the sides of mountains, and the depths of the forests." [18] And if women's existence should not be bereft of nature experience enlightened by science, neither should nature remain untouched by the gentler ministrations of aesthetic and moral ideals.

This attempted Romantic integration of what industrial capitalism had broken asunder was being carried out at a high intellectual level by contemporaries such as Emerson and Thoreau, but the impulse was apparent as well in popular works like Phelps's or Susan Fenimore Cooper's own *Rural Hours*. That nurturing domestic values should be extended into nature over and against the cold calculus of market materialism was a message that Cooper sent forcefully. Many of her remedies for deforestation were aimed at giving homes and farms a more "pleasing character": "In very truth, a fine tree near a house is a much greater embellishment than the thickest coat of paint . . . much more desirable than the most expensive mahogany and velvet sofa in the parlor." The practical effect of these exhortations was limited, needless to say, but Cooper's remedies for the nation's denuded landscapes should not be dismissed as merely a genteel woman gardener's solutions. They signified what was ideologically possible in the antebellum years, given the era's expansionary credo and restrictive gender assumptions — small private improvements: a tree or two planted in the dooryard, a copse left standing in a cleared field, a willow set to droop over a well.[19]

George Perkins Marsh was to confront many of the same ideological boundaries as he rose to the task of instructing his countrymen about the environmental consequences of divorcing material progress from moral progress. Paternal, republican "Duty," defined by rational restraint and commitment to the community good, must counterbalance self-interested and self-aggrandizing "Desire"—or so the Whigs asserted in their stern rhetoric. From this perspective they condemned the wasteful conquests over nature perpetrated by their frontier brethren while righteously absolving their own enterprises of excesses that were at least as profligate and destructive. Marsh's genuinely elitist attitudes, in fact, sharpened his criticism of the short-sighted pioneer mindset. He had his doubts about the reigning Jacksonian faith in the omnicompetence of the unlettered common man, which was a cornerstone of frontier mythology. Marsh's Democratic opponents during the Vermont congressional race of 1843 exaggerated only somewhat when they called him "a man whose veins are bursting with the insolence of aristocracy." He had voiced candidly (and more diplomatically than had his father) his opinion that few men were "both *competent* and *prepared* to decide upon all questions."[20] Civic fathers must instead take the nation in hand and lead it on a principled and orderly path to the future.

In his own capacity as wise disinterested legislator, Marsh opposed the Mexican War of 1846–48 for reasons that were typically Whig and closely linked to his animus against the frontier West. He expressed concerns to his congressional colleagues that the "remote regions" acquired by the war could "never have a common interest with us" and would be "unsuited to agriculture, unable to sustain a dense population, adapted only to the lowest form of civilized life." To Marsh it was more important for the national government to promote the welfare of the existing economy in order to uplift and improve the prospects for his compatriots. Tariffs were essential to protect "the manufacturing capitalist, and the hundreds who depend upon him" ("myself unhappily a manufacturer," Marsh admitted), and internal improvements were necessary to "bind our wide confederacy together." Congressman

Marsh was also instrumental in launching the new Smithsonian Institution as a national museum and research library, a historically significant step toward the creation of a federal scientific establishment, and again exemplifying the Whig belief in didactic institutions as vehicles of progress and national unity. No doubt this promise of the Smithsonian had appeal to Marsh, who had once worried to his fellow New Englanders whether in an expanding nation "the schools of New England will still be nursing mothers to the posterity of her widely scattered children" on the western frontier: "If then we cannot be the legislators of our common country, let it be your care that we become not unworthy to be its teachers, and though we cannot give it law, let us not cease to give it light." [21]

Antebellum political culture, still a fair ideological distance from the modern regulatory welfare state, vested a great deal of faith in the "light" of persuasion to achieve larger social ends. Oratory, especially among the Whigs, was seen as a means toward educating and converting listeners to the speaker's point of view. The sheer force of reasoned argument, the emotive beauty of the language, could change a mind or melt a heart—and obviate the need for coercive laws. The notion was a laudable one, and fully understandable considering the widespread suspicion of governmental power that pervaded antebellum politics. Yet Marsh's unstated confidence in the potency of "light" was belied by the very forces of discord and disunity that thwarted the aspirations of New England Whig reformers to be the "legislators" of their "common country." The slavery issue, sectionalism, ethnic cleavages, the loss of political deference, and, above all, economic self-interest acted to undermine and destroy the Whig Party as a whole in the early 1850s, and no amount of oratory could save it. The implications were troubling: if the nation's political culture could not accommodate moral paternalism as a curb to the passions and appetites of the masses, what then was left except a resort to individual suasion and self-reform?

Scrambling to solve his financial problems, Marsh began a three-year stint as a traveling lecturer in 1854, the same year the Whigs finally collapsed. Like his other money-making schemes, Marsh's turn on the lecture circuit was unsatisfying and unsuccessful. "I shall hang my 'lecturing' on the same peg with my other failures and follies," he told his second wife, Caroline, in 1857. "It must be a long peg and a strong peg to hold them all." For subject matter Marsh drew on experiences from his recent tenure as U.S. ambassador to Turkey (1849–53)—travel descriptions, foreign affairs—along with topics of longer personal interest, such as agricultural improvement. Unfortunately, he seldom could rouse much enthusiasm in his audiences or in himself. Perhaps it was the grind of the circuit, the dull subjects ("The Environs of Constantinople"), or perhaps it was the forum itself.[22] Marsh was no spellbinder, oratorically or in print, but when the subject was important enough, when it was deeply felt, he could rise to the occasion. In Vermont he had been known as a hardy campaigner and formidable opponent (with four terms in Congress to prove it). During a life of many disappointments, he had always found singular contentment in his scholarship and writing, and in *Man and Nature*, he at last discovered his great theme. Lines from the book were still being quoted more than a century after they were written.

Whig political culture instilled Marsh with both a belief in the efficacy of rational argument and the makings of a nascent conservationist analysis, one that he was to explore to its final, universal logic in *Man and Nature*. Many of the values and concerns expressed in the book were Whig values and concerns, as a central passage attests. The condition of the landscape might give testimony to human improvidence and lust for money, as Susan Fenimore Cooper depicted in her own work, but it might also reflect an individual's potential for redemption. The reconciliation of "Duty" versus "Desire" might be revealed in "the establishment of an approximately fixed ratio between the two most broadly characterized distinctions of rural surface," Marsh projected— "woodland [duty] and plough land [desire]." This more environmentally viable balance would "involve a certain persistence of character in all the branches of industry, all the occupations and habits of life," Marsh recognized. It would involve, in short, a fundamental redefinition of American aspirations and behavior. Yet if it were achieved, Marsh declared—his words resonant with Whig oratory—this new relationship with nature would "help us to become . . . a well-ordered and stable commonwealth, and, not less conspicuously, a people of progress." [23] To persuade his countrymen toward this vision of a reformed landscape and a restored republic, Marsh wrote *Man and Nature*. He became an orator of sorts, an advocate, for nature.

MARSH WROTE *Man and Nature* between 1860 and 1864, during the first years of his appointment as American ambassador to Italy, where he was to spend the remaining two decades of his life, stable and secure at last. It was a book of no small ambition. In almost 500 pages of detailed and heavily footnoted text, Marsh surveyed the "changes produced by human action in the physical conditions of the globe we inhabit." He examined the effects of human activities on diverse animal species and a variety of environments ("The Woods," "The Waters," "The Sands"), using examples both ancient and modern.[24] As the title implies, Marsh was required to grapple with fundamental concepts and relationships that had perplexed scientists, theologians, and philosophers for millennia: the dynamics of history; the characteristics of nature; the definition of human nature; the place of human beings within nature.

In some sense, Marsh had been composing the work for nearly twenty years, accumulating experiences, facts, and ideas in a mind that by all accounts was eclectic and encyclopedic. A number of earlier and lesser writings by Marsh from the 1840s and 1850s, for example, provide clues about the culmination of his mature thinking in *Man and Nature*. These minor works were, above all, exercises in methodology, historical methodology, a crucial preparation for him. Whig scholars and orators prided themselves on being empirically and historically minded, and Marsh was no exception. He made his scholarly reputation through his translations of Scandinavian literature, and his admiration for the Northern "Goths" knew no bounds (Norsemen and their possible landings in America being all the rage in this period). Pointedly, it led him to write a "Whiggish" history of the Gothic (or Germanic) contribution to American democracy, the term later applied to a whole genre of historical writing featuring a preconceived narrative of moral and political progress from antiquity to the present. As he observed in *The Goths in New-England* (1843), a book that also allowed him to sing the praises of his Puritan forebears and home region, "The Goths . . . are the noblest branch of the Caucasian race. We are their children. It was the spirit of the Goth, that guided the Mayflower across the trackless ocean; the blood of the Goth, that flowed at Bunker's Hill," and so on, giving New Englanders an "intimate and inseparable connexion with those equal institutions, which are the pride and hope of every true-hearted American." [25] If the racial theme in Goths was tenuous at best, it at least shows Marsh thinking on a broadly comparative and sweeping historical scale, a scale he would widen much further in Man and Nature, as the more generic title itself suggests. For all of its flaws, The Goths in New-England may be seen as a primitive species of universal history, an interpretive approach that effaces national distinctions in pursuit of more encompassing synthetic themes, usually with regard to the countries of the Western world. Ultimately, as his thought matured, universal history became a principle means by which Marsh began intellectually to move beyond the comforting and facile confines of the Whig narrative of progress, which was difficult to reconcile with the story of natural devastation and depletion portrayed in Man and Nature.

Certainly his own life offered evidence enough of the vicissitudinal flow of time and reason to doubt the whole idea of inexorable American and human progress. The "failures and follies" of his "life of incessant flitting," stumbling from scheme to scheme, meant that Marsh was not able to find his professional niche until age sixty, with his appointment as ambassador to Italy. In the interim, notes his biographer, "his personal life was mutilated by tragedy," including the early death of his first wife and a son in 1833. "It was well for me that business drove me into a constant succession of severe labors of a very engrossing character," Marsh later wrote of the aftermath. "This only saved me from madness, for I was never alone for more than a year without bursting into a fit of sorrow, for even my dreams were full of death." If life did not unfold as an automatic success story, and if sickness and death were inherent to existence, then the analogy was there for Marsh, all too cruelly confirmed: could not nations, like individual people, undergo a cycle of birth, growth, and decay, as philosophers from Aristotle to Machiavelli had warned? [26]

Other writings from the 1840s and 1850s reveal him already conceptualizing elements of the major ideas of Man and Nature along these nonprogressive lines. In an "Address to the Agricultural Society of Rutland County" (1847), he cast social development in terms of the transition from savagery to civilization, a common enough conceit of the Victorian era, but one that he unwittingly began to challenge in the same essay. "America offers the first example of the struggle between civilized man and barbarous uncultivated nature," Marsh posited. Everywhere else on earth, the savage was the first to subdue nature by his primitive slow processes. In America, by contrast, "the full energies of advanced European civilization" had made it "the work of a day to win empires from the wilderness," bringing about that "marvellous change, which has converted unproductive wastes into fertile fields, and filled with light and life the dark and silent recesses of our aboriginal forests and mountains." According to Marsh (and conventional assumptions of racial hierarchy), "the arts of the savage are the arts of destruction; he desolates the region he inhabits, his life is a warfare of extermination." Civilization, on the other hand, "is at once the mother and the fruit of peace. Social man repays the earth all that he reaps from her bosom." With the transition to higher stages in social evolution, Marsh concluded, civilization took the savage and transformed him into "a beneficent, a fructifying, and a protective influence, and makes him the monarch not the tyrant of organic creation."[27]

But in the course of advising his audience of farmers on some of the basic principles of conservation, Marsh himself began to subvert these comforting and unproblematic viewpoints. Here in the obscure 1847 "Rutland County" address he articulated many of the proscriptions and warnings that were to be made famous by *Man and Nature.* "Men now begin to realize," Marsh wrote, "that man has a right to the use, not the abuse, of the products of nature; that consumption should everywhere be compensated by increasing production; and that it is a false economy to encroach upon a capital, the interest of which is sufficient for our lawful uses." In light of these strictures, Marsh proposed "certain . . . improvements connected with agriculture," such as "the introduction of a better economy in the management of our forest lands" (later the centerpiece idea of *Man and Nature*). This improvement was necessary because of the "inconveniences resulting from a want of foresight in the economy of the forest" that were "already felt in many parts of New England." By these words Marsh undermined the thrust of his preceding argument that castigated savages in their treatment of nature. New

Englanders, not Indians or slovenly western frontiersmen, were guilty of the "injudicious destruction of the woods," which among other evils washed away soil and led to floods that "fill every ravine with a torrent, and convert every river into an ocean." Throughout the landscape of New England, there were indicators that the consequences of economic development were not automatic progress: "The signs of artificial improvement are mingled with the tokens of improvident waste." Marsh in his youth had seen these tokens, evidences of disruption and decay: the bridges washed out by the Ottauquechee River he knew so well, and, on one occasion, an entire sawmill of his father's also undermined and destroyed by floods. Later in life, as Vermont fisheries commissioner in 1857, he reported that "clearing of the woods" resulted in "the complete change of the vegetable products of the soil and the insects that feed upon them," producing further changes in animal and bird populations that ramified until crops were damaged. In the end, nature was left in the "shorn and crippled condition to which human progress has reduced her." [28]

Marsh's observations of the "changes, which these causes have wrought in the physical geography of Vermont" — apparent now to "every middle-aged man" — eventually were to lead him to the fundamental insight that he made universal in *Man and Nature*. "Man," he wrote, collapsing his earlier dichotomy between civilized cultivator and frontier savage into a single human agency, "has done much to revolutionize the solid surface of the globe." Such revelations of the unintended and unforeseen consequences of human action had a larger impact on Marsh's conception of historical change, which in turn provided him with the interpretive and rhetorical framework, the historical argument, that was to make *Man and Nature* the convincing and classic work it came to be, the "fountainhead" of an intellectual tradition. As he wrote during an uncertain pause in his analysis, qualifying a particular point in terms appropriate to the book as a whole, "the subject is so exceedingly complex and difficult, that it is safer to regard it as a historical problem, or at least as what lawyers call a mixed question of law and fact, than to attempt to decide it upon *a priori* grounds." [29] Any vulgar-Whig assumptions about the progressive course of human history would have to be greatly qualified, if not rejected altogether.

As his reference to the "globe" indicates, Marsh's environmental education in problematic nonprogressive history did not end with the Vermont landscape so familiar to him, but continued abroad during his appointments as ambassador to Turkey in the early 1850s and as minister to Italy beginning in the 1860s. The posts allowed him some leisure to travel, which he and his family did extensively in Egypt, Palestine, Greece, the Levant, the Alps, and throughout Italy and Sicily. He observed everything closely, took measurements, collected specimens and artifacts, as was his eclectic wont. But perhaps one observation would have the greatest significance on the analysis of the yet-unwritten *Man and Nature*: that human influence permeated the environment of the Old World, and "not the pyramids and temples and tombs only— but the very earth." Wherever he went Marsh saw "meadows and hills rounded . . . by the assiduous husbandry of hundreds of generations," quite in contrast to America, where (he assumed) geography was still new, shaped largely by "the action of mere natural forces." More ominously, however, Marsh saw in parts of the Old World "the operation of causes set in action by man" that had "brought the face of the earth to a desolation almost as complete as that of the moon." [30]

Here was the genesis of the idea that was to have considerable influence on subsequent conservationist thinkers: so subtly (and not so subtly) pervasive were the activities of civilization, even before the dawn of industrialization, that the "natural" world might itself be considered to be a human artifact. This central theme of *Man and Nature* was summed up in the book's subtitle, "Physical Geography as Modified by Human Action." Marsh had come to the insight by indirection, inspired by contemporary breakthrough works of geographical theory rather than arriving at it purely by empirical observation. Scientists such as Alexander von Humboldt, Karl Ritter, Arnold Henry Guyot, and other founders of the "new geography" were in this period advocating a *holistic* (organically all-encompassing) approach to the study of nature, with which Marsh wholeheartedly agreed: "It was a narrow view of geography which confined that science to delineation of terrestrial surface and outline, and to description of the relative position and magnitude of land and water," he remarked in *Man and Nature*. "In its improved form, it embraces not only the globe itself, but the living things which vegetate or move upon it, the varied influence they exert upon each other, the reciprocal action and reaction between them and the earth they inhabit."[31]

In essence, the holistic new geography constituted an *ecological* view of the natural world, and more to the point, it furnished a set of analytical tools that were equally valid for the study of humanized environments. As Marsh wrote, the new geographers' most important "inquiry" was "how far external physical conditions . . . have influenced the social life and social progress of man." Marsh himself had pursued this question at rather a crude level in *The Goths in New-England*, hypothesizing that most of the virtues of the northern-dwelling Goths and their Puritan "descendants" derived from their living in cold, harsh climates. His later book, *The Camel* (1856)—by which Marsh hoped to promote the use of camels in the American West—was similarly a paean to an organism wonderfully adapted to its particular environment. But his travels through the ancient human landscapes of Europe and the Mideast, where "every turf is the monument of a hundred lives," led Marsh to reverse the direction of geographical determinism, to stand the new geographers' "inquiry" on its head. What must also be considered, he wrote in *Man and Nature*, is that "man has reacted upon organized and inorganic nature, and thereby modified, if not determined, the material structure of his earthly home." He put the thesis more succinctly in a letter written just after he began the book in 1860: "It's a little volume showing that whereas Ritter and Guyot think that the earth made man, man in fact made the earth."[32]

On the surface, it was hardly a revolutionary insight. After all, the Judeo-Christian tradition presupposed human dominion over nature, and the emerging values of industrial capitalism required and celebrated technological mastery of the environment. Marsh never disputed these assumptions. "Nothing is further from my belief that man is a 'part of nature' or that his action is controlled by what are called the laws of nature." Man, he wrote in the language of antebellum evangelicalism, "is a moral free agent working independently of nature"—and therein lay his capacity not only for good and self-perfection but also for evil and self-interest. Marsh held fast to his conventional Christian beliefs on human nature, and so the true innovation and potency of his "inquiry" becomes clear only if one focuses on the characteristics he ascribed to

"Nature," which, "left undisturbed, so fashions her territory as to give it almost unchanging permanence of form, outline, and proportion." [33]

The key descriptive words that Marsh applied to "undisturbed" natural laws and processes, used throughout Man and Nature, were the Enlightenment- and Romantic-inspired "balance," "stability," "equilibrium," and "harmony." Like many other naturalists of the mid-nineteenth century, he adhered substantially to the comforting pre-Darwinian mechanistic conception of nature formalized earlier by Linnaeus, which was not necessarily contradictory of the more organic and holistic views of the natural world proffered by the "new geography." [34] Marsh may have avoided in his writings any overt "machine" metaphors for nature, but the words and analogies that he did employ indicated his confidence in its ultimate order and benevolence. In fact, even as he acknowledged the presence of competition and violence in natural processes—a primary focus of the contemporary Darwinian scientific vanguard—Marsh maintained his faith in the mechanistic checks and balances that operated under natural law toward a greater harmony and equilibrium.

Tellingly, for his own metaphors and analogies, Marsh sometimes drew on classical liberal economic assumptions, just as had many other observers of nature's "economy" from Thomas Malthus to Charles Darwin. The premise of the classical school of economics was that the human economy also worked according to immutable and predictable natural laws. The sum of individual economic activity and competition, it was believed, resulted in progress and social harmony. Furthermore, the economy automatically self-adjusted to redress scarcity and oversupply; demand always rose to counterbalance excess production. Although Marsh had plentiful evidence from his personal business failures that these "laws" of economics were somewhat tenuous, he nevertheless was influenced by them—they were too deeply a part of the worldview of the solid Whig citizen. Marsh saw these laws at work in an idealized "nature undisturbed," abstracted from the ubiquitous presence (and blunders) of humankind. As he wrote in Man and Nature, "without man, lower animal and spontaneous vegetable life would have remained undisturbed in type, distribution, and proportion." This "permanence of form" occurred because species always "multiply their kind in just proportion, and attain their perfect measure of strength and beauty, without producing or requiring any change in the natural arrangement of surface, or in each other's spontaneous tendencies, except such mutual repression of excessive increase as may prevent the extirpation of one species by the encroachments of another." For it was everywhere the case, Marsh understood, that "the reproductive powers of species, which serve as the food of others, are always proportioned to the demand they are destined to supply." Taking a broader view, he declared that Nature was fundamentally innocent and good: "I am not aware of any evidence that wild animals have ever destroyed the smallest forest, extirpated any organic species, or modified its natural character, occasioned any permanent change of terrestrial surface, or produced any disturbance of physical conditions which nature has not, of herself, repaired." In contrast, man and his modifications were "everywhere a disturbing agent," Marsh asserted with the most famous words of the book: "Wherever he plants his foot, the harmonies of nature are turned to discords," for "of all organic beings, man alone is to be regarded as essentially a destructive power."[35] By Marsh's definition, nature was no longer to be considered solely as a dark, waste, chaotic place into which men carried the goodness and light of Christendom; it became instead another field for human sinfulness, or "evil," a word he used quite frequently.

In the final analysis, Marsh was ambivalent about human nature. It was for him simultaneously a "destructive power" and a creative "free agent." This ambivalence grew out of the splaying of his mind between two sets of dualistic assumptions that were all that his wider inherited culture had to offer him. His traditional Christian, Calvinist upbringing centered on man as a fallen being, willful and therefore sinful because he had rejected and been cast from the paradise of communion with God. Yet the Bible also exalted humanity's separateness and superiority over nature, exhorting believers to subdue and discipline the animal passions and appetites within them even as they were to assert superiority over a hostile external natural world. At the same time, the emerging secular culture of Romanticism posited an inverted version of the earthly paradise myth, in which humanity was fallen from communion with Nature, having acquired the curse of self-consciousness, civilization, and objectifying scientific knowledge. To end the resultant isolation of the individual self and the fragmentation of society would require a rational and intuitive recognition of man's lost integration and oneness with nature (see Chapter 2). These two worldviews coexisted in contradiction and tension for Marsh, who was deeply religious though nonsectarian, having rejected his father's Congregationalism ("I have never connected myself to any church").[36] His religious concerns were primarily focused on personal piety and salvation (his own), making his mind more receptive to secular ideas in the realm of the this-worldly. And so Christian and Romantic entangled themselves in his interpretations, and Marsh seldom undertook to resolve them, seeming little aware that they were in conflict. One sees in *Man and Nature* his dark vision of human "crimes" and "improvidence" incongruously interspersed with admiring projections of man's inventiveness, the persistent remnants of his earlier Whig faith in material progress.

Many of his religious and philosophical beliefs did predispose Marsh toward a dualistic (if not, at times, Manichean) conception of the human-nature relationship. But his scientific understanding, and his scientific optimism, qualified this starker conception until it was considerably more ambiguous and sophisticated, if not entirely reconciled in his mind: the closing words of the book still pondered the "great question, whether man is of nature or above her." In answer, the new geography revealed, according to Marsh, the basic "dependence of man upon the aid of spontaneous nature, in his most arduous material works," although those works were themselves testimony that the "grander achievements" of human action did "differ in essential character" from the activities of mere animals, as the effort of "a self-conscious and intelligent will."[37] At those points where it was most subtle, in short, Marsh's holistic interpretive framework could find some middle ground between his disparate worldviews, a middle ground that implicitly (if not consciously) argued that no complete reconciliation of them was possible, because the dualisms and contradictions were inherent in existence: superior yet flawed humankind living interdependently with a conquerable yet nurturing nature, both *of* and *above* it, lesser than the angels, higher than the beasts.

The relationship between "Man" and "Nature" so defined, further questions were of "great present interest," in Marsh's view: "How far can he compensate, arrest, or retard the deterioration which many of his agricultural and industrial processes tend to produce; and how far he can restore fertility and salubrity to soils which his follies or his crimes have made pestilential"—and this from an individual all too aware in his own case how human actions could issue in "follies and failures." Thus "restoration" was also a key word of the book, the restoration of nature's harmonies through the agency of human cultivation. It was a restoration that would depend on the possibility of personal redemption, a restoration that, if undertaken and fulfilled, could become a means toward that redemption. "Our victories over the external world," Marsh wrote, are merely "a vantage ground to the conquest of the yet more formidable and not less hostile world that lies within." Man must impose self-discipline and give up his destructive habits—"improvidence, wastefulness, and wanton violence"—and become instead a "coworker with nature," acting with the (Whig) values of "foresight and wisely guided industry." Such indeed would remain the most fundamental demand of environmental reformers throughout the modern era.[38]

Much of the text of Man and Nature consequently comprised a detailed historical indictment of the "destructive power" of humanity in various environments, with briefer sections of redemptive reform proposals accompanying the lists of charges. To Marsh, the primary damage wrought on the land was deforestation. As a lumberman himself, he had "had occasion both to observe and to feel the evils resulting from an injudicious system of managing woodlands and the products of the forest." Undisturbed, the forest supplied "a constant uniformity of condition most favorable to the regular and harmonious existence" of climate and plant and animal life. But, as Marsh had noted in his "Rutland County" address, "with the disappearance of the forest, all is changed." Marsh believed that the loss of forest cover caused alterations in local temperature and precipitation patterns, but perhaps the worst side effects of denuded hills were soil erosion and flooding. Without a "retentive bed of absorbent earth," he observed, rainwater and snowmelt must "pour down the valleys seaward." In light of Man and Nature's role as an intellectual "fountainhead," it is important to note that deforestation was to remain the chief concern of the conservation-minded in America for the

Woodstock, Vermont, area as seen from Mt. Tom, where George Perkins Marsh explored as a boy. This late-nineteenth-century view shows the results of extensive deforestation. (Courtesy of Woodstock Historical Society Archives)

next several decades. And small wonder: excluding Maine, Thoreau's and Marsh's New England, once heavily virgin forested, was already two-thirds open farmland by the middle of the nineteenth century. An estimated 600,000 cords of wood were needed annually to supply Boston with heat, and as Thoreau was to discover, even remotest Maine was beginning to come under the axe—a voracious appetite for wood and open land that Americans were carrying throughout the eastern United States and that had long ago stripped the Old World bare.[39]

The indictment of man, "with all his rapacity and all his enginery," did not stop with deforestation. There were other types of "extirpation" occurring at his hands as well, which Marsh had earlier occasion to contemplate while he was Vermont fisheries commissioner. The disappearance of "native birds and quadrupeds from particular localities" was the result of man's "direct persecutions" along with his destruction of "forest shelter" and "appropriate food." Aquatic mammals and fish were also victims of "almost all the processes of agriculture, and of mechanical and chemical industry." Very often, humans would unwittingly disrupt the balance of nature by extinguishing a particular species that was predator or prey within an intricate equilibrium of populations,

Present-day Woodstock, Vermont, from the same vantage point. The
forest cover has returned, and the area probably appears as it did in the early
Revolutionary period, before extensive cutting. (Photograph by the author)

thereby "deranging the original proportions between different orders of
spontaneous life." It was essential to remember, Marsh argued, synthe-
sizing the ancient metaphor of the great chain of being with the new
holistic science, that "all nature is linked together by invisible bonds,
and every organic creature, however low, however feeble, however dependent, is necessary to the well-being of some other among the myriad
forms of life with which the Creator has peopled the earth." There was
virtually no knowing what "a circle of disturbance we produce in the
harmonies of nature when we throw the smallest pebble into the ocean
of organic life." [40]

For evidence, Marsh cited numerous historical and contemporary
case studies, tracing (with the help of the holistic approach of the new
geographers) the interdependent complexities of man-made cause and
natural effect, usually *backward* from some unpredicted catastrophic out-
come, in what was nothing less than an early form of ecological analysis. For example, he reported that "not many years ago, the pines on
thousands of acres of land in North Carolina, were destroyed by insects
not known to have ever done serious injury to that tree before." The
reason was that "insects increase whenever the birds which feed upon

them disappear," and the birds had disappeared because "the white man has laid bare a vast proportion of the earth's surface"—eradicating their habitat—and because humans had engaged in "wanton destruction of the robin and other insectivorous birds." Holding "nature undisturbed" as his normative point of departure, Marsh deplored the loss of the woods' "fairest ornament" as regrettable in itself, but he drew a moral from the North Carolina case that was at once decidedly anthropocentric yet ecological at its heart, reflecting his own ambivalence about the human-nature relationship. It was ultimately in the best self-interest of humanity to curtail their rapacity and enginery, Marsh reasoned, because of their very dependence on the balanced operation of natural processes. For "in waging a treacherous warfare on his natural allies," man became "the indirect cause of an evil for which he pays so heavy a penalty," specifically, the loss of valuable timber resources. Marsh continued the metaphor in a more sweeping and ominous generalization about the consequences: Nature in such cases "avenges herself upon the intruder, by letting loose upon her defaced provinces destructive energies hitherto kept in check by organic forces destined to be his best auxiliaries."[41]

Such consequences, of course, unfolded within human history, affecting the fortunes of individuals and of whole societies. Marsh, ever the good empiricist ("the collection of phenomena must precede the analysis of them"), was obliged as a result to revise further the more sanguine Whiggish conceit of progressive historical pattern. His worldview darkening, he became both social critic and secular prophet. He chose his historical lessons carefully, for maximum rhetorical impact: it was no afterthought that the opening sections of chapter 1 concern the "Physical Decay of the Territory of the Roman Empire, and of other parts of the Old World." Analogies between classical history and American destiny were deeply rooted in the literary and political discourse of the day, reaching back to the Revolutionary generation, and they constituted a form of commentary on the likelihood of national exceptionalism: Would the United States recapitulate the history of the virtuous Roman Republic or the decadent Roman Empire?[42]

Marsh's depiction of the height of the empire brought the parallels uncomfortably close to home. Much like antebellum frontier America, the Roman Empire "comprised the regions of the earth most distinguished by a happy combination of physical advantages"; the "abundance of the land adequately supplied every material want, ministered liberally to every sensuous enjoyment." But as Marsh had personally observed of the "present physical condition" of the long-collapsed empire, more than half of its area was today "deserted by civilized man and surrendered to hopeless desolation, or at least greatly reduced in population and productiveness." These same processes that had caused the "melancholy delapidation" of parts of modern Europe had been spread to America by its colonizers in centuries past. With two sections on the "Physical Decay of New Countries," Marsh very directly subverted any of his audience's pretensions to exceptionalism, any notion that America's natural abundance might allow it to escape what seemed a universal human fate. It was true, he recognized, that in the United States (as well as Australia and South Africa) there were "districts yet remaining in substantially their native condition" of "undisturbed nature," but in longer-settled regions (such as New England) "great, and, it is to be feared, sometimes irreparable, injury has been already done in the various processes by which man seeks to subjugate the virgin earth." If some frontier areas had still to be subjugated, there was all the more reason to "prevent the widespread mischiefs" produced by conventional methods of "rural husbandry and of forest industry" that might be carried into them. For otherwise, Marsh predicted, entering an apocalyptic mode that would be familiar to his twentieth-century environmentalist heirs, the bleakest of prospects awaited humanity worldwide:

> The earth is fast becoming an unfit home for its noblest inhabitant, and another era of equal human crime and improvidence . . . would reduce it to such a condition of impoverished productiveness, of shattered surface, of climatic excess, as to threaten the deprivation, barbarism, and perhaps even extinction of the species.[43]

"True, there is a partial reverse to this picture," Marsh averred in the very next sentence, backing away from the implications of this more cyclical vision of history—as he must if he were to avoid again the pitfalls of determinism. Having empirically qualified a more naive progressive model of historical change ("unlimited power and boundless knowledge do not necessarily imply moral perfection"), he now had to embrace the idea of man as a "free agent," constrained but not bound by natural or historical "laws," with the freedom to create a future of progress if he will. This was the essential leap of faith of the advocate, preliminary to politics. The "partial reverse" in which Marsh vested these hopes—perhaps to become a full reverse—included various reforms and improvements that had already been attempted on a small scale in Europe together with his own criticisms and proposals intended for an American audience. That Marsh was so self-consciously an advocate is beyond doubt. "I address myself not to professed physicists, but to the general intelligence of educated, observing, thinking men"—men much like himself; "my purpose is . . . to make practical suggestions." The whole possibility of reform, Marsh strongly believed, hinged on "the diffusion of knowledge on this subject among the classes that . . . own their woods, their pastures, and their ploughlands [and that have] a strong interest in the protection of their domain against deterioration." [44]

Or, to be more precise, Marsh's book was aimed at those classes that should have such a paternal interest. Most fundamentally, the social criticism of Man and Nature was a sustained exhortation to Americans to set aside the flitting life and "slovenly husbandry" of the pioneer, that wastrel figure of the old Whig demonology. The destructive practices of the frontier settler "soon exhausts the luxuriance of his first fields, and compels him to remove his household gods to a fresher soil," just as the "improvident habits of the backwoodsman" were in danger of depleting the nation's forests beyond any capacity for their continued growth and renewal. Marsh laid the blame for these dangers on the general "instability of American life," on the "want of fixedness" that came of undisciplined "Desire." It is impossible not to hear a hint of self-confession (and self-flagellation) in Marsh's summation that environmental restoration would therefore "involve a certain persistence of character in all the branches of industry, all the occupations and habits of life"— this from the man who had worn so many hats himself. His main appeal, implicitly and explicitly, was to his audience's self-interest, with the warning that economic decline at both a personal and a national level must accompany environmental degradation and resource depletion. But Marsh included a moral plea in his argument as well, though not the hand-wringing concern over nature's desecrated beauties and violated harmonies one might expect. Again his orientation was decidedly anthropocentric: he pled on behalf of posterity, citing the "duties which this age owes to those that are to come after it" and the necessity of fathers to manifest a "self-forgetting care" for their "moral and material interests." This long-term planning and practice, which might be an act so simple as the planting of trees, would not only benefit succeeding generations by saving and replenishing resources, Marsh wrote, but would also serve as a "moral check" against the "incessant flitting" of American life, rooting individuals to family acres tended and improved, then passed down. By this "full atonement for our spendthrift waste of the bounties of nature," he counseled, Americans would in the future become "a people of progress." 45

Marsh outlined in *Man and Nature* the reform measures of which this "atonement" would consist, but he was vague about the political or other means necessary to implement them. "On narrow theatres" in America and Europe, he reported, "new forests have been planted" and "inundations of flowing streams restrained by heavy walls"; torrents "[have] been compelled to aid . . . in filling up lowlands," while "ground submerged by encroachments of the ocean . . . has been rescued from its dominion by diking"; swamps and lakes "have been drained," drifting dunes "have been checked," and "seas and inland waters have been repeopled with fish." These expressions of enthusiasm for human manipulation and reclamation of natural landscapes were frequent in the book, a tribute to Marsh's belief that it was "rash . . . to attempt to set limits on the ultimate power of man over inorganic nature." One of the major lessons taken from *Man and Nature* by contemporaries and later readers, especially the Pinchot school of utilitarian conservationists, was its vision of "great material advantage from stimulating her [nature's] productive energies in provinces of her empire hitherto regarded as forever inaccessible, utterly barren." Reforestation was of particular importance, and Marsh devoted special emphasis to its benefits:

It is hoped that the planting of the mountains will diminish the frequency and violence of river inundations, prevent the formation of torrents, mitigate the extremes of atmospheric temperature, humidity, and precipitation, restore dried-up springs, rivulets, and sources of irrigation, shelter the fields from chilling and from parching winds, prevent the spread of miasmatic effluvia, and, finally, furnish an inexhaustible and self-renewing supply of a material indispensable to so many purposes of domestic comfort.[46]

Significantly, however, in making these proposals, Marsh cited numerous *European* authorities and model projects, where "legislation . . . upon sylviculture" had advanced considerably further than in frontier America. There were simply few, if any, precedents for him to choose from in the United States. Federal laws to conserve forest stands for shipbuilding purposes extended back to 1799, but it was not until 1827 that President John Quincy Adams acted to create the nation's first tiny naval forest reserves. Congress passed a broader law in 1831 that forbade the removal of timber from all public lands, but the measure was unenforceable and universally ignored. In Europe, by contrast, scientific and institutional ferment was proceeding apace, and the results seemed to Marsh "worthy of imitation." He referred specifically to the work of such figures as the French forester Jules Clavé and the naturalist Friedrich Pfeil, regarded as one of the founders of German forestry. In both France and the German states, substantial scientific forestry efforts dated to the early part of the nineteenth century, and customary regulation of forest use extended back several centuries more. Marsh was no doubt aware that Prussia had established a forest department as long ago as 1820, or that in the following year a forestry academy was founded in Berlin. France laid down its *Code Forestier* in 1829, and in 1860 legislation was enacted there to begin watershed control.[47]

Although Marsh's focus on Europe might be attributed simply to his residency and travels during the writing of *Man and Nature*, it is indicative of something larger: his quandary over the legal, legislative, or alternative means toward natural resource "restoration." Marsh well knew that European statist, interventionist models could not be adopted in frontier, laissez-faire America, where resources seemed limitless and there was no sentiment that might favor government interference with free economic individualism—the highest social good for both American political parties. In Europe, the problem of scarcity was greatly more pressing, and there was a continuing tradition of centralized, intrusive, activist government (royal, municipal, ecclesiastical, and otherwise). As a consequence, Marsh wrote, "all [European models] must be more or less modified to harmonize with American nature, and in our general social life." [48] But this qualification still left him with the quandary over means, a dilemma that was to continue to face generations of conservation advocates: To what degree could conservation practices be left to the discretion of the individual landowner, and to what extent did such measures require public intervention and regulation? Individuals could be counted on to put their personal greed and self-interest ahead of the good of the environment and the community, or they might abuse the land out of plain ignorance. Conversely, public regulations could be by turns onerous, or, if unenforced, ineffective, particularly if there were no concomitant change in attitude and practice on the part of landowners. Already, in this originative book of American conservation, Marsh was grappling with such issues.

Ostensibly, he seemed to place himself firmly in the camp of self-reform and individual responsibility. "For prevention of the evils upon which I have so long dwelt," he declared, "the American people must look to the diffusion of general intelligence on this subject, and to the enlightened self interest . . . not to the action of their local or general legislatures." As to why Marsh seemed to have so little confidence in government institutions, therein lies a tale, both biographical and ideological. His four terms in Congress during the 1840s meant that Marsh was hardly a neophyte in the ways of political corruption, and he no doubt encountered his share of intrigue in the early 1850s as minister to Turkey. But it was over the several years' interim between his Turkish and Italian appointments, when Marsh returned to America, that his political education took place in earnest. Besides the legal proceedings over his bankruptcy, he became involved in a bitter feud over congressional reimbursement for extra diplomatic service he had rendered in Greece while still in Turkey. The dispute was finally resolved in his favor, yet it dragged on for year after poisonous year. Meanwhile, casting about as usual for some source of income, Marsh was appointed to a variety of posts in the Vermont state government, including, most importantly, state railroad commissioner (1858–59). He had become an enemy of railroad corporations ("whom I loathe with all my soul") after the demise of the mismanaged Vermont Central helped to ruin him. During his two stints as commissioner he wrote damaging reports on the public and private corruption of companies operating within the state, and he made numerous recommendations to the legislature for reforms. None of his proposals was ever enacted, and railroad lobbyists worked hard though unsuccessfully against his election to a second term. They did succeed in having his salary cut in half, and they later placed a much more pliable commissioner in his seat when Marsh left for his ministerial post in Italy. "There has never been a time since I was a member that influences were brought to bear so directly on members and so overpoweringly as during the session of the legislature just passed," a state representative told Marsh in his last year as commissioner.[49]

Thus disenchantment—and one might say, realism—with regard to the democratic political process necessarily made its way into the argument of *Man and Nature*. Government was "liable, as are all things human, to great abuses," Marsh wrote in a long footnote at the end of the introduction. "The multiplication of public placeholders . . . is a serious evil." Yet, although his misgivings were clearly very strong, leading him in that earlier frustrated moment to trust conservation reform solely to the "enlightened self interest" of the very same American landowners who were laying the country waste, Marsh conceded that some form of public oversight was crucial. It was the old Whig talking, albeit now as a Republican, in principle sympathetic to the Radical wing that foresaw an activist posture for government on issues like the assimilation of the freed Southern slaves, but that was conflicted over the paternalistic ramifications of such a role for the state. Marsh resolved his quandary by seeing government intervention as the choice of a lesser evil. Government corruption, "foul as it is," he wrote, "does not strike so deep as the rottenness of private corporations." Less than enamored with the virtues of the private sphere, which was rapidly becoming an absolute article of faith for most moderate and conservative Republicans, Marsh, in fact, could manifest a certain enthusiasm over a government role in such matters as "public facilities of intercommunications and commerce" (roads, canals, railways, currency) "in which the nation at large has a vastly deeper interest than any private association can have." He went so far as to suggest outright government ownership and control of these facilities, far beyond the pale of the Whig/Republican platform of government grants and charters to private developers. His somewhat aristocratic temperament, his lukewarm opinion toward the common man, his personal frustrations as a regulator, and his vision of a "well-ordered commonwealth" all forced Marsh into dissent from the doctrine of laissez-faire:

> The apophthegm, "the world is governed too much," though unhappily too truly spoken of many countries—and perhaps, in some respects, true of all—has done much mischief whenever it has been too unconditionally accepted as a political axiom. The popular apprehension of being over-governed . . . has had much to do with the general abandonment of certain government duties by the ruling powers of most modern states.[50]

That one of those duties should be the replenishment and protection of America's natural resources Marsh never unequivocally states in *Man and Nature*. Yet certainly his main qualm over legislative action was not a basic philosophical objection but rather a fear that it would not be effective enough. "Enlightened self interest" brought about by the diffusion of general knowledge remained in his mind an all-important means toward conservation. In relying on changed individual attitudes, he was very much a part of the antebellum evangelical culture of reform, which was based on a politics of personal conversion—the pricked conscience, the melted heart, the improved behavior. Nevertheless, Marsh's more Calvinist view of human nature undermined a complete confidence in the individual responsibility of the "absolute irresponsible owner of his own land." As shown by his thoughts on the pioneer settler and back-woodsman, his concern over private evils extended not only to soulless corporations but to avaricious individuals as well. "It is a great misfortune to the American Union that the State Governments have so generally disposed of their original domain to private citizens," Marsh lamented, for otherwise these lands would still be under state jurisdiction and, presumably, protected from the depletion they were now suffering.[51]

Marsh's emphasis on "enlightened self interest" devolved from his recognition (and prophesy, as latter-day environmentalists were to learn) that Americans' strong belief in the absolute rights of private property was to remain a very serious obstacle to any and all regulatory intervention. Handing out the public domain to private individuals would only exacerbate matters, and the wisest course was to retain those lands and resources under government control. (Some years later Marsh proposed that all natural waters in the arid West be declared the "inalienable property of the State" in order to avoid water monopolies and irrigation disputes.) He had, moreover, the evidence of his eyes from abroad, where "enlightened individuals in most European states, governments in others, have made very extensive plantations" of new forests. He cited the particular case of France, which had "set herself energetically at work to restore the woods in the southern provinces." Yet even there, "government has moved with too slow and hesitating a pace, and preventive measures do not yet compensate destructive causes."[52] This was not so much a rejection of government action as it was a call for more: the typically alarming rhetoric of the environmental advocate.

WHEN IT WAS first published in 1864, *Man and Nature* sold more than one thousand copies of its first edition, a very respectable number for a work of "geography." The book did not have much of an immediate impact on the public at large. Marsh's chief biographer overstates somewhat when he declares that the work "inaugurated a revolutionary reversal of American attitudes toward resources."[53] In the post–Civil War period, there was still a huge trans-Mississippi frontier to settle (and close, the map at last filled-up), a vast transcontinental railroad system to build (and overbuild, causing depressions), an enormous herd of bison to hunt (and extinguish, wasting most), and a modern urban-industrial complex to construct (and expand, and expand). All of this history would have to happen before a substantial number of Americans would begin to take notice of the ideas expressed in *Man and Nature*, which would begin to strike home sometime around the turn of the century. The "revolution" in attitudes that Marsh's work contributed to was a very real but slowly unfolding one.

Warnings about the problems of deforestation and species extinction did not originate with *Man and Nature*. Historians have discovered references and discussions of these issues dating back to the 1780s in the United States. Commentators as diverse as Benjamin Rush, James Madison, John James Audubon, and Susan Fenimore Cooper pointed to the disturbing national trend of forest depletion decades before *Man and Nature* appeared. Since the early years of the nineteenth century, agricultural improvement societies in New England and elsewhere had urged their members to replant or maintain forest cover out of concern for productivity, climate, and watershed. Yet a loose comparison to Charles Darwin's *On the Origin of Species* (1859) helps to illustrate the larger historical significance of Marsh's *Man and Nature*. The idea of evolution had been discussed and debated in European scientific and philosophical circles for two generations or more before *On the Origin of Species* was published. But Darwin's book (among other achievements) synthesized both argument and evidence behind evolution in a way no one else had previously. Though *Man and Nature* was certainly not of the stature of *On the Origin of Species*, which in time transformed science and virtually all areas of Western thought, it has assumed much the same place in the canon of environmental writing. No book before it had ever treated the subject of environmental abuse in such a comprehensive, systematic, and compelling fashion.[54]

The initial practical impact of *Man and Nature* may have been limited, but over time its influence multiplied and ramified. The book was first embraced by the small group of scientists and foresters who comprised the American forestry movement, which was the progenitor of what was to become known after 1900 as the "conservation movement." Most directly, *Man and Nature* was incorporated into a report to Congress that led to the establishment of a national forestry commission in 1873, itself a precursor to the U.S. Forest Service, the first important conservation agency set up two decades later. Several state forestry commissions founded in the 1870s were also attributable in part to Marsh's consciousness-raising efforts, and within a decade after his death in 1882, the first large-scale state and national forest reserves were created (see Chapter 3). *Man and Nature* remained in print until 1907, standing virtually alone in its category, then was reissued in 1965. Over the years readers continued to discover it and seek it out. Gifford Pinchot, the chief of Theodore Roosevelt's Forest Service and leader of the conservation movement in its first national incarnation, called Marsh's work "epoch making." Lewis Mumford, writing in 1931, was the authority who described the book as a "fountainhead." And thirty years later Stewart Udall, secretary of the interior in the Johnson administration— writing just as the 1960s floodtide of national environmental concern was about to swell—referred to *Man and Nature* as "the beginning of land wisdom in this country." [55]

To be the "fountainhead" of the "precursor" to the "beginning" of an "epoch," the environmental epoch—perhaps that is as much as any single individual could hope to achieve with a written work, particularly one that was, it is no cliché to say, ahead of its time. None of Marsh's other books is remembered, except as part of the bibliography that includes *Man and Nature*; Marsh remains at best a footnote in the history of Scandinavian studies. His terms as a congressman and state official were unremarkable, and his diplomatic service in Turkey and Italy was solid but hardly brilliant, nothing to make him a historical figure. Yet so much of that experience shaped the writing of the one book that was to be remembered. After the Civil War, Marsh lived out the rest of his life quietly at his post in Rome, working on corrections and revisions of *Man and Nature* (even on the very day he died in 1882) and spending summers vacationing at the school of forestry at Vallombrosa, where the views reminded him of Vermont. He walked and climbed in the Apennines as long as his health allowed, which was right up to the end. Although his book is filled with matters practical and scientific, occasionally a more personal and emotive response to nature glows through, reflective of the experiences he had had as a boy in Vermont and which he still sought out in the forests of Italy. As he paused to note in the chapter entitled "The Woods," "He who has enjoyed that special training of the heart and intellect which can be acquired only in the unviolated sanctuaries of nature, 'where man is distant, but God is near' "—"his regret at the dwindling area of the forest solitude will be augmented." Marsh was writing of himself, but he might easily have been referring to his contemporary, Thoreau, whose works he admired. Thoreau would have understood his regret, during a lonely walk in his final days, of not finding "a single compatriot among the forest growths" of Vallombrosa, any tree native to New England. But when Marsh died his coffin was borne down the mountain by an honor guard of foresters.[56]

CHAPTER TWO

Henry David Thoreau

In Wildness is the preservation of the World.

"Walking, or The Wild"

Henry David Thoreau
(Courtesy of the Concord Free Public Library)

MURMURING THE famous last words "moose" and "Indian," Henry David Thoreau preceded Marsh to the grave by twenty years, having rarely in his lifetime ventured beyond the confines of his hometown Concord except to search for "forest solitude"—and the odd teaching job, which was as high as his worldly ambitions reached. Yet if his was a shorter and more circumscribed it was also a profounder life than Marsh's, a life that subsequent generations regarded in legendary terms. Of Marsh it might be said that having failed to make a success in business he was handed by plain luck what amounted to a leisured expatriation abroad, where scholarship and criticism flourished with refuge from the "evils" of the reckless country he had left behind. But this expatriation, inadvertent and undeclared, carried no social stigma or personal price for him; it was merely that Marsh had found his professional niche, and his home, in a diplomatic post. Thoreau, however, was an expatriate at home, among and against his Massachusetts neighbors, not a few of whom considered him an "oddity" and a loafer. In his own eyes, the eyes of the "majority of one," he lived "deliberately," in accordance with an unconventional and personally demanding ascetic morality, a lifestyle often subversive of received wisdom ("The greater part of what my neighbors call good I believe in my soul to be bad"). He was able to live "deliberately," he believed, because he traveled both literally and subjectively in Nature, the place where he found refuge: the Concord countryside nearby; the "unviolated sanctuaries" of the "dwindling" forests of New England; and the rich conceptions of nature within his own mind.[1]

Nature was an idea so replete with scientific, philosophical, political, and ethical meanings for Thoreau that most of his foreshortened eccentric life was required to construct and understand it. Indeed, on his deathbed, his final two words were indicative of his intellectual and spiritual submergence in nature, or so his biographers would like to think—and so Thoreau, who strove self-consciously to be legendary, would have it thought of him. Julian Hawthorne, the son of one of Thoreau's famous literary neighbors, later wrote of his boyhood friend with much perceptiveness: "Truly, Nature absorbed his attention; . . . it was her way of working, her mystery, her economy in extravagance; he delighted to trace her footsteps toward their source, and to watch her growths and developments. He liked to feel that the pursuit was endless, with mystery at both ends of it."[2]

One discovery that Thoreau did make during this endless pursuit of nature was his ideal of the wilderness. Therein resides his central significance to the tradition of American environmental advocacy, a legacy carried forward in subsequent decades by heirs like John Muir, Aldo Leopold, Robert Marshall, and Benton MacKaye. They read their Thoreau, as have generations of other nature lovers. His writings defined for them the credo and the value of solitary nonexploitative experience of the pristine natural world. In the twentieth century, when his fame and influence were the greatest, Thoreau was to be recognized as the archetype of the Romantic loner-naturalist and the patron saint of the environmental movement, known simply as "Thoreau," a single-name appellation like the great classical writers of old.

He had no active, public, recorded life such as Marsh's. His biographers write instead of small, private, personal acts and events. He was born in 1817 as David Henry Thoreau, and on graduation from Harvard College in 1837 he reversed his names for reasons that are still unknown, though much speculated on. For three years (1838–41) he conducted a private school at Concord with his older brother, John, whose tragic death by lockjaw in 1842 affected Thoreau for a long period afterward. From 1841 to 1843 he lived in the household of his early mentor, the Transcendentalist philosopher Ralph Waldo Emerson. Then, from 1845 to 1847, he dwelled alone in his famous solitary experiment at Walden Pond, during which he completed his first book, *A Week on the Concord and Merrimack Rivers* (1849). In 1846, he spent a night in the Concord jail for failure to pay taxes in protest of the Mexican War; two years later he delivered on this subject his most noted and influential essay, "Resistance to Civil Government" (later retitled "Civil Disobedience"). Also in that year he published part of what was to be the important "Ktaadn" section of his posthumous book, *The Maine Woods* (1864), based on a series of trips he made to the Maine wilderness. In 1854, after working on many revisions, Thoreau published *Walden*, his greatest and most widely read work, in which he recounted and reflected on his experiences in Nature as discovered at the pond's shore. Thereafter, into the late 1850s, he studied scientific natural history and became increasingly outspoken in the antislavery cause until his death in 1862, apparently from tuberculosis.[3]

All in all Thoreau led a quiet existence, yet he has come to be revered as a daring and heroic though humble, gentle, and sensitive soul. And, in fact, who Thoreau was and what kind of personality he had are questions of importance to more than fans or biographers: answers to these questions relate directly to the environmental ethic that he took his lifetime to develop. This ethic posited a relationship to nature that hinged fundamentally on the individual emotive sensibility, a projection onto nature of personal psychological, aesthetic, and religious yearnings. With his pioneering inward and outward explorations—*Walden*, *The Maine Woods*, "Walking"—Thoreau began to cultivate this sensibility in Americans and to instruct how nature might fulfill it. Contrary to legend, he was not an otherworldly hermit but rather an individualist who cherished his solitude, a solitude in nature. He lived most of his adulthood in his parents' household, and he enjoyed the company of children, who could find him immensely entertaining. He never married and "did not appear to feel the *sex*-attraction" (according to a neighbor), though a certain sensuality is expressed in some of his writings. He was an odd, difficult, lonely, introverted, sarcastic, and complicated man, tortured at times, driven at others. For twenty-six months he may have lived "deliberately" at Walden Pond, but for much of his lifetime Thoreau lived at a loss. Whether he could find solace and refuge in Nature, what Nature could provide him that society could not, what values and metaphors he believed were embodied in wilderness that were essential to preserve—Thoreau made his lonesome "saunterings" in search of answers to these queries, pressing and immediate for him personally, and of lasting concern to the tradition he helped to found. Most of these "saunterings" appeared first in the thousands of pages of his private journal, but his one strongest social impulse, though expressed impersonally and universally, caused him to extract, revise, synthesize, and poeticize his myriad observations into books, lectures, and essays, and thereby made him an advocate: the desire to be read.[4]

"For my part," Thoreau confessed in his most important wilderness lecture, "Walking, or The Wild" (1851), "I feel that with regard to Nature I live a sort of border life, on the confines of a world into which I make occasional and transient forays only, and my patriotism and allegiance to the state into whose territories I seem to retreat are those of a moss-trooper," seeking "a life which I call natural."[5] The sources of this "border life" of Thoreau's, so strange and so evocative, may be traced through the strata of influences that constituted and shaped his withdrawn personality: his family, the town of Concord, and the Transcendentalist movement.

THERE IS ostensibly little in Thoreau's early biography that might have predicted his later fascination with "the Wild," little to distinguish him from thousands of other sons of New England middle-class families coming of age during the industrial revolution. The Thoreaus moved several times after his birth because of his father's repeated business reverses, until settling finally near relatives at Concord in 1823. John Thoreau Sr. was a shopkeeper and small manufacturer, and his wife, Cynthia, kept boarders to raise the household income closer to a respectable status. Reportedly John was honest, well-liked (of a "social nature," his son remembered), good-tempered, and docile ("wholly unpretending"), while Cynthia was ambitious, outspoken, and independent, the dominant presence of Thoreau's home life. She was actively involved in the local Congregational church, charitable society, and Bible society, and she was a founder of the Concord Women's Anti-Slavery Society—"a born reformer," according to one of her son's biographers. She scrimped to send her children to the best local schools, where Henry got his first instruction in the classics, a standard course of study for the time and an important influence on his own philosophy. Thoreau was the most promising of the children scholastically, and so he alone was sent to Harvard in 1833 by his mother's ambition and his father's improved fortunes. Earlier, a relative had staked claim to a graphite deposit in New Hampshire, and John Sr. had fallen into the pencil-making trade by the mid-1820s, establishing a small factory in Concord. He, like Marsh, was one of the "quietly desperate" men trying to make a living in the new economy, a man farmless and patrimonyless, with "pecuniary difficulties the greater part of his life," pushed forward by his wife.[6]

How these basic dynamics of the Thoreau family impacted on young Henry to mold his character and thought has been the subject of considerable analysis by scholars. It is probable that his placid father's less than successful ventures, combined with Thoreau's own experience of lofty things at Harvard and his mother's high goals for him, resulted altogether in a long-term crisis of vocation and identity. He felt cast adrift. In 1833, when he was sixteen years old (to cite one emblematic episode), he built a boat that he named "The Rover" and put it to water on Walden Pond. This was the summer before he entered Harvard College, and he spent much of his spare time floating alone. He would row to the center of the pond, lie back in the boat—"dreaming awake," as one of his biographers describes—and drift aimlessly until the currents carried him to a random point on shore. At times like these, he later reflected, drawing one of his typically ironic and paradoxical morals, "idleness was the most attractive and productive industry." Thoreau lived a life that could become material for such epigrams. In his forty-five-year lifespan, he never held what could be labeled a steady job, even as he carried on his quest for a deliberate and authentic existence. "I delight to come to my bearings," he observed in *Walden*, "not to live in this restless, nervous, bustling, trivial Nineteenth Century, but stand or sit thoughtfully while it goes by." It seems, however, that Thoreau never did come to his bearings. "Here I am thirty-four years old, and yet my life is almost wholly unexpanded," he wrote in his journal as late as 1851. "There is such an interval between my ideal and the actual in many instances that I may say I am unborn."[7]

As his words from *Walden* indicate, there were more than familial influences involved in this prolonged identity crisis of Thoreau's. The larger culture of Jacksonian democracy, given reign on the wide-open stage of a frontier country, seemed to lay out before his generation of young men the vista of limitless individual possibilities. Most mundanely, that vista might offer the prospect of economic mobility and opportunity, but more disturbingly, it might also present the burden of protean self-creation (as the Transcendentalists argued). "This is the only way, we say," Thoreau wrote in *Walden*, referring to life choices; "but there are as many ways as there can be drawn radii from one center." Traditional values and institutions that might have provided order and guidance within this personal and social flux were themselves being undermined. "You may say the wisest thing you can old man," Thoreau wrote, perhaps more than rhetorically addressing his own father (and forefathers), but "I hear an irresistible voice which invites me away from all that." To complicate further the career plans of young college men like Thoreau, the Panic of 1837 struck the country in the same year that he graduated, throwing into still greater doubt any conventional paths to success and respectability. As he concluded of life in the new secular and industrial age, the transition toward the modern that he and his contemporaries lived through, "one generation abandons the enterprises of another like stranded vessels."[8]

This transitional crumbling of older fixity and authority was nowhere more evident than in the New England religious establishment. The dwindling of ecclesiastical power there, the latest to occur in America, must also be considered as contributing directly to Thoreau's life "at a loss." Massachusetts did not disestablish the Congregational Church until 1833, and its symbolic coincidence with Thoreau's most impressionable years of education surely left an imprint on him, for disestablishment was at once indicative of the anti-institutional, individualizing tendencies of antebellum spiritual life as well as a hallmark of modern secularization, the decline of conventional theologies. In Concord, Thoreau's own mother was involved in a local Congregational church schism (over the Trinity) manifesting the emergence of the non-Christian Unitarian Church. More radically, Thoreau's future mentor, Ralph Waldo Emerson, experiencing something of a spiritual and vocational crisis himself, quit his Unitarian pulpit in Boston and moved to Concord to begin proselytizing an even newer philosophy, Transcendentalism. Thoreau thus reached maturity in a community that was still outwardly and observantly pious yet without formal or doctrinal religious unity. He inherited out of the Congregational remnants of the old Puritanism a strongly religious sensibility, a yearning for the transcendent, but without a sufficient orthodoxy, a strict and fulfilling enough creed, to give it expression. As a boy his schoolmates called Thoreau by the nickname "Judge," a reflection (according to his biographers) of his innate stoicism and solemnity.[9] But if he seemed a born moralizer, Thoreau as a young man had yet to define his morality.

Emerson and others of the Transcendentalist circle who moved to Concord brought the makings of it with them. Thoreau was extremely fortunate in this intellectual mountain coming to Mohammed. It made his hometown a very enriching place to live, the center of New England's great antebellum literary renaissance, an outburst of creativity from the 1830s to the 1860s that included Emerson, Fuller, Hawthorne, Melville, Stowe, Dickinson, and Thoreau himself. Concord as a *place*, a personal landscape—"my native soil"—that came to be intimately known and exhaustively explored by Thoreau had already been educating him for some years. "Mr. Thoreau dedicated his genius with such entire love to the fields, hills, and waters of his native town," Emerson wrote of his friend's "fancy for referring everything to the meridian of Concord." As Thoreau once declared in his journal, "I think I could write a poem called 'Concord.' For argument I should have the River, the Woods, the Ponds, the Hills, the Fields, the Swamps and Meadows, the Streets and Buildings, and the Villagers. Then Morning, Noon, and Evening, Spring, Summer, Autumn, and Winter, Night, Indian Summer, and the Mountains in the Horizon." The natural environment and humanized landscape of his locality became the subject matter of much of Thoreau's work, as he observed the impact of industrial and commercial expansion on nearby forests and on the equally fragile remnants of colonial community life in his hometown. He was inspired as well by what he called "the *arrowheadiferous* sands of Concord," the artifacts and other traces of Native American tribes that had once lived in the region. "There is scarcely a square rod of sand exposed, in this neighborhood, but you may find on it the stone arrowheads of an extinct race," he wrote. "Such are our antiquities. These were our predecessors." In all of these "familiar and surrounding objects" of Concord, Thoreau "lived the deepest and . . . the most at home": "Here I have been these forty years learning the language of these fields that I may the better express myself." [10]

These twin yearnings of Thoreau's, toward "living deeply at home," or, more concisely, *integration* (the experience of oneness with the world), and toward *self-expression*, have long been identified as two of the fundamental impulses of the culture of Romanticism, of which Transcendentalism was the major American variant. Romanticism, a designation given by scholars to the broader cultural and intellectual transformation of the trans-Atlantic Western world during the first half of the nineteenth century, arose out of the novel experience of free, liberated individualism amid the collapsing hierarchies and verities of revolutionary Europe and America. "We are the changing inhabitants of a changing world," Emerson wrote in 1827. "There are new men, new lands, new thoughts," he added in his major essay *Nature* (1836), of particular influence on Thoreau: "Let us demand our own works and laws and worship."[11] As older social bonds and cultural beliefs were eroded, new ones had to be forged—such was Emerson's prescription, and Thoreau's aspiration.

In previous centuries, a unitary order was believed to reign throughout the social, natural, and supernatural world. Earth lay at the center of harmonious celestial spheres, and humanity lay in God's eye. Every soul and creature had its allotted place in a chain of being, progressing from the lowliest worm upward through the higher animals, to semi-angelic (or semi-brutish) man, and culminating in the godhead, creator and mover of all things, as the Church and Bible taught. Similarly, human society fell into a pyramid of ranks and degrees of eminence and dependence, from the slaves and servants at the base up to the commoners, nobles, and the king at the apex. So too each household and clan was arrayed under a patriarch, with men over women, eldest over youngest, and family members over domestics. Every single individual was enmeshed and enfolded within and in all ways constituted by his or her position in this order, an order of superiors and inferiors, orthodoxy and authority, custom and tradition, faith and superstition. Romanticism emerged in the aftermath of intellectual, cultural, political, economic, and social challenges—modernizing revolutions—that had broken down this order. The Reformation undermined the authority of the One Church and gave new emphasis to individual faith and conscience. Science displaced humanity from the center of the cosmos, which furthermore was discovered to have a law-governed, automatic, clocklike regularity, without need of divine intercession. Early modern commercialism and capitalism legitimized and encouraged individual acquisitiveness and mobility. Kings and aristocracies were overthrown, and slavery was questioned, leveling the old hierarchies still further. By the late eighteenth century, a monumental break in history was perceived to have taken place, relegating this older, medieval order irretrievably into the past to the extent that the formerly accepted way of things was now known as the ancien régime. By the turn of the nineteenth century, the individual (specifically, the white male individual) was left to fend for himself, so to speak, to find purpose and meaning in the absence of all of the encompassing institutions, associations, and relationships into which his ancestors had been born. By comparison, his world now was fragmented, incomplete, changeful—and permanently so unless some new principle of unity were discovered. As the German idealist philosopher G. W. F. Hegel wrote early in the century, "When the power of unification has disappeared from the life of man, when opposites have lost their living relationship and reciprocity and gained autonomy, the need for philosophy arises." [12]

Romantic artists and intellectuals like the Transcendentalists confronted this modern problem of existence at a time when industrialization and democratization were transforming advanced Western societies at a still greater rate and degree. As Emerson observed, newer social bonds and modes of personal identity were being created, which were more abstract and isolating yet more fluid and open than those of the ancien régime, centering on the nuclear family, the nation, the denomination, the party, the occupation, and the self. Legitimacy and belief—the sources of truth as America and other Western countries were coming to accept them—were also in transition and conflict. Reason and science were supplanting faith and revelation, secular philosophy was rivaling theology, conscience was bypassing churchly authority, and the ballot, rather than the wise edicts of the king, was now equated with the public good. In this era of tremendous flux, many traditional institutions and truths appeared to be corrupt and onerous to artists and intellectuals of the Romantic avant garde, who pressed forward the process of their erosion by training criticism on basic preconceptions and by imagining new forms, values, and ideas that showed the old ways to be obsolete. The ancien régime did not pass away easily in this period, however; its last great manifestation in America, the slave system of the South, required several decades of political agitation and a civil war to abolish.

Slavery, the Christian church in general, and the Bible in particular became principle objects of criticism by members of the Transcendentalist movement, Thoreau included. These elements of the traditional world appeared to them not only as hopelessly outmoded but as positively hurtful (if not ultimately evil) in their inhibition of the greatest good in the Transcendentalist's eyes: this-worldly self-realization, the attainment of one's unique inner potentialities and abilities. Yet if Thoreau and his fellow Romantics revolted against most of the institutions of the ancien régime, they also found equally objectionable much in the emergent values and behaviors of the modern, pushing, clattering bourgeois industrial world, even as their philosophy itself embodied in divergent and spiritualized form its central individualistic ethos. As a result many of the Transcendentalists, and Thoreau most extremely, lived in radical detachment and estrangement from conventional society, isolated and withdrawn from institutions and community, from the whole external world beyond their individual consciousnesses, to a profoundly felt and understood degree. "It is impossible for me to be interested in what interests men generally," Thoreau confessed in his journal. "Their pursuits and interests seem to me frivolous. . . . The most positive life that history notices has been a constant retiring out of life, a wiping one's hands of it, seeing how mean it is, and having nothing to do with it."[13] It was out of this condition of *alienation* (a third major impulse of the Romantic mentality) that Thoreau and the Transcendentalists sought *integration* and *self-expression*, which were simply the means for overcoming this intolerable state, for reconnecting with the world and finding a "home" there, on terms that did not compromise one's personal ideals and were not the terms of the "mass of men"—the terms, in other words, of an authentic, realized, "deliberate" life.

Borrowing from European progenitors and counterparts—Kant, Coleridge, Carlyle, and others—Emerson and the more prominent Transcendentalist theorists conceived this individualized and isolated condition of modern man as a problem of consciousness and epistemology: How did the solitary human mind obtain knowledge and truths about the world at large, the world outside and beyond it? The very framing of the question pointed to the crisis of authority and belief as it was manifested in philosophical, scientific, and theological areas of thought. In philosophy, the query represented the Romantic and Idealist reaction against the "skeptical philosophy of Locke," Emerson wrote in 1842, which "insisted that there was nothing in the intellect which was not previously in the experience of the senses," that the mind was originally blank and essentially passive. Similarly, scientific empiricism treated nature as the discrete, distant, and separate object of an observing mind, again positing an isolating gulf between the self and the world. While these varieties of empiricism were gaining legitimacy as the only reliable sources of truth, traditional sources, such as biblical revelation, were being undercut by literary and scholarly critiques that uncovered the historical and human (rather than the divine) origins of the Gospels. Intellect, creativity, and spirituality had seemingly been explained out of the realm of experience by the skeptical, empiricist worldview, just as they were being marginalized by the materialism of commerce and industry. Yet the Transcendentalists, or those individuals who would become part of the movement, still yearned for them. Emerson's famous vocational crisis of the 1830s was such a crisis of belief. He had become "a faint, heartless supporter of a frigid and empty theism," he admitted, even though his "faith is not less." A similar mentality afflicted Thoreau, adrift in his life at a loss: "I feel ripe for something, yet do nothing, can't discover what that thing is. I feel fertile merely." [14] Their impulse was to find a new ground of meaning and purpose, a new moral order to enfold and unify with the individual self as the ancien régime once had, albeit on the modern terms of freedom and individuality.

English Romanticism and German Idealism provided a solution to this crisis and to the problem of consciousness and epistemology, a solution that Emerson and his erstwhile disciple Thoreau were already predisposed to accept because of their American cultural and intellectual inheritance. They were participants with Marsh in the antebellum context of evangelical reform, with its assumption of self-perfectibility by the moral free agent, making ethical choices of his own free will. They too had grown up within the political culture of Jacksonian democracy, with its celebration of the common man. This democratic ideal (crucial to belief in self-government) had its intellectual roots in part within the Scottish Common Sense philosophical school of the late eighteenth century, whose writers were still widely read in the antebellum period. Their most influential idea was that every individual is endowed with an innate moral sense, the inborn ability to discern right from wrong. So the epistemological solution that the Transcendentalists garnered from

Coleridge and Kant must have had a familiar ring to it: "There was a very important class of ideas," Emerson wrote, "which did not come by experience, but through which experience was acquired," for "these were intuitions of the mind itself." To Emerson and other Transcendentalist philosophers, these "intuitions" organized experience of the world and made it comprehensible. They comprised an inner moral sensibility, one that enabled individual perception and revelation of the divine—because the intuitions themselves were divinely endowed. The individual consciousness was therefore an active, free, creative, and spiritual force, with little need for traditions or institutions to nurture its growth and development. "Man begins to hear a voice . . . that fills the heavens and the earth, saying, that God is within him," Emerson rejoiced not long after leaving his pulpit and before moving to Concord. "I find that this amazing revelation of my immediate relation to God, is the solution to all the doubts that oppressed me." For with this revelation the solitary mind moved toward the attainment of *integration*, reconstructing a new world of meaning and certainty out of the collapsed fragments of the old, so that "the world lies no longer a dull miscellany and lumber-room," Emerson wrote in *The American Scholar*, "but has form and order; there is no trifle; there is no puzzle; but one design unites and animates the farthest pinnacle and the lowest trench." [15]

To Emerson and the Transcendentalists, this consciousness of the divine in the world and within the self was most directly evoked by the contemplation of nature. Human institutions were corrupt and misleading. The personal God of Christian revelation was remote and mythical. Consequently, there remained only one seat in the world, in this world, for order and morality, for the beautiful and the good: *Nature*, whereby the divine revealed itself directly to the soul. This was the chief philosophical lesson that the young Thoreau was to learn from the Transcendentalists, a belief that was further reinforced for him through his predilection for pantheistic and animist Eastern religions. Emerson's *Nature* appeared in 1836, his *American Scholar* in 1837, and Thoreau read them both while still an undergraduate at Harvard. After graduation, he returned to Concord, where Emerson made him a member of his luminous salon, and Thoreau in turn acted as guide for his mentor in the world of nature beyond the salon, out in the Concord woods. There Emerson's "solution" to doubt and meaninglessness was made manifest. His spiritualizing doctrines obliterated the alienating distance between the self and the external natural world described by science, by the biblical concept of dominion, and by the workaday utilitarian treatment of nature as economic raw material. Emerson bespoke *integration* between humanity and Nature: "[B]ehind nature, throughout nature, spirit is present; one and not compound it does not act upon us from without, that is, in space and time, but spiritually, or through ourselves: therefore that spirit, that is, the Supreme Being, does not build up nature around us, but puts forth through us. . . . As the plant upon the earth, so a man rests upon the bosom of God." This condition of integration was experienced most fully in moments of philosophizing and poetic creation about nature (just as Emerson himself was doing in the above passage), because Nature itself symbolized spiritual truths, a conclusion that Thoreau took also from his reading of ancient Hindu works upholding (as one contemporary interpretation put it) "the unity and identity of all things in the Deity." Demonstrating that he had learned his lessons well, the mature Thoreau wrote to his journal in 1852: "My thought is part of the meaning of the world, and hence I use a part of the world as a symbol to express my thought." A subsequent entry, written late in life, revealed how deeply he had internalized Emerson's own terms and concepts: "Why, the roots of *letters* are *things*. Natural objects and phenomena are the original symbols or types which express our thoughts and feelings." Here was the central philosophic and aesthetic faith of Romanticism, that one's innermost self-expression, one's "thoughts and feelings," given natural forms (through metaphor and allegory), could literally attain a universal significance—could become a "rivet in the machine of the universe," as Thoreau exclaimed in *Walden*, articulating his personal achievement of integration: "This earth which is spread out like a map around me is but the lining of my inmost soul exposed." [16]

AS IMPORTANT as Emerson's Transcendentalism was in shaping Thoreau's thought, it would be a mistake to treat Thoreau as a mere disciple, or to assume that Transcendentalism encompassed all of his interests and insights. A mutual friend later recalled, "It was a quiet joke in Concord that Thoreau resembled Emerson in expression, and in tones of voice." Yet in deeper matters, "Thoreau was an imitator of no mortal." In time, observed another friend, "he ceased to be illustrator and personifier, or in any sense derived. His movements, which had been projectile, a recognition of the elder's . . . wholesome methods, now went far beyond them." Thoreau once described himself as something more than a Transcendentalist: "The fact is I am a mystic, a transcendentalist, and natural philosopher to boot"—and, one might add, a teacher, a surveyor, a local historian, and a skilled amateur scientist.[17] Far more than Emerson and the Transcendentalists proper, Thoreau confronted the natural world in ways other than the philosophic and poetic. He was a realist who believed that nature was actual and external to the mind, and increasingly during his lifetime, the comprehension of nature in itself rather than as a symbol in support of idealist or religious yearnings became his preoccupation. This is certainly not to say that Thoreau abandoned his profound desire for self-expression and integration. His attempts to understand and experience nature in the concrete wrought powerfully on his philosophy and poetry, and on his politics. Moreover, Romantic concepts and folk-agrarian ideals both educated him toward his own more radical constructions of the meaning and utility of nature. Nevertheless, his excursions to Maine and throughout eastern Massachusetts in the 1840s and 1850s, as well as his residence at Walden Pond, were to reveal to him a nature that could not always be grasped in a scholar's study or a scientist's notebook, a nature whose evasion of human purposes was the essence of its importance to him. These excursions led Thoreau to "the Wild."

It is clear that as a "natural philosopher" Thoreau understood that nature had no intrinsic meanings other than those given to it by humans. As he wrote, "Nature must be viewed humanly to be viewed at all. . . . The moral aspect of nature is a jaundice reflected from man." This was an essentially modern conclusion, which appeared repeatedly on rare but significant occasions in his writings. For us it may also be seen as a conceptual starting point for charting other, more conventional attitudes and definitions that he consciously and unconsciously projected onto his environment. Often these projections were decidedly benevolent and anthropocentric in character, despite (and probably because of) his discomfiting recognition of nature's absolute value neutrality.

"Let us wander where we will," Thoreau wrote in his journal, "the universe is built round about us, and we are central still." Floating down the lazy Concord River with his brother John in 1838—the first of his excursions—he could speak with confidence of "the grand security and serenity of nature": "She is very kind and liberal to all men." Several years later, out with his guides in the wilder woods of Maine, Thoreau still perceived himself to be in "blissful, innocent nature." Tellingly, he would sometimes personify his intimate Romantic relationship to the natural world: "It is as if I always met in those places some grand, serene, immortal, infinite, encouraging, though invisible companion, and walked with him." Or, variously, the never-married Thoreau marveled of himself "how rarely a man's love for nature becomes a ruling principle with him, like a youth's affection for a maiden, but more enduring! All nature is my bride." This literal passion for things natural was able to carry him into the condition of complete integration that he fervently sought, or so Thoreau believed: "The seasons and all their changes are in me. . . . Almost I believe the Concord would not rise and overflow its banks again, were I not here. . . . The perfect correspondence of Nature to man, so that he is at home in her!"[18]

Two elements of the Romantic conception of nature were to be crucial to Thoreau's idea of the wilderness and to his arguments for its preservation. The first devolved from the experience of integration— that humans were, or should be, in an *organic* relation to the natural world, part of a greater whole. The organic as metaphor was the central trope of Romantic artists and intellectuals. It shaped their very perceptions of reality, which was seen by them as holistically structured, complexly interrelated, metamorphically transformative, and incrementally evolutionary over time. Thoreau's own view was that "there is nothing inorganic," no aspect of reality that was not plastic and growthful: "The earth I tread on is not a dead, inert mass; it is a body, has a spirit, is organic and fluid to the influence of its spirit." Beyond its purely conceptual significance, the organic was also a normative, reconstructive way of imagining reality, a way to reintegrate Emerson's fragmented "lumber-room" of the world into a greater whole incorporating the self with all other objects and selves. When applied to humankind and nature, as Thoreau would have it, an organic relationship was a symbiotic relationship. "What is the relation between a bird and the ear that appreciates its melody?" Thoreau inquired. "Certainly they are intimately related, and the one was made for the other. It is a natural fact. . . . I see that one could not be completely described without describing the other."[19] In short, they were both elements of a greater and irreducible organic whole.

But as these words imply, the description of the organic, holistic character and interdependencies of nature could be problematic, which Thoreau well understood. In confronting its complexity he was provoked (like Marsh) to a critique of the limits of contemporary science. For Thoreau, the dry methods and narrow, static categories of taxonomic science were clearly insufficient: "The man of science, who is not seeking for expression but for a fact to be expressed merely, studies nature as a dead language." By "expression," of course, Thoreau meant an *aesthetic* experience or utterance, which to his mind was both a way of knowing and a way of relating to nature—a more profound, nonreductive, and nonexploitative way. This second of his Romantic insights with relevance for a wilderness ethos was illustrated by two famous incidents he describes in his account of the Maine woods. The first concerned his discovery of the phosphorescent "light that dwells in rotten wood," which was so suggestive of the living, organic, even animist quality of the natural world. The experience evoked this response: "I let science slide, and rejoiced in that light as if it had been a fellow creature. . . . A scientific *explanation*, as it is called, would have been altogether out of place there. That is for pale daylight. Science with its retorts would have put me to sleep. . . . It suggested to me that there was something to be seen if one had eyes."[20]

Broadened and deepened senses were needed to perceive the living, holistic totality of the natural order. Thoreau prescribed which "eyes" were most appropriate in an earlier set of reflections on "how base or coarse are the motives which commonly carry men into the wilderness," a fulmination against hunters and lumbermen brought to the fore by his party's killing ("murder") of a moose for sport. It was here that Thoreau explicated his long-influential concept of "highest use," that "every creature is better alive than dead." Science too often treated a glowingly organic nature in an abstract and reductive manner, as did the purely instrumental goals of the lumbermen, who reduced and destroyed the great intrinsic value of the forest wilderness and were "content to behold it in the shape of many broad boards brought to market." Against this exploitative worldview Thoreau posited the "eyes" of the poet—"he it is who makes the truest use of the pine" and who "understands its nature best," its "living spirit," and "will rather preserve its life than destroy it." An aesthetic approach to the environment was, according to Transcendentalist doctrine, revelatory of the "true and highest use" of nature because it was revelatory of the divine in the natural world; and because the aesthetic revealed the divine to the poetic soul, it was integrative and therefore created symbiosis. As Thoreau wrote of the glowing pieces of wood, "For a few moments I enjoyed fellowship with them." He summed up his concept of "highest use"—typically—as a personal ethic: to bring to the woods "a pencil to sketch or sing" rather than "an axe or rifle" was to pursue "employments perfectly sweet and innocent and ennobling," for "our life should be lived as tenderly and daintily as one would pluck a flower."[21]

There were other eyes besides those of the poet that might apprehend and follow this ethic. Thoreau's Romantic conception of nature was complemented and buttressed by a strong belief in many of the myths and values of folk life, frontier culture, and agrarian republicanism. To be "viewed humanly," he believed, natural scenes "must be associated with humane affections, such as are associated with one's native place, for instance." In this preoccupation with the indigenous, Thoreau the self-avowed "New Englander" reprised the actual environmental history of his region, which since the 1600s had witnessed a succession of cultural complexes shape the landscape. The communal, hunting-and-planting subsistence economy of aboriginal New England tribes, ruled over by the animate cosmos of the Corn Mothers and tended by the women farmers of each village, had been displaced with the arrival of European colonists and their institution of private property. Yet until the late eighteenth century, this colonial environmental regime had itself been considerably traditionalist; a rich body of folklore, woodcraft, and superstitions guided seasonal production and daily life. A "moral economy," often patrolled by women, set strictures on personal profit at the expense of the common good. Precapitalist barter networks among farmwives radiated throughout each community, and a common area for grazing, hunting, or firewood gathering could be found outside many towns.[22]

The ultimate extent to which both the Native American and colonial environmental complexes were then shunted aside after the advent of industrial capitalism is evident in Thoreau's own bifurcated assumptions about nature and gender. In this area of his thought he largely failed to break free of conventional prejudices. He was unable to recognize the centrality of native and colonial women's earlier roles in fostering less exploitative, more symbiotic economies for the New England landscape. Perhaps because of his personally confused sexuality (which was by turns heterosexual, homoerotic, and indifferent), Thoreau was also too quick to dismiss contemporary women as fellow nature lovers, the very people who might have been his strongest allies (Susan Fenimore Cooper, for example). The beauty and divinity of the environment were precisely those values that married women were being instructed to coax from home and garden, or to seek out in woods and pastures. Rhetorically at least, Thoreau adjudged such women as too "tamely bred" to grasp the larger natural world that their influence had been banished from. "Ladies" personified for him stifling social convention. But it is important to remember that Thoreau's own clinging to the household of his mother and sister belied this supposed alienation from bourgeois domestic virtues (recall his weekly dinners at the family table during his sojourn at Walden). In addition, on at least one occasion, Thoreau wrote admiringly of a young woman in the Concord area who planned to "live free" through her own personal retreat into nature. She "appreciates and can use that part of the universe as no other being can," he remarked; she was, in other words, on her way to becoming an authentic individual through nature. More fundamentally, Thoreau's search for alternative environmental ethics in the cultures of Native Americans and the New England folk signified his quest—like that of other male artists and intellectuals of the Romantic era—to reclaim the organic and holistic world of the Corn Mothers. Although vanquished by male-dominated industrial expansion, it survived in enough remnants for him to appropriate. Thoreau said more than he realized when he referred to nature with feminine pronouns, or when he spoke of making "her" his "bride." [23]

Preeminently for Thoreau, the straggling bands of local Native Americans represented a practicing embodiment of the kind of integrated, symbiotic, low-impact lifestyle that he upheld as the ideal. In the course of amassing over 3,000 pages of notes on the subject, he declared that Native American culture "reveals another and wholly new life to us," and he wondered "why, then, make so great ado about the Roman and the Greek, and neglect the Indian?" The primary lesson of his Maine woods encounter with the phosphorescent wood chips was how profoundly his Native American guides appreciated their beauty and mystery, in the face of which the white man's science "evaporates completely, for it has no depth": "Nature must have made a thousand revelations to them which are still secrets to us." Although he deplored their hunting habits and was disappointed in some individual Native Americans whom he knew personally, Thoreau's assertions of the superiority of Indian life and lore was indicative of his estrangement from middle-class American society in general. Native Americans provided him conceptual sanctuary and examples of alternative values and lifestyles. "I have much to learn of the Indian, nothing of the missionary," he declared of things natural. "In proportion as I understood the language, I saw them from a new point of view," in a "new light." Above all, the Indian was important because he "stood nearer to wild nature than we," dwelling within it in the proper and higher condition of "intimacy." By comparison to white bourgeois existence, Thoreau concluded, "the Indian's earthly life was as far off from us as heaven is." [24]

Nevertheless, Thoreau's pointed praise of Native American culture should not be taken as a blanket condemnation of white civilization, but merely of its modern corruption. As Susan Fenimore Cooper spoke of in her *Rural Hours* (a book that he is known to have read), Thoreau also found among the humbler farm and town folk of his locality examples of humans living well with their environment. He mythologized them into the likeness of the hardworking, virtuous Roman farmers of Virgil's

Georgics, which remained perhaps his favorite classical work. He took inspiration as well from American agrarian myth and history, as shown in his *Week on the Concord and Merrimack Rivers*, where he pauses to celebrate

> rude and sturdy, experienced and wise men, keeping their castles, or teaming up their summer's wood, or chopping alone in the woods, men fuller of talk and rare adventure in the sun and wind and rain, than a chestnut is of meat; who were out not only in '75 and 1812, but have been out every day of their lives; greater men than Homer, or Chaucer, or Shakespeare, only they never got time to say so. . . . Look at their fields, and imagine what they might write, if ever they should put pen to paper.

Romantics have long been distinguishable by their nostalgia about the traditionalist folk, who were exemplars of the integrated world that Romantics hoped to establish in modern terms. The art with which New Englanders could shape their landscape, melding into it, did not escape Thoreau's notice when he floated past it or put ashore. The "old gray structures" of some canal locks, for example, "with their quiet arms stretched over the river in the sun," seemed to him like "natural objects in the scenery." The "lock-men's houses" were "humble dwellings, homely and sincere, in which a hearth was still the essential part," with a "small patch of corn and beans" and "some running vine over the windows," situated "high on a leafy bank." Admiring them, Thoreau exclaimed in his most idealistic Romantic mode, "I have not read of any Arcadian life which surpasses the actual luxury and serenity of these New England dwellings." The tiller of a famous bean field himself (featured in *Walden*), he could soar equally high in his praise of agrarian pursuits, as he wrote in his journal: "What noble work is plowing, with the broad and solid earth for material, the ox of fellow-laborer, and the simple but efficient plow for tool! . . . You turn over the whole vegetable mould . . . and put a new aspect on the face of the earth. It comes pretty near to making a world." In Thoreau's eyes, the two great republican virtues of this heroic agrarian existence were among the chief human virtues, the pursuit of which finally led him to the bank of Walden Pond (where he wrote *Week* with its mythologization of the folk) to "live simply and eat only the crop which he raised, and raise no more than he ate, and not exchange it for . . . luxurious and expensive things," but instead become "more independent than any farmer in Concord."[25]

Thoreau's embrace of the homely folk and agrarian values of simplicity and independence gave him a certain sympathy for life on the frontier, even as his emerging nonexploitative wilderness ethic implicitly rejected it. In *The Maine Woods* (1848, 1864), which is considered to be Thoreau's most environmentally enlightened work, it is at first surprising to come across passages of homage to pioneer aspirations, quite in contrast to Marsh's demonization of them:

> The mode of clearing and planting is to fell the trees, and burn once what will burn, then cut them up into suitable lengths, roll into heaps, and burn again; . . . for a first crop the ashes sufficing for manure, and no hoeing being necessary. . . . Let those talk of poverty and hard times who will in the towns and cities; cannot the emigrant who can pay his fare to New York or Boston pay five dollars more to get here . . . and be as rich as he pleases, where land virtually costs nothing, and houses only the labor of building, and he may begin life as Adam did?

At Walden, although he was actually living on land Emerson owned, Thoreau established his "economy" in terms of "squatter's rights," and he did a fair amount of tree-felling and field-clearing himself—all in quest of the ultimate freedom and self-reliance out of American frontier mythology, the political economy that he believed prerequisite to Romantic integration and self-expression.[26]

Yet this same project of Thoreau's also reconfigured frontier values into something radically beyond (and in contradiction to) their mainstream meanings. In *The Maine Woods*, his wonderment at the large expanse of landscape there "virtually unmapped and unexplored," where "still waves the virgin forest of the New World," was not the avidity of the claim-locater, promoting a vision of well-tended homesteads. Rather, the source of the Maine forest's daunting attraction was its very emptiness, "grim and wild . . . like a desolate island, and No-Man's Land," where "prevail no forest laws but those of nature": "No clearing, no house." Thoreau rarely if ever used the word "frontier," preferring instead his inversely defined "wilderness," all of the biblically enjoined pitfalls of which—its paganism, its anarchy, its barbarism—he reconceived as moral wellsprings and assets, particularly for alienated free-spirited loners like himself. "I love Nature partly because she is not man, but a retreat from him"—a telling genderization of nature for a lifelong bachelor to make. "None of his institutions control or pervade her," Thoreau continued in this 1853 journal entry. "None of the joys she supplies is subject to his rules and definitions." Paradoxically, the value of wild lands was destroyed rather than increased by permanent human occupation. The only way to reap the value of the wilderness was to become a "sojourner" there, leaving behind, however briefly, all "worldly engagements": "When I would recreate myself," Thoreau wrote in his essay "Walking," "I seek the darkest wood, the thickest and most interminable and, to the citizen, most dismal swamp. I enter a swamp as a sacred place, a *sanctum sanctorum*." [27]

Thoreau might have found, and usually did find, this Transcendentalist comfort in "desolate" and "dismal" wild places. He had his belief in natural symbolism and symbiotic integration to keep him company there. But the bleak prospect of empty wilderness itself worked a transforming influence on his thought, carrying his conception of nature beyond even the radicalizing conclusions of the Romantic worldview, and—when he could muster courage to behold it—beyond containment within any human concerns. It was the final chilling biocentric logic of his understanding that "Nature must be viewed humanly to be viewed at all" and that "she is not man, but a retreat from him"—not his "bride," but rather, an alien "other." Some scholars have suggested that Thoreau's benevolent, anthropocentric conceptions of nature became complicated by the violent death of his brother John from lockjaw in 1842. The historian Henry Adams witnessed the death of his own sister from the same cause in 1870, and his reactions may provide some clues to the full implications of Thoreau's response. After seeing the "fiendish torture" to which tetanus subjected his sister, it seemed to Adams that "he had never seen nature,—only her surface,—the sugarcoating that she shows to youth." With black bitterness, Adams wrote of his sister's death that "Nature enjoyed it, played with it, the horror added to her charm, she liked the torture, and smothered her victim with caresses." Thoreau himself reportedly exhibited symptoms of lockjaw "from his sympathy with the sufferer," so profoundly did the shock of his brother's sudden illness affect him. In the immediate aftermath of his brother's demise, he confessed to being "denaturalized," a repulsion that manifested itself on the practical level as a loss of all interest in his usual outdoor pursuits. Although Thoreau of course eventually did return to the outdoors, a family friend recalled that twelve years later he "started, turned pale, and could hardly overcome his emotion when some reference to John was made."[28] Perhaps a more subtle and persistent "denaturalization" remained with him besides his grief. In effect, it meant an undermining, in his eyes, of nature's kindly anthropocentrism and a fuller revelation of the meaning and *experience* of its biocentric character.

There are, for example, his radically biocentric thoughts in an oft-quoted passage from an essay recounting his 1846 excursion to Maine, where he took time to climb alone up to the violently turbulent summit of Mt. Ktaadn, clouds roiling and streaming around his perch on bare rock. "[W]e have not seen pure Nature, unless we have seen her thus vast and drear and inhuman," he noted, following out this train of thought until he was carried away from his Transcendentalist faiths into an abyss of meaninglessness—yet closer to "actual" nature:

This was that Earth out of Chaos and Old Night. Here was no man's garden, but the unhandseled globe. It was not lawn, nor pasture, nor mead, nor woodland, nor lea, nor arable, nor waste land. It was the fresh and natural surface of the planet Earth, as it was made forever and ever, . . .— so Nature made it, and man may use it if he can. Man was not to be associated with it. It was Matter, vast, terrific, —not his Mother Earth that we have heard of, . . .—the home, this, of Necessity and Fate. There was clearly felt the presence of a force not bound to be kind to man. . . . What is this Titan that has possession of me? Talk of mysteries! Think of our life in nature, —daily to be shown matter, to come in contact with it, —rocks, trees, wind on our cheeks! the solid earth! the actual world! the common sense! Contact! Contact! Who are we? Where are we?[29]

On this particular trip, Thoreau found it a "relief" to descend again into the cultivated valleys where nature might "smile" tamely. But in other years he revisited "pure Nature" as he had seen it on Ktaadn, confronting and shrinking from it at Walden and during trips to the seashore of Cape Cod in the early to mid-1850s. In the famous chapter in *Walden*, "Spring," Thoreau included images of a "vulture feeding on the carrion which disgusts and disheartens us" and of "a dead horse in the hollow by the path to my house, which compelled me sometimes to go out of my way." His solace, his "compensation" for this look at a violent and destructive *Darwinian* nature, became apparent to him only from a far distant perspective, a self-annihilating immersion in natural processes that was integration of a sort, though hardly nurturing and fulfilling: "Nature is so rife with life that myriads can be afforded to be sacrificed and suffered to prey on one another; that tender organizations can be so serenely squashed out of existence like pulp. . . . The impression made on a wise man is that of universal innocence. Poison is not poisonous after all, nor are any wounds fatal." Significantly, Thoreau had used much the same monistic, naturalistic language in correspondence with Emerson written soon after his brother's death: "How plain that death is only the phenomenon of the individual or class. Nature does not recognize it. . . . It is as common as life." Despite what classical Stoic philosophy and modern Darwinism had taught him, Thoreau did "recognize" death, and his fragile and sometimes facile equanimity toward it was not easily maintained, especially when the "tender organizations" squashed were his fellow men. Looking out on the "wild and unfathomable" ocean from the vantage of a "wild, rank" Cape Cod beach strewn with the shipwrecked "carcasses of men and beasts together . . . rotting and bleaching in the sun and waves," he knew what he saw: "There is naked Nature,—inhumanly sincere, wasting no thought on man." Again he sought "compensation" by attempting to domesticate this vista, analogizing it with more comforting and familiar places. "A pond in my native town, only half a mile long, is more than one hundred feet deep. . . . The ocean is but a larger lake." Yet in the end it threatened to overwhelm him, his frames of reference, his philosophy:

As we looked off, and saw the water growing darker and darker and deeper and deeper the farther we looked, till it was awful to consider, and it appeared to have no relation to the friendly land, either as shore or bottom . . .—over that ocean, where, as the Veda says, 'there is nothing to give support, nothing to rest upon, nothing to cling to,' I felt I was a land animal.

The man in a balloon even may commonly alight on the earth in a few moments, but the sailor's only hope is that he may reach the distant shore.[30]

So too Thoreau maintained his belief in the "moral" meanings "reflected" onto nature from humanity, from himself. In his posthumously published account *Cape Cod* (1865), he was a "land animal" very literally. The majority of the work turns its back on the ocean and surveys the local history and landscape of the Cape's narrow peninsular arm. In a broader sense, Thoreau ventured to "pure nature" only occasionally in person and in his writings. For the most part he stayed conceptually ashore on the firm ground of Transcendentalism, folk-agrarianism, and (as will be seen) science. He staved off the implications of biocentric indifference to man by stolid pronouncements of a faith in anthropocentrism, incongruous yet reassuring. He could convince himself on occasion that "naked Nature" had no value separable from human desires: "What is Nature unless there is an eventful human life passing within her?"[31] And he might have further reassured himself that even an acknowledgement of the natural world's biocentric obliviousness to man was an insight of the human consciousness. But Thoreau's exposure to the ultimately "untameable" and autonomous reality of wild Nature left its imprint on all areas of his thought—his larger understanding of nature, his personal ethics, his politics in general, and his preservationism in particular. Not only in empty wilderness but in all of these realms of his concern, Thoreau would conclude, "the Wild" did or *should* operate as animating principle.

Ironically, in his later years Thoreau expressed misgivings over self-perceived constrictions and limitations entering into his thinking. Rather than remaining free, open, poetic, and transcendental, he wrote, "I fear that the character of my knowledge is from year to year becoming more distinct and scientific; that, in exchange for views as wide as heaven's cope, I am being narrowed down to the field of the microscope. I see details, not wholes nor the shadow of the whole." An editor of Thoreau's journal reports that, in fact, vast "deserts of writing" filled the final volumes, "minute notations of things measured and counted, mostly in the lifeless style of professional scientists." It is noteworthy too that Thoreau obtained employment around Concord as a surveyor in the 1850s; no occupation would seem to be more cold and calculating in its approach to landscape—this was the "dry knowledge" he referred to in the quotation. One might speculate that Thoreau's greater reliance on scientific methods of explanation as a way of relating to nature (in spite of his continued criticism of them) occurred because of his shocking encounters with the chaotic scenery of Ktaadn and Cape Cod, that consequently he needed the sense of certainty provided by laws, classifications, and formulae, that, in other words, he needed a knowable Nature, just as he found it in the smiling, cultivated valleys. Yet Thoreau's self-consciousness about the pitfalls and limits of scientific knowing would seem to indicate that he possessed a more complex and ambivalent attitude toward science: it was for him both more and less than a prop for certainty. "Science," he wrote in a comparatively rare moment of frank enthusiasm, "sees everywhere the traces, and it is itself the agent, of a Universal Intelligence." His invention of a superior process for making pencils in his father's workshop is often cited as exemplifying this more positive attitude toward science and technology as well as an adeptness in their use, in spite of his reputation as champion of threadbare primitiveness. Moreover, he was a member of Boston's Society of Natural History, and he collected local specimens for the renowned Harvard scientist Louis Agassiz. Thoreau read works of scientific natural history voraciously (including Agassiz, Lyell, Linnaeus, and Darwin) and seems to have been contemplating his own massive study of the Concord environs as a successor to his great work, Walden. Though the book was never finished, Thoreau compiled and organized ten years of observations into hundreds of pages of description, charts, and lists so detailed and intricate that one scholar has called the project nothing less an attempt to capture the "ecology" of the area.[32]

Science, then, for Thoreau could be a means toward apprehending the order of nature and thereby uncovering the divine. Its incisive tools, increasing his understanding of his locality, could lead him into a state of integration. But science never seemed sufficient in itself for these purposes; to Thoreau it missed the spiritual and especially the aesthetic dimensions of reality, which required the supplemental insights of folklore, poetry, and philosophy. In Thoreau's view, many of the tools of nineteenth-century science (as Marsh also discovered) were still blunt instruments. They might dissect and label individual facts and phenomena and fill the mind with wondrous detail, but they could not capture "wholes nor the shadow of the whole"—living, organically interconnected, ecological systems at work. In a central passage of *Walden*, Thoreau sought to convey one such "whole," and he made it another occasion to criticize science—even as science had given him the habits and techniques of observation to penetrate and appreciate the complexity of what he was seeing. The passage is from the chapter "Spring," and its theme—culminating the description of a sudden eruption of intricate formations of sand out of a thawing bank of clay—is that "there is nothing inorganic":

> As it flows it takes the forms of sappy leaves or vines, making heaps of pulpy sprays a foot or more in depth, and resembling, as you look down on them, the laciniated lobed and imbricated thalluses of some lichens; or you are reminded of coral, of leopards' paws or birds' feet, of brains or lungs or bowels, and excrements of all kinds. It is truly grotesque vegetation. . . . When the flowing mass reaches the drain at the foot of the bank it spreads out flatter into strands . . . gradually becoming more flat and broad . . . till they form an almost flat sand, still variously and beautifully shaded . . . till at length, in the water itself, they are converted into banks.

> I am affected as if in a peculiar sense I stood in the laboratory of the Artist who made the world and me,—had come to where he was still at work, sporting on this bank, and with excess of energy strewing his fresh designs about. . . . You find thus in the very sands an anticipation of the vegetable leaf. No wonder that the earth expresses itself outwardly in leaves, it so labors with the idea inwardly. The atoms have already learned this law, and are pregnant by it. The overhanging leaf sees here its prototype. . . . The whole tree itself is but one leaf, and rivers are still vaster leaves whose pulp is intervening earth, and towns and cities are the ova of insects in the axils.

Scientific knowledge did not suggest these holistic analogies and divine presences, Thoreau reasoned. To conventional science, the earth was "a mere fragment of dead history, stratum upon stratum like the leaves of a book, to be studied by geologists and antiquaries chiefly." [33]

After the publication of *Walden*, however, Thoreau became in the final years of his life more reconciled with science through his enthusiasm for Darwinism. One suspects that this interest in evolutionary theory emerged not only because it provided him with a potent set of concepts for unlocking Concord's natural history but also because it accorded with some of his deepest philosophical intuitions about ultimate reality. His would be a "science which deals with the higher law." A processive, developmental, organicist metaphor—the trope of the seed—had long permeated Romantic thought in general. Throughout Western culture, the more advanced thinkers were converging on an acceptance of the inherent and constant mutability of reality, and Thoreau was no exception. The earth was a "living earth" of "inexhaustible vigour," he believed, where creation was daily and ongoing, "still at work": "Earth is still in her swaddling clothes, and stretches forth baby fingers on every side. . . . There is an incessant influx of novelty into the world." Although Thoreau might have found daunting a nature indifferent to humans, he upheld its changeability as something sublime and liberating: "The very globe continually transcends and translates itself, and becomes winged in its orbit." [34]

Two of his last writings, both natural history studies, embodied this insight—"The Succession of Forest Trees" (1860) and the larger, unfinished manuscript into which it was incorporated, "The Dispersion of Seeds," part of a book-length project that Thoreau was revising at the time of his death. "We find ourselves in a world that is already planted, but is also still being planted as at first," he concluded at one point in his observations. "The consequence . . . is that almost every part of the earth's surface is filled with seeds or vivacious roots of seedlings of various kinds. . . . The very earth is a granary and a seminary, so that to some minds its surface is regarded as the cuticle of one great living creature." Despite his concern over being narrowed by science, Thoreau had discovered a natural world of on-going Darwinian processes by what was essentially an *ecological* method of scientific investigation, his effort to understand the workings of the Concord landscape as an organic whole. Like Marsh, he was especially attracted to the holistic method of Alexander von Humboldt. Using this method, he learned that wind, water, birds, animals, and humans were all agents that dispersed seeds and were implicated in the transformation of the surrounding forests. "Hence, we see how the character of a primitive oak wood may gradually

change from oak to pine," he noted, "the oaks gradually and succes-
sively decaying and not being replaced by oaks but by pines." Here was
no "mere fragment of dead history" but a glorious confirmation of one
of the fundamental truths of existence—where it should be confirmed,
in living nature.[35]

Thoreau's longstanding reservations over the limitations of science
and his intuition of processive changeability in nature were ultimately
reconciled within his concept of the "Wild." While he had been con-
ducting his research on the woods of his neighborhood, more qualms
about science had cropped up to give him pause. "I fear this particular dry knowledge may affect my imagination and fancy, that it will not
be easy to see so much wildness and native vigor there as formerly," he
wrote in 1858. Yet the end result of this dry knowledge, painstakingly
tabulated and cross-referenced, had proven that Concord's landscape
was profoundly mutable in ways he had not previously grasped, the very
oaks temporary residents. More grandly, he had now seen with his own
eyes the evidences of a Darwinian universe involved in "a sort of constant *new* creation." In his 1851 essay "Walking, or The Wild," Thoreau
had avowed that "Nature is a personality so vast and universal that we
have never seen one of her features." By the end of his life, he had
seen one or two—but there were more, many more, beyond his grasp,
hidden in the 700 pages of ecological field notes and charts in his possession. He still had no reason to revise the conclusions of "Walking,"
that the world was "infinitely wild," because it could never be known
completely, only partially: "The universe is wider than our views of it."
It therefore provided an unlimited setting for novel experience—for *freedom*. This insight explains Thoreau's startling contention that "a man's
ignorance sometimes is not only useful, but beautiful" because ignorance by this definition was personal potential for knowledge and experience, human potential in an open-ended universe—the "Wild."[36]

IN ITS OPEN-ENDED vastness and mutability, its wildness, nature
thus symbolized to Thoreau the *spiritual* truth of freedom, including,
above all, human freedom. Necessarily, this concept of freedom under-
lay Thoreau's political philosophy and activism. His politics, in turn,
shaped his proposals regarding wilderness preservation and natural re-

source use, inspiring and circumscribing them at the same time. For what Thoreau most valued in nature was not easily translated into laws and institutions.

Freedom for Thoreau had both a personal and a political meaning. In the personal realm, it was synonymous with self-expression and self-realization. Just as he marveled at the multitudinous and variegated forms in which nature might express itself, Thoreau stood in awe of the plasticity of human nature, the limitlessness of personal growth. Thoreau's was a deeper radicalization of the basic faith in opportunity and progress that was central to antebellum democracy. "The world is a fit theatre today in which any part may be acted," he wrote. "There is this moment proposed to me every kind of life that men may lead anywhere." Consequently, "I am freer than any planet." In Thoreau's estimation, Nature and human nature were essentially free, but all human institutions, wherein men acted not individually (each according to his unique nature) but en masse and therefore falsely, must stand contrary to freedom: "He [humankind] is constraint, she [Nature] is freedom to me."[37]

Followed as a personal ethic, this doctrine eventuated in Thoreau's strange uprooted "border life." Despite his agrarian beliefs, for example, he turned down his one chance to purchase a farm in 1841 because, he argued, "I must not lose any of my freedom by being a farmer and landholder." Later, while at Walden, he felt "more independent than any farmer in Concord" because he was "not anchored to a house or farm" of his own. He purposefully cultivated "simplicity" if not outright poverty because material possessions similarly encumbered the individual, "owned" the individual, diverting him from the elemental and higher things of existence. "By poverty," Thoreau wrote, his "diffuse and vaporous life" became "solidified and crystallized," or, switching to an organic metaphor, it became egg- or seedlike, a "silken web or chrysalis . . . which shall ere long burst forth a more perfect creature." The freedom that Thoreau celebrated and tried to enact was not just a negative one of absence of constraint (the conventional laissez-faire) but, within this wide-open context, a positive freedom of self-realization. "I desire that there may be as many different persons in the world as possible; but I would have each one be very careful to find out and pursue his own way." [38]

Thoreau's devotion to these freedoms defining his personal autonomy fed his self-absorption in outdoor pursuits and made him extremely averse to formal organizations. It is probable that his attitudes toward freedom would have remained at an abstract and philosophical level, that he would have remained always apolitical and withdrawn, in the absence of issues that might force him to react publicly, that is to say, politically. In 1842, he wrote from a transcendental distance, "The sudden revolutions of these times and this generation have acquired a very exaggerated importance. They do not interest me much." [39] But within five years of writing these words Thoreau was to be forced into politics, although it required the most blunt expressions of state power to provoke him—the slavery issue and the slavery-extending and imperialist Mexican War. Thoreau's uncompromising opposition to the slave system loomed constantly in the background of his thoughts on freedom, giving many of his political ideas shape and direction. For him, the great sin of slavery was much the same as that perceived by evangelical abolitionists: it abrogated the God-given moral free will of the slave's soul, denying the possibility of self-perfection. To Thoreau's non-Christian censure, it was the consummate violation of the "higher law" of freedom built into the very substance of Nature and human nature. Human bondage destroyed individual opportunity arising out of the condition of negative freedom, and in this way it foreclosed the positive cultivation of the unique inner self. Worse still, the enforcement of the slave system brought down government oppression even on free citizens, as Thoreau and his Massachusetts neighbors discovered to their outrage, with federal measures like the Fugitive Slave Law (1850). This law and others heated the nation's political atmosphere toward the conflagration of civil war and produced fevers in the minds of radicals like Thoreau, who, already alienated in his antisocial "border life" and accustomed to assuming his every thought had cosmic significance, responded by framing a starkly drawn politics of the autonomous individual conscience, the politics of the "majority of one."

Some have described Thoreau's general political leanings as libertarian, if not anarchist, in orientation. The motto "That government is best which governs least," so often ascribed to Thomas Jefferson as the central ideal of antistatist Jeffersonianism, actually leads off Thoreau's essay "Resistance to Civil Government," which goes further to propound governance "not at all." A careful reading of Thoreau's political philosophy will not reveal an extreme anarchist, but certainly a proponent of minimalist, localistic, nonintrusive, and strictly "expedient" government, performing those functions that citizens could not do better individually and, when and where they can, withering away. Thoreau was in favor of practical functions such as publicly maintained roads, public schools, and a public library. The latter two were designed to promote the "education, cultivation, [and] civilization" (or self-realization) of the individual, to the still unforeseen end of creating a self-sufficient citizenry fully capable of individual self-government, without external authority. Yet Thoreau's acquiescence in political community, even the relatively benign form known to the township, could be dissolved in controversies surrounding burning moral issues like slavery. As the self-described "majority of one" he rejected majoritarianism—particularly for national issues, which necessitated the largest display of mass democracy. "There is but little virtue in the action of masses of men," Thoreau believed, because to act morally one had to examine one's individual conscience, where (according to Transcendentalism) the divine "higher law" was inscribed and regarding which there must be no compromise.[40] Human laws framed by vote were creatures of compromise, as was the act of abiding by them, which most men did out of blind patriotism, mere apathy, or under threat of brute coercion.

Physical force was the primary basis of "civil government," Thoreau thought. He had reached this conclusion after being jailed for failing to pay taxes he declared to be supporting the Mexican War, and after years of hiding runaway slaves in flight from authorities via the Underground Railroad, which had a stop at his mother's house. To Thoreau's mind these means of personal "direct action" were the most legitimate form of political activity because they were "from principle," free and voluntary expressions of the "higher law" that superseded any law enforced by the state. "I think that we should be men first, subjects afterward," he wrote in "Resistance to Civil Government." As he had noted in Walden,

"It is not desirable to cultivate a respect for the law, so much as for the right." (Reportedly, he sheltered escaped slaves at Walden Pond as well.) Catalyzed by his rejection of duly legislated yet unjust slave laws, Thoreau's apolitical Transcendentalism, with its conception of an autonomous moral intuition, was thus transformed—politicized—into an ideology of the sovereign individual. The *individual*, rather than the *people* collectively, was "a higher and independent power, from which all [of the state's] own power and authority are derived," he declared. Against this sovereignty the will of the majority had precedence only because "they are physically the strongest"—and majoritarian democracy, which tolerated slavery, had no other claim to legitimacy than this, which was no claim at all. "Action from principle" dictated that each individual must personally resist the operation and enforcement of the unjust laws of the state, as Thoreau instructed in the most famous words from "Civil Disobedience": "If the injustice is part of the necessary friction of the machine of government . . . then, I say, break the law. Let your life be a counter friction to stop the machine." [41]

This ethic, as Thoreau knew, was an assertion of the "right of revolution," but it was the extreme to which belief in natural and transcendental freedom carried him when confronted by slavery. Appropriately, he found a metaphor in nature—the competitive Darwinian "state of nature" that human brutality exemplified—to express the fundamentally antagonistic relationship between the self and the mass democratic State:

[The state] is not armed with superior wit or honesty, but with superior physical strength. I was not born to be forced. I will breathe after my own fashion. Let us see who is strongest. What force has a multitude? . . . They force me to become like themselves. . . . I perceive that, when an acorn and a chestnut fall side by side, the one does not remain inert to make way for the other, but both obey their own laws, and spring and grow and flourish as best they can, till one, perchance, overshadows and destroys the other. If a plant cannot live according to its nature, it dies; and so a man. [42]

To resist further these "forces" acting upon him, Thoreau sought out as a "resource and a background" his most potent natural symbol of freedom, the wilderness. Nature, intrinsically free, was freest and "wildest" here, where it was uncluttered by human constructs. In coming to understand the social and political importance of wilderness (illuminated by slavery's dark light, by the pallid glow of bourgeois conformity, and the harsher glare of state coercion), Thoreau elaborated arguments advocating the general value of wilderness that would remain persistently persuasive for later generations of preservationist heirs. "I wish to make an extreme statement," he wrote in the opening of his essay "Walking, or The Wild," which rhetorically goes beyond even the trenchantly libertarian vein of "Resistance to Civil Government." He imagined a space of "absolute freedom and wildness," where the individual was abstracted out of membership in society and treated as "an inhabitant, or a part and parcel of Nature." This realm of absolute negative freedom was "a place beyond the jurisdiction of human governments," he wrote, and he added to this basic definition in his journal: it was "a room all to myself," or, variously, "a prairie beyond your law . . . a prairie for outlaws." This was the place, Thoreau vowed, "to which I would migrate,—wild lands where no settler has squatted," because "hope and the future for me are not in lawns and cultivated fields, not in towns and cities, but in the impervious and quaking swamps." This image of wilderness, of a landscape utterly void and empty save for a lone and "absolutely free" individual, was surely a "retreat from man." And with this image Thoreau offered so radical a definition of "absolute freedom" that in comparison virtually every other form of "freedom and culture merely civil" seemed oppressive. "Give me a wildness whose glance no civilization can endure," he wrote.[43] Wilderness, for him, was not only "free," it was also—in a personal, social, and political sense—liberating and subversive.

In such images, Thoreau conjured remote spaces off the map like that where a Maine Indian guide dwelled, places that expressed his own disenchantment with American oppression, "places where he might live and die and never hear of the United States." By this radicalized tangent his conceptualization of wilderness intersected with frontier mythology, celebrating not the line of settlement but the vast emptiness beyond it. Yet Thoreau did on occasion invoke more conventional interpretations of the frontier in his public utterances, especially those relating to American exceptionalism, to persuade his audience about the importance of wilderness. In his lecture "Walking," for example, he made his famous declaration, "Eastward I go only by force, but westward I go free," alluding to the myth of America as a New World of freedom distinct from the tyrannies of the Old. He continued in words that would have been familiar to nineteenth-century listeners: "I must walk toward Oregon, and not toward Europe. And that way the nation is moving, and I may say that mankind progresses from east to west . . . we go westward into the future, with a spirit of enterprise and adventure." He then clinched his argument with allusions to classical and racialist history that Marsh would have appreciated and that played directly to the patriotism of his audience:

> The West of which I speak is but another name for the Wild; and what I have been preparing to say is, that in Wildness is the preservation of the World. . . . Men plow and sail for it. From the forest and wilderness come the tonics and barks which brace mankind. Our ancestors were savages. The story of Romulus and Remus being suckled by a wolf is not a meaningless fable. The founders of every state which has risen to eminence have drawn their vigor from a similar wild source. It was because the children of the Empire were not suckled by the wolf that they were conquered by the children of the northern forests who were.[44]

By retaining contact with wilderness, Thoreau insisted, Americans (the descendants of the children of the northern forests) could fulfill their redemptive, world-historical destiny. He shared and believed in these myths, but like Marsh, he held that the attainment of progress, the realization of exceptionalism, would require his countrymen to reform their treatment of the natural world.

Yet, as was noted earlier, Thoreau's conception of wild nature, with its Transcendentalist meanings, could not be entirely contained within the conventional terms of frontier mythology. The Wild of which he spoke was not necessarily another name for the West. Others saw in the West a Promised Land of progress and opportunity, a space for homesteads and townlots on newly cleared grids of acres, a former realm of pagan darkness now brought under Christian dominion. This was the ordained mission that the Puritans had bequeathed to contemporary expansionist Americans, their motives never pure, as many a used-up landscape testified. Commerce had always commingled with faith, and faith had waned, or rather, commerce had supplanted it as the object of devotion. Thoreau's West, not the rhetorical one for lecture audiences but the one he saw for himself, was a different place, a weed-choked, virgin-forested setting for the "highest use" of aesthetic self-development, where humans could "witness our own limits transgressed," a "Holy Land" where the divine already resided, if sojourners would seek it out, glowing in phosphorescent wood.[45]

Furthermore, Thoreau's understanding of nature as *innately* wild, as a mutably organic force of "inexhaustible vigor" within any thicket not under human cultivation, shifted his attention away from equating the wilderness with the westering frontier proper and toward the woods and streams closer to home, interspersed with villages and fields. "It is vain to dream of a wildness distant from ourselves," he wrote in his journal in 1856. Everywhere nature afforded solitude and was "not yet subdued by man, its presence refreshes him," Thoreau observed in "Walking." And because it was ever changing, "it will never become quite familiar to you." He recalled of one of the farms that he had "contemplated purchasing" that he was "attracted solely by a few square rods of impermeable and unfathomable bog" in a corner of it, adding: "I derive more of my subsistence from the swamps which surround my native town than from the cultivated gardens in the village." He noted also that "there are square miles in my vicinity which have no inhabitant" and that he could "easily walk ten, fifteen, twenty, any number of miles, commencing at my own door, without going by any house." In his journal he came closer to the crux of the matter, as his concept of the "Wild" defined it: "I shall never find in the wilds of Labrador any greater wildness than in some recess in Concord, i.e. that I import into it." The observation of the wild in one's neighborhood was all a matter of looking at the world in the right way, of living within it poetically, and choosing "to front the essential facts of life." Thoreau did not even have to leave his door to experience the wild—he could find it within individual human nature "living deep," feeling the "primitive vigor of Nature in us," a state of being he articulated to his "Walking" audience through wilderness used as pure metaphor: "Life consists with wildness. The most alive is the most wild. . . . One who presses forward incessantly and

Thoreau's Cove, Walden Pond, nineteenth-century view
(Courtesy of the Concord Free Public Library)

never rested from his labors, who grew fast and made infinite demands
on life, would always find himself in a new country or wilderness, and
surrounded by the raw material of life." [46]

Perhaps Thoreau lifted his idea of wilderness out of the physical
world and into the metaphorical and spiritual, into the "interior and
ideal world," not only because of his mystical Transcendentalism but
also because of his naturalist's realism: he recognized that the physical
settings of wildness, remote and nearby, were disappearing. This idea
too would differentiate him from the mass of adherents to frontier mythology, for whom no end to open land was ever in sight—as his compatriot Marsh, who castigated them, well understood. Marsh arrived
at his conclusions primarily through the comparative study of diverse
foreign historical landscapes, but appropriately, Thoreau came to his
independent insights through observation of his locality, as he charted
some of the consequences of the early industrial revolution upon it.
One of the very coves of Walden Pond, for example, had been landfilled
to buttress an embankment for the railroad to Concord from Boston,
and when Thoreau lived "deliberately" there in the mid-1840s his cabin
was a scant 500 yards from the tracks. In 1853 he wrote of a newly constructed house in Concord that had done "irreparable harm to a large

section of country for walkers. It obliges us to take still more steps after weary ones, to reach the secluded fields and woods." Saddened over the absence of large wild animals from his neighborhood three years later, he expressed considerably deeper concern in a journal entry:

> [W]hen I consider that the nobler animals have been exterminated here . . . I cannot but feel as if I lived in a tamed, and, as it were, emasculated country. . . . Is it not a maimed and imperfect nature I am conversant with? Do not the forest and the meadow now lack expression? . . . I am reminded that this my life in nature . . . is lamentably incomplete. I listen to [a] concert in which so many parts are wanting. The whole civilized country is to some extent turned into a city. . . . I wish to know an entire heaven and an entire earth. All the great trees and beasts, fishes and fowls are gone.

Thoreau admitted that "Primitive Nature is the most interesting to me," but to his dismay he had observed on his trips to the northern woods that "Maine . . . will soon be where Massachusetts is. A good part of her territory is already as bare and commonplace as much of our neighborhood."[47]

In the course of mapping this "emasculation" of his region's landscapes, Thoreau arrived at a further rationale—an *ethic*—for wilderness that defined its value in a way even more radically divergent from the expansionist mentality than his Transcendentalism, folk-agrarianism, and libertarianism had carried him. For these keystones of his thought necessarily upheld wilderness in its relation to humans. His naturalist's eye and sympathy, however, furnished Thoreau with an inverted, biocentric perspective on the destruction he was witnessing, and nonhuman reasons why it must be stopped. "In order to avoid delusions," he wrote, "I would fain let man go by and behold a universe in which man is but a grain of sand." If on some disoriented and confused (yet insightful) occasions this biocentrism afforded him a fearful glimpse of indifferent "pure Nature," or gave him the solace of a self-annihilating philosophical naturalism wherein good and evil evaporated, it also allowed him to treat nature as an *inherently* moral and value-laden entity— a Transcendentalist's Nature with the symbolizing human consciousness abstracted out of the picture: "Man is but the place where I stand, and the prospect hence is infinite. It is not a chamber of mirrors which reflect me. When I reflect, I find that there is other than me." [48] For the purposes of wilderness advocacy, this "other than me" was a nature good in itself.

Just as he had reconstrued moose hunting into the "murder of the moose," Thoreau interpreted the cutting down of a very large and old pine tree near Concord in 1851 not as the creation of lumber but as the needless death of a living being. "A plant which it has taken two centuries to perfect, rising by slow stages into the heavens, has this afternoon ceased to exist," he mourned in his journal. "Why does not the village bell sound a knell? I hear no knell tolled." In the instant that the huge tree began to lean and fall, Thoreau recounted that the lumbermen (whom he called "manikins," emphasizing their inhumanity) could be seen "fleeing from their crime." The sight may have been particularly affecting to Thoreau because seven years earlier he had accidentally set fire to these same woods he so loved, a campfire having leaped out of control, finally burning 300 precious acres. It was one of the most mortifying experiences of his life ("I was a 'damned rascal,'" according to some of the owners), and although he very humanly tried to absolve himself ("These flames are but consuming their natural food"), it left him "a guilty person,—nothing but shame and regret." Sometime after the pine was killed he observed sadly of the Concord area that "every larger tree which I knew and admired is being gradually culled out and carried to the mill. . . . I miss them as surely and with the same feeling that I do the old inhabitants of the village street." [49]

By thus recasting the pursuits of hunting and lumbering into forms of "crime" and "murder" and by calling for a humane treatment even of trees, Thoreau was demanding their right as living entities to exist independent of human needs. The "true and highest use" of a tree or a wild animal, he argued, should be governed by the same "higher law" that provided guidance regarding antislavery and any other moral issue. Thoreau put this argument forward, virtually alone among all his contemporaries, during a period when the sphere of ethical inclusion was also being expanded to encompass the subordinated slaves of the South. Thoreau framed his equation of human rights and nature's rights, elevating the moral claim of the latter, in a central passage of *The Maine Woods*. Standing firmly on the fundamental doctrine that "every creature is better alive than dead," he declared: "The pine is no more lumber than man is, and to be made into boards and houses is no more its true and highest use that the truest use of a man is to be cut down and made into manure. A pine cut down, a dead pine, is no more a pine than a dead human carcass is a man." [50]

The thrust of these unsystematic pleas of Thoreau's on behalf of a heightened moral status for the natural world, with his implicit and explicit invocation of a language of criminality, ethics, and rights, culminated in two demands for reform. The first was workaday and attitudinal: the "highest use" of the pine, Thoreau believed, a use that recognized its inherent right to a full and free existence, would require a human-nature relationship of "reverence and humility," the "dainty" treatment of nature intuited and practiced by the poet, the Indian, and the folk. Yet, having few "delusions" about the moral fiber of his fellow modern countrymen, "Judge" Thoreau also groped toward more certain means of saving nature from its "vandalic proprietors," as he frankly suggested on one occasion (1857) when he was outraged at the destruction of a clump of favorite bushes: "[I]f some are prosecuted for abusing children, others deserve to be prosecuted for maltreating the face of nature committed to their care." Although in cooler moments he stopped short of advocating actual jail terms, the libertarian Thoreau was nevertheless compelled by "expediency" (and his own overriding moralism) to propose outright civic and legal protection of wild nature. Most men, he concluded late in life, "do not care for Nature and would sell their share in all her beauty, as long as they may live, for a stated sum—many for a glass of rum. . . . It is for the very reason that some do not care for those things that we need . . . to protect all from the vandalism of a few." [51]

Ostensibly, this argument might seem an odd one for an archindividualist critic of majoritarianism to make, invoking the authority of the community ("we") and, by extension, the power of government, to restrict the actions of individuals. It is clear, though, that the localistic Thoreau derived a measure of communitarian values from a belief in traditional neighborliness ("the duties of neighbors") and that he perceived wanton and self-interested destruction of flora and fauna to be violations of its informal strictures. Hence his anger over ill-placed house construction and the chopping down of familiar trees and bushes, all of which defaced a landscape that in some ancient sense "belonged" to everyone in the community. These sentiments of Thoreau's were rooted in the traditionalist concept of the village "common," an area of unfenced, unowned land in which each town member had a vested but not a proprietary right. More generally, the "common" also connotated a set of vaguer customs that allowed neighbors the right of ingress and egress on another's land, including the temporary run of it for hunting and fishing. These practices of the "common" were a survival of the ancien régime of Old World medievalism ("certain savage liberties [that] still prevail in the oldest and most civilized countries") that, as Thoreau well understood, were fast disappearing in bourgeois-commercial New England and elsewhere in America. As an avid walker of the countryside he was keenly aware of the rise of privatism: "It is true we as yet take liberties and go across lots . . . but we naturally take fewer and fewer liberties every year, as we meet with more resistance." He foresaw a time when "a few will have grounds of their own, but most will have none to walk over but what the few allow them." There seemed to be only one place in his vicinity where there was "an extensive 'common' still left"—the river: "Without being the owner of any land, I find I have a civil right in the river—that, if I am not a land-owner I am a water-owner. . . . In relation to the river, I find my natural rights least infringed on." [52]

Manifestly, Thoreau viewed the curtailment of common rights not just in communal terms but primarily as infringements on his individual liberty. The ruinous development and commercialization that "simply deform the landscape" and made it "more and more tame and cheap" precluded the direct solitary experience of wild nature necessary for self-realization. In this sense, the "expedient" of public protection of the land against individual destructiveness was no radical break from his libertarian predilections. Instead, it was another application of the basic maxims of good government as Thoreau defined them in "Resistance to Civil Government": government was essentially "an expedient by which men would fain succeed in letting one another alone," and at its best it could reveal "how successfully men can be imposed on, even impose on themselves, for their own advantage." To Thoreau these maxims were not contradictory, and to be sure, they reflected the widely held liberal-republican concept that government, the rule of law, was necessary to safeguard individual rights—from other individuals. In this sense, law and order was merely one service most expediently performed by government rather than by individuals. "Practically and as a citizen" Thoreau also saw why certain other public "impositions" (taxes for roads, schools, libraries) increased the opportunity and enlightenment of the individual and were to the common "advantage" of all individuals.[53] To this set of fundamental individual advantages (or interests) under public responsibility he would "fain" add the protection and preservation of natural areas from exploitation, so that all could enjoy the liberty and self-fulfillment of confrontation with the "Wild."

The phrase "natural rights," which Thoreau used to imply more than one level of allusion and meaning, may be tapped further to sum up the political philosophy of *preservationism* that he largely originated. In this particular usage, he knew that readers in his time would connect the phrase to John Locke's idea of inherent human rights and liberties that preceded and superseded government and what Thoreau as a Romantic understood as universally free and undetermined human nature. Most directly he intended the phrase to assert his "civil right" (and older "commoner's" right) to wilderness, where human nature in its integration and symbiosis with wild Nature was at its freest and most protean and closest to the divine. Yet this experience (and its degree of "absolute freedom") would be unobtainable unless some recognition was made of "natural rights," in the biocentric sense of *nature's* rights, to unspoiled health and beauty in autonomous existence apart from human economic activity—"some life pasturing freely where we never wander." In a late journal entry dated 1861, Thoreau applied these doctrines to a dispute involving the private ownership of the forbidding summit of Mt. Washington: "I think that the top of Mt. Washington should not be private property; it should be left unappropriated for modesty and reverence's sake, or if only to suggest that earth has higher uses than we put her to."[54]

The means, the public means, by which all of these "natural rights" must be guaranteed were suggested in various brief passages of Thoreau's writings, wherein he helped to originate the idea of local and national public nature parks. Certainly, publicly owned urban parks were not unknown in the United States, and by the last years of Thoreau's life, their design was entering a golden age under the leadership of famed architect Frederick Law Olmsted (see Chapter 3). But Thoreau had something rather different in mind than the carefully crafted and welcoming landscapes offered by Olmsted and his counterparts. He seems to have derived his most direct inspiration for the forest park idea from several older strands of custom and tradition, according to which the human presence in a designated area of land might be regulated and restricted. The tradition of the common was most familiar to him as a New England villager, and its influence was most evident in his hope for the establishment of local, municipal forest parks: "Each town should have a park, or rather a primitive forest, of five hundred or a thousand acres, where a stick should never be cut for fuel, a common possession forever, for instruction and recreation. We hear of cow-commons and ministerial lots, but we want men-commons and lay lots, inalienable forever. . . . All Walden Wood might have been preserved for our park forever." While his reference to the commons tradition emphasized that the parks were to be public, democratic institutions, Thoreau clearly envisioned a common unlike any other, one that was not designated for collective exploitation, but quite the opposite. He turned to another early model of land regulation to underscore this point—the private game parks of European gentry, aristocrats, and royalty. As he wrote in The Maine Woods, "The kings of England formerly had their forests 'to hold the king's game,' for sport or food . . . and I think that they were impelled by a true instinct. Why should not we, who have renounced the king's authority, have our national preserves . . . our forests, not to hold the king's game merely, but to hold and preserve the king himself also, the lord of creation,—not for sport or food, but for inspiration and our own true recreation?"[55]

Thoreau invoked the "old forest laws" precisely because he conceived the preserves as freely open institutions. These laws had the reputation of being strict and exclusivist, if not harsh, in their enforcement, far more so than the more vague and equitable communal customs governing the common. They decreed whom might hunt wild animals, chop wood, or simply gain access to a meadow or forest adjoining an estate;

wardens patrolled expressly to preserve herds of deer and other game. In *Walden*, Thoreau quoted an account of these laws which noted that "the encroachments of trespassers . . . were 'considered as great nuisances' . . . and were severely punished." So Thoreau's analogy of a royal-style preserve for the nation may have been carefully chosen: all too well acquainted with the damage perpetrated on the common landscape of his neighborhood by his own neighbors, and cognizant as well of the frontiersman's unrestrained practices of squatting and wastefulness, he knew that the parks proper might furnish a more thoroughgoing protection necessary to save woods and wildlife from everyday destruction—"or shall we . . . grub them all up, poaching on our own national domains?" he queried rhetorically.[56] This new form of common, in an unprecedented departure from communal tradition and expansionist history, would be reserved for "highest use" only.

Despite his deep understanding and persuasiveness of the need for them, Thoreau did not (or could not) take his notion of local and national preserves beyond this level of rhetoric, toward any concrete proposal. Certainly he never had any intention of organizing support for their creation—a fair enough evaluation of his efforts, given that reform organizations for a variety of other causes were by his time permanent fixtures of the process of American politics. In later years, John Muir, his most immediate heir to the preservationist cause, would understand the necessity of political action and pursue it. Thoreau was limited in his vision and activity for much the same reasons that Marsh was: there were as yet few if any precedents in America for government activism on behalf of saving natural resources, and European models could at best be grafted domestically only in principle, if at all (which Thoreau discovered with his idea of democratized royal game parks). As was true of forest conservation, federal efforts on behalf of preservationism had been quite meager during the antebellum period. The fate of the nation's first small natural "reservation" is instructive of the ideological barriers still to be overcome: Congress remained much more interested in distributing public lands than in saving them, and Americans much more dedicated to possessing than merely "visiting" them. In 1832, the Hot Springs Reservation was established in the Arkansas Territory when Congress withdrew from private settlement approximately four sections of public land (2,529 acres) surrounding the rare natural feature. The area was "left unappropriated" because (as a lawyer who later attempted to appropriate it observed) "the hot springs were too valuable for an individual to own" — prized for their medicinal powers rather than their scenic appeal, yet with resort potential nevertheless. Consequently, the tiny reservation was besieged for decades by prior claimants and squatters whose lawsuits reached the Supreme Court in 1876. The Court rejected their claims, but Congress rescued them the following year by authorizing a commission to grant or sell off the reservation's lands to those with plausible cases. The original tract was thereafter whittled down to slightly more than 900 acres, although in a brief bow to public spiritedness (1878) Congress directed that bathhouses and free baths be made available to all visitors. In time, the private lots of the city of Hot Springs engulfed and intermingled with the remnants of the reservation, which was not substantially expanded until the 1930s.[57]

Surely the larger legal and political climate of Thoreau's day, carving up the Concord countryside and whittling the Hot Springs reserve, would have presented difficulties for the most devoted preservation activist. Yet Thoreau was not to be that activist. It was above all his own personal political philosophy and experience that hindered him from developing a specific preservationist agenda. Romantic assumptions had convinced him of the efficacy of "self-reform" as the primary means to social change. Human nature was free and malleable and could will itself toward the good. Each individual had to place himself in right relation to the divine "higher law," and then harmony and progress would result. "The true reform can be undertaken any morning before unbarring the doors. It calls for no convention," Thoreau believed. "I can do two thirds of the reform of the world myself." [58] Thus he remained aloof from any organized form of politics — parties, reform groups, or even the radical alternative of Brook Farm, an experimental utopian enclave full of eccentric individualists like himself.

Thoreau did nonetheless seem to recognize some degree of public interest and collective role in establishing parks and protecting forests. True to his notion of self-reform, his proposed means for acquiring parklands was for "any owners of these tracts [who] are about to leave the world without natural heirs . . . to abandon their possession to all" and "give a forest or huckleberry-field to Concord." This plea for individual beneficence was also made on behalf of the larger public good, of the obligations one incurred: "A town is an institution that deserves to be remembered." Thoreau's more suggestive statements on this theme appeared in the final pages of his late, unfinished manuscript "The Dispersion of Seeds." Years of surveying the Concord woods and dealing with local landowners seem to have had their effect on him, since the subject he took up was forestry. Contrary to the stereotypical view of Thoreau the jealous lover of pristine nature, he cared deeply about the cultivated rural environs of his neighborhood, in accordance with his embrace of folk-agrarian values and lifestyles. Forestry practices would allow his thoughtlessly exploitative neighbors to live more symbiotically with the processes and cycles of nature. "The history of a woodlot is often, if not commonly, here a history of cross-purposes," he wrote, "of steady and consistent endeavor on the part of Nature, of interference and blundering with a glimmering of intelligence at the eleventh hour on the part of the proprietor." Yet "if we attended more to the history of our woodlots" and learned the sequence and means of succession, Thoreau asserted, "we should manage them more wisely." The implication was that proper individual "management" of private forestland would occur, as Marsh was also concluding, primarily through self-reform. But Thoreau underscored that the common membership that landowners shared in the local ecosystem of Concord required some acknowledgement of collective responsibility. The "dispersion of seeds" ignored all property lines, and what one farmer did on his woodlot could unintentionally affect woodlots adjoining and distant. Why, Thoreau asked, should we "be dependent . . . on these windfalls from our neighbor's trees, or on accident? Why not control our own woods and destiny more?" As he had earlier implied with his resort to tough "old forest law" to protect his imaginary nature preserves, Thoreau here again decided that it might be "expedient" for government—local government—to take a hand where self-reform fell short, so that "men would fain succeed in letting one another alone." He ended the manuscript with the story of a local farmer who clear-cut and sold his woodlot of white pine, then burned off the oak seedlings that had sprouted under the pine canopy to plant the ground in rye, with the expectation that the oaks would regrow at his convenience. "A greediness that defeats its own ends," Thoreau exclaimed of the barren field, "for Nature cannot now pursue the way she had entered upon. . . . I am chagrined for him. That he should call himself an agriculturist! He needs to have a guardian placed over him. . . . Forest wardens should be appointed by the town—overseers of poor husbandmen." [59]

This traditionalist localism of Thoreau's (the main source of his narrow public-mindedness) made him amenable to membership in a political community encompassing his rural neighborhood and to positive measures in support of their education, livelihood, recreation, and husbandry. But it was insufficient to frame public policy on a larger national scale, with its clashing heterogeneous interests and shady compromises. This was impure "politics" that Thoreau despised and withdrew from, although it was politics as the rest of the country knew and practiced it. Indeed, Thoreau was much of his life so apolitical, so nature-solipsistic, that with a few exceptions his writings contain no sustained or very profound meditation on civics and government; the one significant exception was his essay "Resistance to Civil Government." Self-reformism and apolitical indifference led him to accept the basic shape of established government even as he found in great moral issues like war and slavery rationales not for structural change but for rejecting established institutions radically and completely. "Seen from a lower point of view," he wrote in "Resistance," "this State and this American government are, in many respects, very admirable and rare things, to be thankful for . . . ; but seen from a point of view a little higher . . . who shall say what they are, or that they are worth looking at or thinking of at all?" [60]

This ideological volatility, bursting suddenly from obliviousness to white-hot rejection, was a product of Thoreau's application to conventional politics his concept of innate and absolute freedom—the "Wild." It was an awesome outgrowth of thought tended in his wooded otherworldly solitude, which was undomesticable. When he carried its message to his fellow citizens, it translated into an individual "right of revolution," which could be (and has been historically) a powerful weapon of dissent against unjust laws and regimes. But the "Wild's" very absolutism could also lead one beyond all social contracts and moral restraints,

as when Thoreau himself endorsed the actions of the antislavery ter-
rorist John Brown, the perfect exemplar of his political philosophy and
its troubling final logic. As Thoreau admitted in an 1859 address, "even
though he were of late the vilest murderer," Brown was still a "transcendentalist above all," an "Angel of Light" who followed the injunctions
of his own self-defined "higher law" (which unfortunately made mas-
sacre an "action from principle"). Brown's martyrdom served only to reinforce Thoreau's disgust for institutional solutions: reform and justice
must remain "private and individual" pursuits, he wrote afterward.[61] In
the end, these conclusions stranded his preservationist agenda, such
as it was—in unpublished journal entries and passages in posthumous
books—a legacy that had to await the future.

IN THE CLOSING paragraphs of *Walden*, Thoreau recounts a New
England folktale that may be treated as emblematic of his life's work.
It is the story of "a strong and beautiful bug which came out of the dry
leaf of an old table of apple-tree wood, which had stood in a farmer's
kitchen for sixty years, . . .—from an egg deposited in the living tree
many years earlier still . . . which was heard gnawing out for several
weeks, hatched perchance by the heat of an urn. Who does not feel
his faith in a resurrection and immortality strengthened by hearing of
this?" Thoreau wondered, and continued: "Who knows what beautiful
and winged life, whose egg has been buried for ages under many con-
centric layers of woodenness in the dead dry life of society . . . may unexpectedly come forth from amidst society's most trivial and handselled
furniture, to enjoy its perfect summer life at last!"[62] Whether or not
Thoreau himself used it as a fresh way to restate the hackneyed author's
solace that "I write for posterity" (his first book had sold poorly), the
tale of the applewood bug is a fitting analogy for the subsequent history
of his influence on American society and culture.

Thoreau was not a political man in any pragmatic sense, and he certainly was no policy maker. His advocacy was that of an ethicist, a poet,
a teacher, a philosopher, or, combining all of these roles together, a minister and a prophet of the "Wild" (or so his admirers have beheld him).
"I am doing my part to educate my fellow-countrymen now," he once
commented revealingly of his self-perceived purpose.[63] His writings, in

other words, were not intended solely for himself or the universe. But to call Thoreau a prophet is to acknowledge that, like Marsh, his influence lay beyond his own era; it is to recognize that it lay on future audiences, those living in oppression and anonymity who were to find his ideals of freedom and individuality alluring, those existing under the denaturing effects of urban-industrialism who were also to become receptive to his words. In fact, should one choose to label Thoreau in general as a philosopher, it is arguable that, other than the twentieth-century reform theorist John Dewey, he has been the most widely influential in American history.

Ironically, a large measure of Thoreau's impact on later generations was to be in the political realm. To some, he supplied a powerful liberating solvent for breaking up obsolete systems of domination. It has long been acknowledged that the tactics of two of the greatest grassroots uprisings of modern times, the 1940s movement for Indian independence from British imperial rule led by Mohandas Gandhi, and the 1960s civil rights movement in America headed by Martin Luther King Jr., owed much to the inspiration of "Resistance to Civil Government." (Regarding what policies and programs they might pursue once self-rule was attained, however, "Civil Government" was silent; it was a solvent, merely.) Thoreau became as well over the decades an icon for all manner of libertarians and nonconformists. The commune dwellers of the 1960s, for example, embraced his celebration of a lifestyle of antimaterialistic simplicity. And in the role of patron saint of American environmentalism, Thoreau has shaped and continues to shape the values and goals of a movement that has been one of the most important in post–World War II American politics. His issue, wilderness preservation, was to become the nexus around which the modern movement proper was to coalesce, thanks especially to the efforts of admirers John Muir and Aldo Leopold and the respective organizations that they each cofounded, the Sierra Club (1892) and the Wilderness Society (1935). If twentieth-century Americans have been able to enjoy the experience of solitude in wilderness, it is a privilege attributable in part to the shared passion for wild nature that Thoreau helped to inspire in these two individuals. Muir, of course, became famous for his own solitary sojourns in wild nature, and Leopold, a federal conservation bureaucrat and academic known at the time only to professional peers, purchased a weedy neglected farm in Sand County, Wisconsin, during the same year in which the Wilderness Society was formed. That intimate spot of "native soil" became the setting for the "wide travels" through nature he wrote about in his acclaimed book A Sand County Almanac (1949), which was to be considered the so-called bible of the modern environmental movement.[64]

Preservationism for the purposes of recreation and self-renewal in nature was to comprise part of the mainstream of twentieth-century environmentalist thought and politics, the anthropocentric mainstream. But Thoreau was also to be cited perennially as moral authority for the more radical proponents of a biocentric agenda. His influence was most directly passed down through his first biographer, the British ethicist Henry S. Salt, who left a prestigious post at Eton to live the simple life in rural Surrey and who was the author of the widely-read Animals' Rights in Relation to Social Progress (1892). Others, too, out on the ever more extreme ramparts of the defense of nature, were to find Thoreau speaking to them in new and confirming ways from across a hundred years: deep ecology polemicists for "biocentric equality," tree spikers protecting forests ("A people . . . would begin by burning the fences and let the forest stand!"), and monkeywrenchers sabotaging rampant development ("I for one am with thee," Thoreau once told the fishes of the Concord River, blocked from swimming upstream by new construction, "and who knows what may avail a crowbar against that Billerica dam?").[65]

Some of Thoreau's radical descendants, however, were to judge him less than radical, if not rather tame, a man whose conception of the "Wild" could be found on the banks of a pond scarcely a mile outside town, adjacent to railroad tracks, and whose mother weekly sent him treats to eat—a man famously given pause by exposure to raw nature on Mt. Ktaadn, a place crowds of backpackers would later smile on. It is true that Thoreau in his "border life" conducted himself somewhat more diffidently than the brave persona of Walden might suggest. He needed human company even as he craved solitude; he had deep bonds to his hometown despite his alienated criticisms of it; he yearned for the physical and spiritual challenges of wilderness but at bottom preferred the poetic life of the mind among Concord's literary circle. Thoreau realized that as crucial as wilderness was to the individual and the nation, it could never be all-sufficient for the "deliberate" life, that it could not serve as a "permanent residence," as he wrote in *The Maine Woods*: "A civilized man . . . with his ideas and associations, must at length pine there, like a cultivated plant," if he were to remain in its "barrenness" for too long—a cryptic description, this "barrenness," perhaps allusion to Nature's awful indifference, threatening at the edge of consciousness to disperse such Muses to be found within it, or perhaps reference to that "absolute freedom" in the wild that, unfortunately, opened only onto empty space. As his late-expressed interest in forestry indicated, Thoreau's true idyll was instead a "partially cultivated country" like the Concord environs where he lived his "border life," "our own woods and fields,—in the best wooded towns . . . with the primitive swamps scattered here and there in their midst, but not prevailing over them." This was, he concluded, "the perfection of parks and groves, gardens, arbors, paths, vistas, and landscapes." [66]

Still other twentieth-century heirs of Thoreau, most particularly the regional planner Benton MacKaye, who wrote and lived alone in a rustic cabin in the small village of Shirley Center, Massachusetts, were to agree with this conclusion. MacKaye posited in *The New Exploration* (1928) that cosmopolitan, rural, and wilderness experience were all essential elements of the total human environment, each a necessary backdrop for the good life. Always, Thoreau had emphasized, there must be opportunity available for the poet, "from time to time," to "travel the logger's path and the Indian's trail, to drink at some new and more bracing fountain of the Muses, far in the recesses of the wilderness"—and then return to civilization. Surprisingly, amid all the defiant affirmations of individualism that pervade Thoreau's writings, a *social* vision did exist quietly and for the most part implicitly (in his homebody self, in his "wide travels" around Concord), a utopia of sorts, set within a mixed and varied "partially cultivated" landscape. Emerson had once inspired Thoreau to describe it: "In his world every man would be a poet, Love would reign, Beauty would take place, Man and Nature would harmonize." [67]

THERE HAS BEEN considerable puzzlement among scholars as to why Thoreau's last two large-scale projects, his natural history of Concord and what may have been a study of the region's Native Americans, were never completed. Did the Muses finally elude him? Were his famous last two words, naming the long-vanished subjects of books never to be written, expressions of regret? Seven hundred pages of lists and charts, 3,000 pages of notes had been accumulated daily over many years— yet there was no finished work to show for it, only a vast record of observation, reflection, and speculation about Nature and its inhabitants, a record of the endless process of thinking. "The Dispersion of Seeds," creditable as it may have been as a pioneering work of American ecology, contained very little poetry and virtually no flights of metaphorical fancy, just as Thoreau feared. Perhaps there was some personal, emotional reason, one now lost to posterity, why he could not write the successor to *Walden*, his life's great work. Or it may be that over the years Thoreau's understanding of the "Wild" had come to subtly preclude, in his own mind, any capture of the *whole* of nature, even of local nature, in a fixed, final statement.

"I am still a learner, not a teacher," he wrote in an 1856 letter; he was now "feeding omnivorously, browsing both stalk and leaves." He had hopes that by his holistic methods he would "be enabled to speak with the more precision and authority by and by,—if philosophy and sentiment are not buried under a multitude of details." There was the problem: "We can never begin to see anything as it is so long as we remember the scientific term which always our ignorance has imposed on it," Thoreau noted as he looked at the "constant *new* creation" around him. "Natural objects and phenomena are in this sense forever wild and unnamed by us." Years earlier, floating on the Merrimack River with his brother John, he had caught a glimpse of this insight—applied then more generally and profoundly, an insight disturbing enough so that it must be relegated to one of the numerous rhetorical eddies of the fluidly formless book about their trip:

> The frontiers are not east or west, north or south, but wherever a man *fronts* a fact, though that fact be his neighbor, there is an unsettled wilderness between him and Canada, between him and the setting sun, or, farther still, between him and it. Let him build himself a log-house with the bark on where he is, *fronting* IT, and wage there an Old French war for seven or

seventy years, with Indians and Rangers, or whatever else may come between him and the reality, and save his scalp if he can.

Confronting a "constant *new* creation" from his solid if (when he cared to look) precarious philosophical ledge, Thoreau discovered an affirmation of his "border life" of freedom and independence, his life adrift and at a loss. He was "still unborn" at death, according to the doctrines of wild Nature, and his life had been "perfectly symbolical of the path which we love to travel in the interior and ideal world": "Is not our own interior white on the chart?" [68]

CHAPTER THREE

John Muir

I care to live only to entice people to look at Nature's loveliness.

Letter from Yosemite Valley, October 7, 1874

John Muir

(Courtesy of the Bancroft Library, University of California, Berkeley)

IN THE THREE decades after the Civil War the impulse of American environmental advocacy moved west and grew up with the country. It was carried there—to the West, and to maturation—by two men who had themselves grown up on the frontier, John Muir and John Wesley Powell. The journey began, literally and figuratively, in 1867, the year in which Muir set off on his "thousand-mile walk" from Kentucky to the Gulf of Mexico, and when Powell led his inaugural expedition into the Rocky Mountains of Colorado. These first forays heralded two pathbreaking careers that were to take environmental concern out of the books and salons of a few learned devotees and into the realm of national policy and politics.

Before beginning his solitary walk of 1867 Muir quit his machinist job in Indianapolis, said good-bye to his family in Wisconsin, and, "joyful and free," packed a small satchel with poetry (Milton and Burns), the New Testament, a botanical plant press, and a journal inscribed with his change of address, "John Muir, Earth-planet, Universe." His intention, he wrote, was "simply to push on in a general southward direction by the wildest, leafiest, and least trodden way I could find," gathering specimens, sketches, and observations along the trail, recording everything in his journal. Muir was a native Scotsman and a pacifist, and he had spent some time in Canada to avoid the Civil War draft. As he approached thirty years of age he was still unsettled, "utterly homeless" and "disengaged from all the grave plans and purposes and pursuits of ordinary orthodox life." He had been nearly blinded by an industrial accident in mid-1866, and on recovery Muir became determined "to devote the rest of my life to the study of the inventions of God." His consequent walk to the Gulf marked the first of many years of "long continuous wanderings" in nature; it was his induction into the "University of the Wilderness."[1] By April of 1868, Muir was to debark from a ship in California and hike straightway over the Coastal Range into the Sierra Nevada and his new home, the ill-protected state park at Yosemite Valley, where he began a forty-year career as wilderness interpreter, journalist, and lobbyist.

Powell, late of the Union Army, had meanwhile brought his small party to Pike's Peak and the highest reaches of Rockies in the previous year, after tireless months of promoting the idea to the Smithsonian

Institution, the War Department, Congress, various railroad companies, the Illinois legislature, the state Industrial University, and the Illinois Natural History Society museum, where he was secretary. With army rations, borrowed equipment, and the monetary contributions he had received, Major Powell and his group of mostly amateur scientists collected specimens for the museum and measured topography as best they could before the aid ran out. Unfazed, and with lessons learned from boosting this initial minor effort, Powell afterward organized the more elaborate "Colorado Scientific Exploring Expedition," going once to Washington in 1868 to lobby on its behalf before returning to the headwaters of the Green River in Wyoming. From there he and his boat mates started the first successful American descent of the Colorado River and its canyon system the following year, an exploration that was to make Powell nationally famous, and ultimately influential in the burgeoning federal scientific establishment.[2]

The maturation of environmental concern beyond the prescient yet unrealized intellectual foundations laid by George Perkins Marsh and Henry David Thoreau meant its *institutionalization*. Two definitions of the word may be connected to these formative late-1860s experiences of Muir and Powell and to their subsequent careers, spanning from the 1870s to the 1910s. Appearing already in Muir's journal account of his first important "wandering" is the persona who was later to achieve fame among contemporaries as a heroic pathfinder and comforting authority within wild nature, educating his readers in the lessons of the "University of the Wilderness." His spiritual and aesthetic pleas on behalf of wilderness preservation, taken from the journal and published as books and articles of broad appeal, were to make wilderness an *institution* in the sense that it was to acquire an enduring value in the public mind. Additionally, Muir was to help to create a political organization, the Sierra Club, to secure for wild areas protected legal status—and concrete institutional form—as national parks, forests, and monuments. Powell by this latter meaning was also to assume a quite deliberate role as institution builder, marshaling around himself personnel and support just as he had in his first and most modest expedition proposals, but to the larger end of establishing the permanent new agencies, laws, and political mechanisms essential to overseeing proper natural resource development in the American West. He was to attempt to gain for his own scientific bureau, the U.S. Geological Survey, a key role in that oversight, because he believed science must have such a role. His several Washington trips of the late 1860s reveal that Powell had early grasped the centrality of the federal government to the future disposition and administration of the West's remaining frontier abundance.

For in these years there could still be found blank spaces on a map of the United States. The empty grids depicting the plateaued basin of the Colorado River attracted Powell's interest and ambition. So too Muir could anticipate a leafy, untrodden path through the neofrontier of the post–Civil War rural South, where railways and other modern conveniences had been scarce even before they were destroyed in wartime. At Yosemite many of the towering granite monoliths surrounding the valley were still unnamed, and Muir would name them. Powell and his survey were also to have this rarest privilege of the New World explorer, drawing and correcting maps of the Grand Canyon; later some of his men were to discover the last unknown river and the last unknown mountain range in the contiguous United States. Yet both Powell and Muir were part of the first generation widely to recognize that America's existence as an unmapped frontier country was coming to an end. Earlier prophets like Thoreau had foreseen the limits within the confined landscape of industrial New England, with its shrinking forests and harnessed rivers. Marsh, in his travels, had looked upon the ruins of foreign nations without frontiers. By the time of Muir and Powell, the thirty-year period before 1900 in which the industrial revolution descended on America with full force, the wildest remnants of the frontier were receding to the remote canyon depths and alpine heights of the far West. Seeking them out, the two men reported back to their contemporaries on fragile, besieged places of unparalleled beauty and on vast, spare, inhuman landscapes of rock where conventional practices and assumptions became obsolete. Those reports began to find an audience among thoughtful Americans concerned with the dread coincidence of a vanishing frontier and an explosively expansive urban-industrial complex. Nature as spiritual balm and nature as renewable resource came to be seen as one solution to growing middle-class worries over modern decay, disorder, and corruption.

The West of Muir and Powell provided the first setting in which preservation and conservation were made issues of national policy and debate because so much of the disappearing western frontier lay in the public domain, under the control of the national government. Well before the two institution builders entered the scene, the trans-Mississippi landscape had already become the subject of federal legislation. During the Civil War a substantial part of the older Whig agenda of government-sponsored internal development (dear to Marsh's heart) was at last enacted by a wartime Congress packed with "free soil" Republicans in the most activist legislative session that would occur until the early twentieth century. The 37th Congress voted into law three measures of monumental importance for the distribution of the western domain. The Morrill Land Grant Act (1862) set aside for each state one 30,000-acre parcel of public land multiplied by the number of members of its congressional delegation to fund the establishment of state agricultural and mechanical (A&M) universities. The Homestead Act (1862), as its name implies, gave every settler a free 160-acre plot if the settler agreed to live on it for five years and make improvements. The Pacific Railroad Act (1862) and subsequent subsidy measures began an even larger federal land-giveaway program, granting thousands of acres per mile of railroad construction to aid corporations in its financing. Although these landmark laws together distributed over 225 million acres of western land, they did not exhaust Congress's generosity. The Timber Culture Act (1873) and the Desert Land Act (1877) set equally easy terms for acquiring or purchasing a homestead, while the General Mining Law (1872) allowed prospecting and mining on all lands in the public domain.[3]

Through these and other legislative measures, clearing the way for the hope and greed of thousands of individuals, families, and companies, the frontier disappeared. It was with epochal tones that historian Frederick Jackson Turner announced its closing in his long-remembered 1893 essay. "[T]he frontier has gone," he wrote, "and with its going has closed the first period of American history." Turner and his disciples were to make large claims for the frontier as a liberating and democratizing historical force. According to their heavily mythologized definition, the frontier was the area of free land where the oppressed of Europe might flee to make a fresh start, acquire the physical means of economic independence and individualism, and learn the practices of local democratic self-government. Its disappearance thus had ominous implications for the nation's future. Increased governmental centralization and coercion seemed to be one of the likely consequences. "The defense of the pioneer democrat began to shift from free land to legislation," Turner later noted, "from the ideal of individualism to the ideal of social control through regulation by law."[4] In fact, the 1890s did witness the small beginnings of the modern era of activist regulatory government at the federal level. Although Turner's argument has been greatly qualified and controverted by other scholars emphasizing political, cultural, and economic change in the shaping of American institutions and values, his thesis retains a certain utility in the history of the emergence of conservation, as an artifact of the contemporary anxiety over a closed frontier and in a more direct application for which the careers of Muir and Powell provide evidence and illustration.

Both Muir and Powell were involved in the watershed transformation of American political culture that Turner described, which is often depicted as a shift from the "old" liberalism of the nineteenth century to the "new" liberalism of the twentieth. Most generally, the orthodoxy of nineteenth-century laissez-faire liberalism upheld the ideal that government might facilitate individual economic activity but must not constrict it in any way. Individuals must be "allowed to do" in the economic realm—hence, for example, the massive hand-out of western frontier lands, with few strings attached, by which individuals (whether small farmers or large corporations) pursuing their acquisitive self-interest might create wealth and push forward national progress. The new liberalism arose when some groups of Americans began to perceive that the result of this unrestrained capitalist economic activity was not social progress but social chaos: a widening extreme between rich and poor, an increase in misery and degradation, a rise in the monied corruption of public officials, and a growing propensity for class conflict. In their view, capitalist self-interest had to be restrained and regulated if it were to be constructive rather than anarchic; furthermore it must be regulated in the public interest, a very old yet also very new concept in American politics, as compelling as it was amorphous. The "public interest" was vague and elastic in that it could be defined to include any number of diverse segments and sectors of American society, in contrast to the specific and narrow interest of the regulatee (consumers versus meatpackers, for example). But it was politically transformative in its recognition that the United States had outgrown the old liberal conception that the country was simply an aggregation of independent, competing individuals. In the eyes of new liberal commentators, the nation was now perceived in more collective, interdependent, and social terms, consisting of large corporations, organizations, groups, and blocs. In the final analysis, the only entity with the power and authority to adjust and harmonize the conflicting interests of this complex national polity, according to new liberal thinking, was the federal government.

During their surveys and explorations of the West, Muir and Powell observed how unconstrained economic activity exploited and corrupted frontier landscapes and societies. Their response was to appeal to the "public interest" for measures to preserve environment and democracy alike. Turner's thesis was therefore this much correct: the threatened disappearance of the last wilderness patches and poor man's homesteads on the frontier did precipitate these first historic efforts for federal environmental activism. Muir was to cite the public interest—the universal need for beauty, purity, and spirituality—in seeking federal intervention to protect natural wonders from the narrow and exclusive use of those interested only in quick profit. Powell, for his part, would promote disinterested, federally sponsored scientific expertise in the public service as the surest means to compiling an objective evaluation of the nation's natural abundance and to charting a blueprint for settling the inhospitable West in an environmentally viable and soundly democratic manner. The "common interest" rather than "personal gain" must be the guiding principle on the last frontier, Powell argued.[5] In spite of these new liberal leanings, however, neither Powell nor Muir embraced their personal political roles, or the necessity for federal intervention, without some ambivalence. They retained much contemporary distrust and disgust for politics, and they could not imagine a national government on the subsequent scale of the twentieth-century welfare state. Their efforts were to be important yet limited initial steps toward the institutionalization of preservation and conservation as national policy goals.

But before Muir and Powell came to understand the urgency for such federal and public action, they first had to learn about the value and nature of the landscapes that were to become the objects of their advocacy and concern. Before their life courses converged in the new political culture, Muir and Powell each separately went exploring.

JOHN MUIR'S early life, which was to eventuate in his "long continuous wanderings" through the western wilderness, seemed unlikely to predict the mature man who was to become something of a national institution himself. Those early years are usually portrayed as a succession of liberating escapes: from the harsh schoolmaster's regime he experienced as a boy in Scotland to the comparative freedom of a New World frontier farm in Wisconsin; from the endless backbreaking labor of the farm to enlightened undergraduate studies at the state university; from the threat of induction into military service to the safe haven of Canada; from maiming factory work to the aimless pastoral existence of the part-time naturalist; from the zealous Calvinism of his father's religion to the softer natural theism he discovered in Transcendentalist literature and the wilderness itself. Taken together these episodes suggest a formlessness to Muir like that of Thoreau—with whom he is inevitably compared—a disengagement from "ordinary orthodox life" that could be the precondition for a radically liberated if somewhat lonely and eccentric existence. Undoubtedly, a certain "wildness" did infuse Muir's character. He was given to climbing trees at night to better experience the thrill and power of thunderstorms. As a mountaineer, there were few cliff-faces or glacial snowfields that could daunt him. In fights between humans and animals, he rooted (rhetorically) for the animals. He was employed as a shepherd and sawmill laborer well into his thirties, presenting to the world a rather shabby bearded figure who lived in a hut and took long treks alone into the mountains. His literary career took off in the early 1870s, but his income was modest until he married money and respectability in 1880 at the late age of forty-two.[6]

Thereafter began, incongruously, a decade-long interlude during which Muir became a gentleman farmer, living in his relatives' house, overseeing their lands, and turning the horticultural dabblings of his father-in-law into a more efficient and commercial operation. Muir hagiographers are sometimes puzzled by this interregnum of domesticity and conventionality, yet there was always a great deal of the conventional Victorian in Muir, and it set limits to his "wildness." Many habits of the Victorian mind, Muir's Victorian mind—his secularized Christian worldview, his belief in evolutionary progress, his faith in objective science, his genteel aesthetic and literary tastes—were to guide him in the wilderness and allow him to interpret it for a mainstream audience who read him avidly because they shared these comfortable assumptions. But just as his years as a gentlemanly farmer were only an interregnum, ending after his entry into the first preservationist battles of the 1890s, so also were there "wilder" (and more private) dimensions of Muir's thought, biocentric dimensions, that led him over the safe ledge of contemporary orthodoxies, compelling him toward cultural criticism and politicization.

Muir had arrived at Yosemite Valley in 1868 with much of this complicated sensibility already in place. According to most of Muir's biographers, the chief breakthrough in his moral and intellectual development occurred with his presumed liberation from the strictures of his father's Christian dogma. The biblical declaration in which God gives man "dominion" over the earth and charges him to "subdue" it to his purposes (Genesis 1:26–28) has long been singled out by environmental writers as evidence for Christianity's supreme culpability in sanctioning the exploitation and destruction of nature. Muir's rejection of his father's beliefs fits neatly into the widespread (and uncritically accepted) interpretive assumption that preservationism and biocentrism are absolutely antithetical to Christian views of the natural world. There is no doubt that conquerors of the wilderness have looked to biblical authority to justify their actions. Yet like all cultural and intellectual traditions, Christianity has been historically an ambiguous and multivalent body of values and ideas from which all manner of inspiration might be drawn. Its conception of the human-nature relationship cannot be reduced to a single Bible verse. In fact, Muir's own life and writings reveal that Christian influences other than the oft-quoted "anti-natural" commandment of Genesis powerfully shaped his perceptions of the wilderness and its value. He was no biblical literalist, surely, nor was he conventionally religious in any practical sense of the word. But an idiosyncratic form of Christian belief, a *Christian naturalism*, comprised part of the ideological bedrock of his preservationism, a faith "naturalized" and secularized by the two other essential cores of his thought, Transcendentalism and science.[7]

During the years prior to 1867–68, for example, there is considerable evidence that religious practice was still prominent in Muir's everyday life, long after his departure from the family household. His father, whom Muir once called "semi-fanatical," was a stern and devout Campbellite circuit rider (as was Powell's father, for the Methodists) who insisted on frequent prayer and church attendance, intensive Bible study, and strict observance of the Sabbath. In more reflective moments, Muir would probably have agreed with the line from the Robert Burns poem that "carefully he bred me in decency and order," because his father's regimen was only somewhat more severe than that followed by millions of other families in evangelical nineteenth-century America. Although he left home in 1860 to pursue a career as an inventor and enroll at the University of Wisconsin (his father had always frowned on his scientific curiosity), Muir apparently found religion a hard habit to break, despite the oppressive rigor of his youthful instruction. A college roommate later recalled him (c. 1862) as "a high-minded Christian gentleman" who lived among shelves of homemade inventions and lab equipment: "While he was not a very regular attendant at church, he read his Bible regularly, said his morning and evening prayers each day, and led the kind of life all this implies." According to an early biographer, correspondence shows Muir to have been a "tender and solicitous religious adviser" to Union soldiers training at a camp near the university. As of 1865 he was wondering about "the Creator's plan concerning us [himself]" and asserting that "eternity, with perhaps the whole unlimited creation of God as our field, should satisfy us."[8]

The John Muir who arrived at Yosemite with these heavenward aspirations was clearly a deeply religious person, and he remained so in an unconventional way for the rest of his life. Into the early 1890s his journal and letters contain numerous direct allusions to Scripture and occasional opinions on religious practice (such as infant baptism). He refers to "our Savior" in the very sequence of Gulf Walk journal entries that have been presumed to describe his permanent break from nature-destroying Christianity—a slip due perhaps to his reading of the New Testament he carried with him. But it is nonetheless true that after his college years Muir's spiritual beliefs cannot be interpreted without considering the profound impact of the Transcendentalist philosophy and natural science that he was exposed to there. The fundamental transformation that these secular influences wrought was expressed most succinctly in an important and necessarily muddled 1866 letter that Muir wrote from Canada to a college mentor, in which he voiced some misgivings over the implications of nature study for his Christian faith, even as he was still doubting the sufficiency of a faith rooted solely in nature, where Transcendentalism and science seemed to be leading him:

> [A]lthough the page of Nature is so replete with divine truth it is silent concerning the fall of man and the wonders of Redeeming Love. Might she not have been made to speak as clearly and eloquently of these things as she now does of the character and attributes of God? It may be a bad symptom, but I will confess that I take more intense delight from reading the power and goodness of God from "the things which are made" than from the Bible. The two books harmonize beautifully.[9]

Muir's solution to this spiritual dilemma, a solution that was to have much significance for his ethics of biocentrism and his rationale for preservation, is evident in the passage's final, abruptly qualmless assertion. He would consider nature to be a direct source of divine revelation, speaking to him of the Christian God. Indeed, as his confidence in the harmony of the natural and biblical indicates, he was to discover that nature was not "silent" regarding fallen humanity and divine redeeming love but completely expressive of them.

Well before his exposure to Transcendentalism and university science, the youthful Muir had been predisposed toward this embrace of natural revelation. His family's "sudden plash into pure wildness" after emigrating to the prairies of Wisconsin left a sharp impression on an eleven-year-old boy accustomed to the iron strictness of Scottish schools and paternal piety. As most every would-be community of saints back to the Puritans have found, discipline and subordination were not easily maintained on the American frontier. Muir recalled his boyhood hikes and romps in the "glorious Wisconsin wilderness," stolen from work, as a "baptism in Nature's warm heart" quite in contrast to other modes of education and edification he had known: "Nature streaming into us, wooingly teaching her wonderful glowing lessons, so unlike the dismal grammar ashes and cinders so long thrashed into us." His father's eventual withdrawal from farmwork to devote himself full-time to religious study, leaving all of the responsibilities of the farm to his young sons, underscored very palpably for Muir the potential *unworldliness* of Christianity, detached and cloistered, needing this-worldly engagement and explication. Then there were Muir's legendary teenage inventions—whole clocks carved from wood, of his own rather novel design; homemade thermometers, precise and delicate; a timing mechanism to tip him out of bed each morning upright and awake on his feet: these were expressions of a mind enraptured by the measurability and orderliness of the physical world. They were also the artifacts and means by which Muir showed his growing independence of his father, helping him to develop a wee-hour schedule of reading and tinkering. One of the books that Muir read while sitting up late in his automatic clockwork room was *The Christian Philosopher*, by Thomas Dick, the thesis of which was (in the author's words) "to illustrate the harmony which subsists between the system of nature and the system of revelation, and to show that the manifestations of God in the material universe ought to be blended with our view of the facts and doctrines recorded in the volume of inspiration." Taking these words to heart, Muir connected himself to the intellectual tradition associated with its more renowned expositor, the Reverend William Paley, author of *Natural Theology* (1802).[10]

Muir's science courses in college served not to undermine but to confirm his belief in natural theology, or so the elderly Muir remembered in his autobiographical *Story of My Boyhood and Youth* (1910). He recounts an episode when a fellow student pointed out the similarity between the internal structure and chemistry of two ostensibly disparate types of plants by having him taste their leaves. " 'Now, surely you cannot imagine that all these similar characters are mere coincidences,' " the student observed. " 'Do they not rather go to show that the Creator in making the pea vine and locust tree had the same idea in mind, and that plants are not classified arbitrarily? Man has nothing to do with their classification. Nature has attended to all that, giving essential unity with boundless variety.' " This particular lesson imbued Muir with "wild enthusiasm" for botany because now he saw that flowers were "all alike revealing glorious traces of the thoughts of God, and leading on and on into the infinite cosmos." This belief of Muir's in a divine design revealed by objective science (an idea reaching back to the Enlightenment and earlier), which he called the "Scriptures of Nature," was to lead him to two important conclusions: that nature existed autonomously, apart from human desires and perceptions (as his fellow student implied), and that behind nature there was a purposeful, knowable Creator directing its construction and processes.[11]

Muir was to learn from Transcendentalism a further set of more spiritual insights into nature, insights that also affirmed for him the truth of natural revelation. His acceptance of Transcendentalist doctrines, however, was selective, delimited by Christian naturalism. Muir cannot be seen (as some interpretations have had it) as merely a lesser and latter-day Transcendentalist disciple of Emerson and Thoreau (and as Emerson himself, after meeting and corresponding with Muir, seemed to want). Certainly he admired both men extravagantly and was strongly influenced by their words and deeds. When Emerson visited Yosemite Valley in 1871, Muir later wrote that his "heart throbbed as if an angel direct from heaven had alighted on the Sierran rocks." After he himself stood on the bank of Walden Pond during a pilgrimage to Concord in 1893, Muir acknowledged a kinship: "No wonder Thoreau lived here two years. I could have enjoyed living here two hundred years or two thousand." Muir shared with Thoreau and Emerson the basic Transcendentalist faiths that divine spirit permeated nature and that the divine might be grasped through the aesthetic perception of beautiful natural objects. In 1871, he described what it was like to *see* the "genius of the Sierra Nevada": "the hardest rocks will pulse with life, secrets of divine beauty and love will be revealed to you by lakes, and meadows, and a thousand flowers, and an atmosphere of spirit be felt brooding over all." Implicit in this passage was another belief that tied Muir to his Romantic philosophical progenitors: the centrality of the *organic* in the structure of the world, which to him was alive, growing, changeful. Like the Transcendentalists, Muir too sought out organicist experience, the sense of *integration* between the inner human self and external Nature that was the highest form of consciousness. He expresses this yearning in an essay ending *A Thousand-Mile Walk to the Gulf*, in which he writes about the distant Sierras as seen across a wide plain:

> Their spiritual power and the goodness of the sky make them near, as a circle of friends. . . . You cannot feel yourself out of doors; plain, sky, and mountains ray beauty which you feel. You bathe in these spirit-beams, turning round and round, as if warming at a camp-fire. Presently you lose consciousness of your own separate existence: you blend with the landscape, and become part and parcel of Nature.[12]

As more than one critic has noted, the final five words of the passage precisely echo those at the beginning of Thoreau's 1851 essay "Walking, or The Wild."

Yet if Muir, Thoreau, and Emerson had an intellectual kinship, they were first cousins at best. Muir diverged from Transcendentalism above all because he retained a belief in two fundamental Christian precepts. First, he perceived in nature evidence of a benevolent God. Nature was not in itself divine, which was the essentially *pantheist* assumption underlying Transcendentalism—divine in the sense that it embodied love, truth, meaning, goodness, beauty, eternity, oneness, and harmony. For Muir, nature possessed these qualities because of the action in time, the *immanence*, of an omniscient, omnipotent, caring, eternal, and supernatural divine being, the Creator. "We all flow from one fountain Soul. All are expressions of one Love," Muir wrote in 1872, articulating his understanding of immanence. "The rocks and sublime canyons, and waters and winds, and all life structures," he elaborated in an 1873 journal entry, "are words of God, and they flow smooth and ripe from his lips." Divine immanence in nature furnished evidence for omniscience because (as he wrote in 1911, near the end of his life and career) nature represented "God's earth plans and works." Under the gaze of this omniscience "all things in the creation of God register their own acts" (or so Muir had concluded forty years earlier), and all things were "under the tender keeping of a Father's care"—an omnipotent "God playing upon everything, as a man would play on an instrument, His fingers upon . . . every living thing." For the monotheistic Muir, in short,

"Christianity and mountainanity" were "streams from the same fountain."[13]

Acting on these precepts, Muir turned the Transcendentalist quest for integration with nature into a form of worship, as he told his brother in an 1870 letter about Yosemite Valley:

I have not been at church a single time since leaving home. Yet this glorious valley might well be called a church, for every lover of the great Creator who comes within the broad overwhelming influences of the place fails not to worship as he never did before. The glory of the Lord is upon all his works; it is written plainly upon all the fields of every clime, and upon every sky, but here in this place of surpassing glory the Lord has written in capitals.

Taking his notion of immanence one step further, Muir found a new source of grace, of salvation, in nature. "Every purely natural object is a conductor of divinity," he observed in his journal, "and we have but to expose ourselves in a clean condition to any of these conductors, to be fed and nourished by them. . . . Only thus may we be filled with the Holy Ghost." On the "resurrection day," when Muir had first caught sight of the distant glowing Sierras in 1868, he recalled the experience, an experience of integration, as "my baptism in this font" of "God's shoreless atmosphere of beauty and love." In the theology of Christian naturalism, symbiotic integration of the self with holy Nature—being in nature—was analogous to redemption, for these "baptisms will make you a new creature indeed," Muir wrote, paraphrasing the words of 2 Corinthians 5:17 ("Therefore if any man be in Christ, he is a new creature").[14]

Standing in stark contrast to this religious awe that he felt before the majesty of divine creation, and reflecting darkly off of it, was the second of Muir's lifelong Christian preconceptions divergent from the Transcendentalist tradition. Humankind was not possessed each individually of a spark of the divine, as Emersonians believed, and as Muir but rarely declared in his writings. Rather, man was sinful, prideful, and fallen, that is, distant from God—a truth that Muir articulated in terms of the human-nature relationship, where it was "revealed" to him (much as it had been to the Calvinist-raised George Perkins Marsh). Although many environmental writers have interpreted the Bible's coronation of humanity with "dominion" over brute creation as the cultural root of anthropocentric hubris, they have largely ignored the Scriptures' somewhat low estimation of human virtue, a pervasive biblical theme that might potentially undercut any reader's tendency toward conceitedness. Muir's understanding of fallen humanity, drilled into him by his father's religion, was simply reconfirmed and highlighted by what were to him the glorious epiphanies of natural revelation, in comparison to which humankind's place in the cosmos seemed very degraded and anthropocentrism quite unfounded. Thus his radical biocentric ethic was born.

The journal that Muir kept during his 1867 walk to the Gulf, which contained some of his most famous passages, reveals that these views were already matured within him at the very beginning of his career as a naturalist and that he carried them into Yosemite. It is also possible that, in addition to his biblical, Transcendentalist, and scientific influences, the young Muir discovered some biocentric inspiration as well in the poetry of Robert Burns. "On my first long walk from Indiana to the Gulf of Mexico," Muir recalled in 1906, "I carried a copy of Burns's poems and sang them all the way." Burns addresses one poem "To a Mountain Daisy" (1786) and apologizes for crushing it "in an evil hour" when the flower had "Scarce rear'd above the *Parent-earth* / Thy tender form." In a more philosophical vein, "To a Mouse" (1785) expresses regret to a field mouse whose nest had been broken open by Burns's plow: "I'm truly sorry Man's dominion / Has broken Nature's social union, / An' justifies that ill opinion, / Which makes thee startle, / At me, thy poor, earth-born companion, / An' *fellow-mortal*!" Certainly there are echoes of these sentiments in Muir's Gulf journal. Commenting on the injustice of humans defining some animals (such as alligators) as pests requiring extermination, Muir made his opinion of their relative worth more than clear: "How narrow we selfish, conceited creatures are in our sympathies! how blind to the rights of all the rest of creation! With what dismal irreverence we speak of our fellow mortals! . . . They dwell happily in these flowery wilds, are part of God's family, unfallen, undepraved, and cared for with the same species of tenderness and love as is bestowed on angels in heaven or saints on earth." [15]

No fire-and-brimstone preacher ever spoke as poorly of humanity as did Muir when he recommended that instead of using the "cleansing chemistry" of fire to dispose of natural obstacles, "more than aught else mankind requires burning, as being in great part wicked. . . . [T]he tophetization of the erratic genus Homo were a consummation devoutly to be prayed for." The extremity of these pronouncements signified Muir's general departure from religious convention. He rejected official dogma and its purveyors, not religion itself—Christendom, but not Christianity (or his redefinition of it). As he wrote acridly, "It is hardly possible to be guilty of irreverence in speaking of their God any more than of heathen idols." Particularly, Muir belittled any literalist account of man's fallen state when it was depicted as "in some way connected with the first garden" as a burdensome punishment levied by the Creator on His most prized and special and worrisome creature, "Lord Man." In Muir's theodicy, humankind was inherently sinful and fallen for much the same reason long emphasized by Calvinist Christianity: pride and presumptuousness.[16]

Muir transposed this unfashionable doctrine into the biocentric terms of natural revelation. "The world, we are told, was made especially for man—a presumption not supported by all the facts," he wrote. Awakened by his own affliction with malaria during the walk to the Gulf, Muir leveled the hierarchy of beings by wondering pointedly, "Why is the lord of creation subjected to the same laws of life as his subjects?" and "Why should man value himself as more than a small part of the one great unit of creation?" From "the common elementary fund, the Creator has made Homo sapiens," and from "the same material he has made every other creature," Muir observed, borrowing from Darwinism. This commonality of origin suggested the relatively equal worth of all creatures in the eyes of God (who was also egalitarian in a more orthodox sense, i.e., "no respecter of persons"). Muir's assertion of God's omniscience, that "all things in the creation . . . register their own acts," was also a statement of the absolute value of all life. He answered his own rhetorical questions with perhaps the first American declaration of what would later be known (to radical theorists) as the concept of biocentric equality: "And what creature of all that the Lord has taken the pains to make is not essential to the completeness of that unit—the cosmos?

The universe would be incomplete without man; but it would also be incomplete without the smallest transmicroscopic creature that dwells beyond our conceitful eyes and knowledge." [17] As will be seen, by less blunt rhetorical means Muir later sought to instill the same sense of humility in his readers that this passage embodied, which would lead them toward the contrite and melted heart that in his natural theology was the preparation for the "baptism" of redemptive symbiotic integration—the oneness and love of God's nature felt in the wild.

The very radicalness of this biocentrism of Muir's, which devolved from his belief that a monotheistic God was immanent in a natural creation existing "beyond our conceitful eyes and knowledge," outside the purposes and conceptions of proud yet lowly humankind, had important consequences for other areas of his thought. Most pertinently, biocentrism limited the radicalness of any other philosophical explorations he might undertake, especially those pertaining to consciousness and epistemology. Muir's faith in a divine presence and plan within nature was also an empiricist's faith in the autonomous, objective existence of an orderly universe. "This star, our own good earth, made many a successful journey around the heavens ere man was made," Muir noted in his journal, "and whole kingdoms of creatures enjoyed existence and returned to dust ere man appeared to claim them." Muir therefore discounted the role of human consciousness in constructing the meaning of the world, much as his fellow botany student had counseled ("Man has nothing to do with . . . classification"). In the margins of a volume of Emerson's essays, Muir responded to the statement, "The beauty of nature must always seem unreal . . . until the landscape has human figures," by objecting, "God is in it." [18] Thoreau had arrived at his own biocentric perspective as the result of direct and unsettling reflections on the relationship between nature and consciousness (atop Ktaadn and elsewhere), but Muir, safely insulated by his twin objective faiths in God and science, never confronted a similar epistemological crisis. He avoided the problematics of subjectivity. And so Muir diverged still further from his Transcendentalist progenitors, while other Emersonian heirs—especially Friedrich Nietzsche and William James—carried forward the main project of contemporary philosophical speculation, concerning themselves with the function of individual consciousness in the apprehension of moral, aesthetic, and cognitive experience.

A STRONGLY religious sensibility, a faith in scientific empiricism, a radical biocentrism, and (otherwise) a philosophical conventionality— these elements defined the odd-shaped boundaries of the worldview that Muir brought into Yosemite in 1868. They also determined the conception of nature that he acquired there during five years among the Sierra's valleys and peaks. This conception of nature, in retrospect, was to distance Muir further still from the Transcendentalist tradition. More crucially for his preservationist politics, Muir's understanding of nature's operations was necessarily to influence how he perceived and depicted wilderness in his private and public writings, and ultimately, how he convinced his audience of its value and importance. For because of his conception of the natural world, Muir was to achieve this goal in a paradoxical way: he would *domesticate* wilderness—as might be expected of a proper Victorian—making it seem homely and comfortable for all of its God-sculpted beauty and majesty.

Although broadly connected to the genre of ideas identified with Paley's *Natural Theology*, Muir's nature was no scientific throwback to the divinely designed Enlightenment watchworks that had long reassured the educated classes in Europe and America. By the 1860s, no thoughtful understanding of natural processes could ignore the theories of Louis Agassiz, Charles Lyell, and especially, Charles Darwin; Muir read them all in 1870 while living on the Yosemite Valley floor. But it was still possible for him to ignore or skirt the more disturbing aspects of current geological and biological science that might undermine his bedrock faith in the intrinsic harmony and benevolence of divine creation. A less venturesome thinker than Thoreau in many ways, Muir was to conceive a wild Nature such as tourists would want to go to, an understanding of wilderness significant in the subsequent history of environmentalism precisely because of its long-lasting popularity. This understanding was to embody Muir's sense of the sublimity of the Darwinian and Lyellian insights that he first gained during his walk to the Gulf and his years at Yosemite. It was also to incorporate, in unquestioned tension, his faith in the goodness and truth of natural revelation. Reconfiguring

Thoreau's famous dictum, Muir declared during an 1890 journal entry, "In God's wildness lies the hope of the world." [19]

Fundamentally, Darwinism confirmed Muir in his *organicist* view of nature, a perception that had also been instilled in him by naturalist fieldwork and Transcendentalist texts. As has been noted, Muir accepted the Darwinian argument—epoch making in the emergence of ecological science—that humans were intimately a part of the natural world. Because of "our origin in one common ancestor," Darwin once wrote, humans and other organisms were "all netted together." So too did Muir argue (paraphrasing Robert Burns) that other species were "earth-born companions and fellow mortals" with humanity in nature and that "all together [they] form the one grand palimpsest of the world." This "palimpsest," according to Muir, was both unitary and diversified, as only the organic could be: "There is not a fragment in all nature, for every relative fragment of one thing is a full harmonious unit in itself." Moreover, Muir believed that each "unit" of creation changed and developed incrementally over time, that each was involved in and the product of constant natural processes—the central Darwinian organicist concept of *evolution*: natural entities grow, change, and transform themselves in the course of geologically long stretches of time (as both Darwin and Muir learned from Lyell). Muir observed even of the human organism that "such a being is man, who has flowed down through other forms of being and absorbed and assimilated portions of them into himself." Following out the more radical logic of Darwinism, the mature Muir's larger conception of the very structure of matter and space-time was organically processive, if not *animist*, at its core: "Contemplating the lace-like fabric of streams outspread over the mountains, we are reminded that everything is flowing—going somewhere, animals and so-called lifeless rocks as well as water . . . while the stars go streaming through space pulsed on and on forever like blood globules in Nature's warm heart." [20]

Muir's eyes were most fully opened to the Darwinian processiveness of nature by the "elaborate history of seas, and glaciers, and volcanic floods" that he explored during the early 1870s in the complex landscape of California. Most particularly, glaciation—his special area of study, borrowing from the theories of Agassiz—crystallized all that Muir had come to understand about the natural world theologically, philosophically, and scientifically. In an 1871 letter written from Yosemite Valley he told a correspondent that there he had "read God's own mountain manuscripts" and "gathered many faint hints from what I had read as glacial footprints in the rocks worn by the storms and blotting chemistry of ages." These "blurred sheets of glacial writing," Muir later concluded, convinced him that he "had a key to every Yosemite rock and perpendicular and sloping wall": "[E]ach dome and brow and wall, and every grace and spire and brother is the necessary result of the delicately balanced blows of well directed and combined glaciers against the parent rocks which contained them, only thinly carved and moulded in some instances by the subsequent action of water, etc." Muir's scientific findings on California glaciation marked the beginning of his fame as a naturalist and a writer. In 1871, his evidence was presented to the Boston Academy of Sciences, where Muir made important acquaintances in the scientific community, among them the chief American Darwinian, Asa Gray. In 1871–72, glaciers were the subject of the first popular writings Muir ever wrote, articles for the *New York Daily Tribune* and for the California-based *Overland Monthly*, an early publisher of Mark Twain and Bret Harte. These articles were the worldly fruits of his glaciation studies, which were valuable to him on a more deeply personal and spiritual level as well. The powerful erosive forces of liquid and frozen water, acting across thousands of millennia down to the present moment to sculpt the spectacular Yosemite, affirmed for him Darwin's and Lyell's paradigm of constant natural change—as another truth of divine natural revelation. "From form to form, beauty to beauty, ever changing, never resting," Muir marveled of these forces, "all are speeding on with love's enthusiasm, singing with the stars the eternal song of creation." His glaciation studies were thus a scientific "font" for an integrative "baptism" in God's nature, as Muir confessed breathlessly in a letter: "The grandeur of these forces and their glorious results overpower me, and inhabit my whole being." [21]

Yet the study of glaciation also confirmed Muir in his rejection of some of the most radical and unsettling of the findings of Darwinism. He had no objections to Darwin's undermining of the literal biblical account of creation, which had few serious scholarly defenders in the increasingly secular late nineteenth century. Muir himself had moved beyond the Bible's pages for a more direct source of revelation. Certain basic assumptions of Darwinism, however, threatened to subvert the divine truths Muir had discovered in nature. According to Darwin and his interpreters, evolutionary processes such as natural selection occurred by "variations" in the characteristics of species, variations that arose spontaneously and by chance and that tended to produce "an infinite diversity in structure, constitution, and habits." Therefore, change in the natural world was not "well directed," purposeful, or progressive. As Darwin wrote, "Natural selection . . . does not necessarily include progressive development—it only takes advantage of such variations as arise and are beneficial to each creature under its complex relations of life." Consequently, present-day species need not have resulted from a predetermined design, but rather, "variation" alone was a sufficient creative force, given millions of years in which to operate. This it did in the organic realm through the "struggle for survival," a "severe struggle for life" that took place within and among species and individuals competing, often violently, for the same habitat or seeking to adapt to novel environmental circumstances. The winners were those in whom variation had produced the most "useful" and "profitable" characteristics, making them the "fittest" to survive the struggle and pass their superior or more fortuitous traits on to future generations; the losers and their kind, less well endowed by nature, died out. Darwin put it most bluntly in the rough draft for On the Origin of Species: "[T]he doctrine that all nature is at war is most true." [22]

These ideas comprised much of the heart of Darwin's theory, and Muir ignored, rejected, or remained very ambivalent toward virtually all of them. Throughout his life Muir was made uneasy by the evidences of violence and destruction in nature, which he had deemed benevolent because of God's immanence within it. As he once wrote to Asa Gray, "Darwin's mean ungodly word 'struggle' " was simply heretical to him. It is true that one can find passages in Muir's writings that show him hardly shrinking from displays of violence and overwhelming power in nature, but confronting them with ostensible bravery and acceptance. The ocean, for example, affected Muir not as the alien abyss that had disturbed Thoreau but as his first instructor in "wildness." When he was a boy growing up on the North Sea coast of Scotland, he had often watched the "waves in awful storms thundering on the black headlands." Later in life Muir sometimes took pleasure in appalling hosts and fellow hikers by heading outdoors when a storm appeared, "for on such occasions Nature has always something rare to show us," he believed. Climbing up to a high treetop, he was "free to take the wind into my pulses and enjoy the excited forest from my superb outlook." But Muir usually dealt with the moral implications of natural violence by anthropomorphizing it, ascribing motives and emotions to natural entities that were products of his own wishful and qualmish imagination. "We hear much today concerning the universal struggle for existence," he remarked in the course of describing a windstorm, "but no struggle in the common meaning of the word was manifest here; no recognition of danger by any tree . . . but rather an invincible gladness." The sound of a robin's call was a "reassuring voice" to the "awe-stricken" hiker in the high Sierra, saying, " 'Fear not, fear not. Only love is here.' " Muir also explained away struggle, death, and destruction in nature by obtaining a transcendental distance from the unpretty Darwinian process, holistically subsuming these aspects of nature within larger and larger scales out to the universal and "philosophically" encompassing all in what he held to be a greater means for the good. "One is constantly reminded of the infinite lavishness and fertility of Nature—inexhaustible abundance amid what seems enormous waste," Muir wrote in *My First Summer in the Sierra* (1911):

> And yet when we look at any of her operations within reach of our minds, we learn that no particle of her material is wasted or worn out. It is eternally flowing from use to use, beauty to yet higher beauty; and we soon cease to lament waste and death, and rather rejoice and exult in the imperishable, unspendable wealth of the universe, and faithfully watch and wait the reappearance of everything that melts and fades and dies about us, feeling sure that its next appearance will be better and more beautiful than the last.

Thus, Muir had long before concluded, "by forces seemingly antagonistic and destructive . . . has Mother Nature accomplished her beneficent designs."[23]

Muir's other fundamental point of contention with Darwinism is also illustrated in these two preceding passages. Muir believed that God's beneficent nature must have an intelligent, "directed" design; it must be teleological and progressive. A universe evolving by the blind mechanism of chance was abhorrent to Muir, as it was to most of his more thoughtful contemporaries. Many assumed (inaccurately) that "evolution" was a synonym for "progress," especially when Darwinian notions were pressed into service to lend scientific authority to the "natural laws" of human society (and to prove the superiority of its apotheosis, America). "Unbroken evolution under uniform conditions pleased everyone," observed a sardonic Henry Adams, Muir's almost exact contemporary (1838–1915) but his philosophical opposite; "it was the very best substitute for religion; a safe, conservative, practical, thoroughly Common-law deity." As Muir himself jotted in the margins of a book written by natural selection's codiscoverer, Alfred Russel Wallace, "Every cell, every particle of matter in the world requires a Captain to steer it into its place." No other conclusion was possible for a man with faith in the worldly presence of an eternal, omniscient, caring Creator. "Somewhere, before evolution was, was an Intelligence that laid out the plan," Muir reasoned, "and evolution is the process, not the origin, of the harmony." In this belief he was very much in accord with other Victorian gentlemen, though Darwinism led a few, like the unhinged historian Henry Adams, to rather more modernist, and frightening, speculations: "Chaos was the law of nature; Order was the dream of man." [24]

Muir's natural theology and empiricist scientism could never admit to such a conception of nature. He never had the equivalent of Thoreau's disconcerting Ktaadn experience, in which nature did leave the impression that it was chaotic and blankly indifferent. In fact, Muir considered it one of his most substantial scientific achievements to be able to disprove the reigning academic theory of the catastrophic formation of Yosemite Valley, that it had fissured open quite suddenly as a result of earthquakes, floods, or volcanic action. Instead, Muir's studies had shown that the methodical "well directed blows" of glaciers had carved it over millions of years, upholding Lyell's uniformitarian principle—and God's design—that "geologic change is slow, gradual, and steady, not cataclysmic or paroxysmal." Even the earthquakes that would occasionally and randomly jolt Muir sitting in his cabin on the valley's floor seemed just another evidence of spiritual beneficence revealed in the "Scriptures of Nature," as he wrote in an 1872 letter:

> These earthquakes have made me immensely rich. I had long been aware of the life and gentle tenderness of the rocks. . . . Now they have spoken with audible voice *and* pulsed with common motion. This very instant, just as my pen reached "and" on the third line above, my cabin creaked with a sharp shock and the oil waved in my lamp.

There is no rattling the temperament of the true believer. After being stranded overnight during a blizzard on the slopes of Mount Shasta in 1874—"frozen, blistered, famished, benumbed"—Muir made his way happily back to the lowlands to find "my friends among the birds and plants . . . and we felt like speaking to every one of them as we passed, as if we had been a long time away in some far, strange country." With a good night's sleep, he wrote, "next morning we seemed to have risen from the dead." His host's children "came in with flowers and covered my bed, and the storm on the mountain-top vanished like a dream." The best way of coping with such an experience was not to contemplate it at all.[25]

Perhaps the closest that Muir ever came to an experience of Ktaadn-esque disenchantment with nature occurred in 1878, when as a result of his growing reputation he was invited to join a party of the U.S. Coast and Geodetic Survey on a mapping expedition in Nevada and Utah. This survey was one of several then engaged in exploring the mountains and canyonlands of the desert West—among them, the U.S. Geological Survey of the Fortieth Parallel, headed by Clarence King, and John Wesley Powell's own Geographical and Geological Survey of the Rocky Mountain Region. During his years of travel across the vast "Plateau Province" of southern Utah and northern Arizona, Powell had found a certain awe and sublimity in the face of this "strange and weird" landscape of endless, dry, barren, solid rock carved by roaring rivers. Muir, in his part of the Arid Region, had to look harder. "Boo! How hot it was riding in the solemn, silent glare, shadeless, waterless," he remarked in one letter from Nevada. "Strange how the very sunshine may become dreary. How strange a spell this region casts over poor mortals accustomed to shade and coolness and green fertility." Nevertheless, Muir was able to locate enough comforting life-forms to give him some sense of security, as he immediately continued: "Yet there is no real cause, that I could see, for reasonable beings losing their wits and becoming frightened. There are the lovely tender abronias blooming . . . and a species of sunflower, and a curious leguminous bush." But all too soon the pall of the place reclaimed him: "Immense areas, however, are smooth and hard and plantless." Later in their excursion, Muir and two comrades were made "subject" to the "laws of life" in the Nevada desert, "forty miles from any known water": "On Lone Mountain we were thirsty. How we thought of the cool singing streams of the Sierra while our blood fevered and boiled and throbbed! . . . I suffered as never before"—"two days and nights in this fire without water!" He survived to write and mail his ambivalent letter, of course, having spied out just sufficient verdure tucked into the crannies of the wasteland to prevent him from "losing his wits" (as Thoreau had on Ktaadn), or from challenging his worldview: "How treeless and barren it seemed. Yet how full of small charming gardens, with mints, primroses, brier-roses, penstemons . . . watered by trickling streams too small to sing audibly. How glorious a view of the Sink from the mountain-top. The colors are ineffably lovely, as if here Nature were doing her very best painting." [26]

IF MUIR WAS in some ways a less radical thinker than various of his predecessors and contemporaries, it could be argued that he was all the more effective as a popularizer and institutionalizer of environmental ideas. His religious sensibility and philosophical conventionality served him well when he began to seek to persuade a stolid, respectable, middle- and upper-class audience about the value of wilderness and wilderness encounters. For Muir shared a great many of the assumptions and tastes of this audience, despite his early years as a wild man of the mountains. It was for them that he would "domesticate" the wilderness in his popular writings, making of it a familiar and comfortable place. It was they who would comprise the small but influential membership of the Sierra Club in its first years during the 1890s. "As for the old freedom I used to enjoy in the wilderness, that, like youth and its enthusiasms, is evidently a thing of the past," Muir sighed to his wife in 1885, revealing how his life had been confined and tamed by marriage and business responsibilities after 1880. Yet he could also have been giving voice to a broader cultural mood descending on his audience in the fin de siècle: harried and enervated by urban-industrial existence, worried over the unexceptional and decadent direction the country seemed to be taking, they also were to yearn back to a lost national youth in the two decades around 1900. For them and for himself Muir offered (in Thoreau's words, from a work he knew well) the "tonic of wildness."[27] He advocated wilderness as a setting of spiritual renewal and physical reinvigoration, pleading for its value and preservation in words that were to continue to be persuasive in subsequent eras. At the same time, Muir was to renew and reinvigorate his own lagging career, elevating himself personally to the heights of "national institution" through his efforts to build another: the National Park System.

The popularity of Muir and his message, the receptiveness and the very existence of an audience for him, can only be explained with reference to a variety of social and cultural preconditions that had emerged in America by the 1890s. Most fundamentally, between 1860 and 1900 the United States became a more crowded and a more urbanized country. The population grew from 31 million to 75 million, and the percentage of Americans living in urban areas doubled, from only 20 percent in 1860 to 40 percent in 1900. Meanwhile, the nation was expanding across space as well, with twelve new states joining the union during the same period, all of them in the Great Plains and mountain West regions, demonstrating quite palpably the closing frontier announced by Frederick Jackson Turner. But Americans of the day did not need Turner to tell them that an epoch of the national past was coming to an end, that they no longer lived in the primarily rural, small-town, frontier society of Marsh and Thoreau's time. The evidences of a startlingly new world of metropolises, machine wonders, monopolistic corporations, mass production, and mass consumption were everywhere at the turn of the century. Intercontinental and interurban railroad networks shrank time and distance dramatically, as did the telegraph and telephone. The first skyscrapers began to rise above the bridge towers and church steeples of cities like New York and Chicago, while streetcar suburbs sprawled over the countryside. By the 1910s, the automobile—unimaginable in Muir's youth—was to be commonplace. In the city centers, human warrens spread into sub-subdivided old houses and newer ramshackle tenements, filled with wave upon wave of immigrants recently arrived in search of opportunity. Usually they and the native-born found dehumanizing piecework on factory lines, while the luckier or better educated took the new white-collar jobs in business firms and corporate bureaucracies. Those on the shop floor suffered most, and went on strike the most, in the erratic upswings and downturns and cutthroat competition of the period's overheated economy, as often in depression as it was in boom. On more than one occasion (1877, 1886, 1890, 1892, 1896) "industrial *revolution*" would have seemed all too ominously appropriate a catchphrase for this violent age, peopled as it was by robber barons, strikebreaking thugs, wild-eyed anarchists, farmers in rebellion, Southern lynch mobs, and Indian-pacifying militarists. But by the 1890s many Americans also came to believe in the dream that the industrial economy was holding out to them, the luminous obverse of the vast crudities and misery it created: the dream of abundance. Already they could see it materializing, in the grand big-city department stores, in the mail-order catalogs, in the new amusement parks, in their own changing wants and needs. The emergence of this modern consumer economy was to be of signal importance to the cause of conservation, especially so with regard to wilderness preservation.[28]

The earlier, *producerist* economy of the fading rural-frontier America, still dominant as late as the 1850s, had centered on the attainment of subsistence as the chief (and often hard-won) end of the average household's activity, with only surpluses going to market. Such an economy made virtues of hard work, self-denial, frugality, stern sobriety, and other values conducive to a productivity that was family-centered, labor-intensive, low-technology, seasonal, weather-dependent, and locally oriented. "Wilderness," to the producerist mind-set, was a supply of free firewood, game, and lumber, and an uncleared area of future farmland—a repository of raw materials. In a darker sense, wilderness also represented danger to those far-flung families living isolated and unprotected on its edges, danger from Indian attack, from outlaws, from wild animals, from the furies of the weather, from whatever might creep into the barnyard out of the dismal shadows of the surrounding forest. Necessarily then, when typical Americans began to live their lives in towns and cities, when the Indian menace was put down, the bears and wolves hunted out, the unknown horizon cleared and surveyed into sections and quarters, wild nature—confined to ever more remote provinces—did not present so daunting a face. Nature's image was softened further as the basic necessities were made convenient, purchasable items, items of household consumption rather than household production, thanks to farm mechanization, refrigeration and canning technology, and the nationwide transportation network. By the 1890s and early 1900s, mass manufacturing, technological breakthroughs, and the division and specialization of labor had resulted in much-increased productivity, leading in turn to rising national wealth and personal income, and for some classes and occupations, shorter workweeks. In everyday terms, this productivity meant that more and more people had more money to buy an ever greater variety of products (well beyond mere necessities), with more time, more leisure, in which to enjoy them. New values and virtues emerged, definitive of the consumerist ethos and behavior: if producerism might be identified with self-denial and hard work, with the discipline of necessity, then the culture of consumerism upheld self-fulfillment, play, indulgence, self-expression, and individuality, all now attainable through the miracle of industrial abundance and the vista of personal freedom it opened. No longer directly dependent on (or at the mercy of) nature, urban Americans were now free to admire and revel in it. Leisure in the great outdoors was becoming part of a good "quality of life," a key catchphrase of the new consumer ethos.[29]

Of course, in the nascent years of the consumer economy some were more free to enjoy nature than others, than many, in fact. Muir's readership was largely limited to the more affluent and more educated urban middle and upper classes, as were a good deal of the fruits and benefits of Gilded Age economic growth. These classes pioneered some of the basic patterns and habits of consumption that would soon enough be accessible to the masses, albeit transmuted into cheaper, more raucous, more exciting forms, especially true of leisure and amusements. Indeed, it was the desire of the more well-to-do classes to distinguish themselves from the great unwashed democracy that had earlier eventuated in a middle-class lifestyle very much defined by consumption, by a high-toned and respectable status that has come to be known, by the label, *genteel*. To be genteel (a word with the same derivation as "gentleman" and "gentry") meant that one must cultivate good morals and manners and that one should embrace the finer things in life, the beautiful, the learned, the uplifting, the ideal. By exposing oneself to culture (the assumption went), one would be fulfilled and expanded spiritually, and elevated above the squalor and brutality of modern urban-industrial life.

This genteel refinement could be achieved through individual artistic and intellectual expression, but first and foremost it involved consuming productions and reproductions available commercially. The post–Civil War years, for example, were the great era of the large-circulation literary magazines—*Scribner's*, *Harper's*, *The Atlantic*, *The North American Review*, *The Century*—which serialized important new novels, sponsored political exposés, and otherwise shaped and reflected the tastes and opinions of the educated classes. Only "serious" writing, the "best thought" of the day, was appropriate for the men of affairs (and their wives) who comprised the audience. In their reading and in other areas of "art appreciation," especially architecture and design, the trademark Victorian historical-eclecticism of their tastes became apparent, dictated by the fashion-meisters of New York and Boston. The aesthetic emphasis was on geometry, verticality, proportionality, and ornateness —nothing simple and nothing wildly natural. In home and commercial construction classicism was favored and colonial revival became increasingly popular, but anything beautiful and traditional would do, for the point was to place oneself in relation to a timeless order above and apart from the unsettling, chaotic stream of modern daily life. In an era of capitalist go-getting, a sense of permanence and solidity was much sought after, and it was usually found in the haven of the well-appointed suburban home.[30]

That such an effect was achieved by *artifice*, by imitating old styles, by filling parlors with plaster statuary and reproduced paintings, fake flowers, and potted plants, was also part of the point, the "higher" end, of genteel culture. If the Gilded Age (a term itself implying artifice) was to become famous for its Darwinian faith and praxis, for upholding the manly competitive ethic of the "survival of the fittest," Muir's contemporaries were no less troubled and ambivalent than he by the implications of this hard view of the world. Despite all their paeans to the virtue of competition, for example, corporate owners and managers spent most of their efforts trying to reduce and eliminate it, through the market- and supply-controlling means of corporate concentration. Regularity and order were what they sought, as did (understandably) most Americans in their everyday lives.[31]

Darwinian insights, selectively interpreted and misinterpreted, played into this culturewide desire. Humankind was now discovered to be elementally connected to nature. Therefore, human society must operate in accordance with natural laws, meaning laws that were knowable, predictable, and ultimately benevolent. For instance, the law of competition (as "old" liberalism already taught, confirmed now by science) must automatically add up to social harmony and progress. Humanity represented the culmination of evolution, and further progress would lead finally to social perfection. Yet everywhere there were evidences of human degradation and brutishness matching that found in nature; there were barbarous races and tribes that seemed scarcely different from animals. Thus it was concluded that not only were human beings the most evolved of the animals but that some races of humanity were more evolved than others, preeminently, white Anglo-Saxons. They were superior within a hierarchy of being (a very old belief with life still in it) that for all intents and purposes distinguished the white man as proper ruler over all the world—a mastery over savage nature that modern wonders of technology proved completely, as did the "white man's burden" of global colonial empires. Like art, literature, and architecture, technology and government were themselves artifice, that is, uniquely human creations differentiated from natural phenomena. They were products of the higher faculties of reason and intelligence, while nature (and primitive man) were directed by mindless force and base instinct. From these assumptions and presumptions emerged the famous (or infamous) dichotomy animating and recurring throughout Victorian culture: the order of the world could be understood as being divided between civilization and savagery.

Muir's wilderness advocacy both drew support from and subverted this genteel way of looking at nature. But his was not the only or even the first counter-Darwinian conception to soften and "domesticate" savage nature for a genteel audience, to offer it as an alternative to *culture* as a realm for self-cultivation and personal fulfillment. It may be noted that the darker, *savage* interpretation of nature was not unlike the older frontier-producerist view of the wilderness, as a place of danger and peril. An important aspect of national mythology had long held that the wild was a setting for testing manliness, cunning, woodcraft skills, and physical courage. This compelling myth remained while the frontier receded into history and Americans became tenderfooted city dwellers. Many of the activities associated with maintaining a frontier subsistence—especially hunting and fishing—were subsequently converted into forms of (primarily) masculine recreation pursued by hobbyists who needed no extra food but were captivated by the myth. In fact, detached from the harsh necessities of the frontier and identified with fun and sport, hunting, fishing, and woodcraft developed in more pastoral and ethical directions. In accordance with frontier mythology, outdoor sports were assumed to have a bracing, invigorating effect on the mind and body—nature perceived as challenge rather than danger. The temporary character of hunting or fishing trips reduced nature's ominousness further; one always could return to civilization. These comforting perceptions were pastoralized and ethicized still more through the skills needed to fish and hunt, which required that the sportsman understand the habits and habitats of his quarry, that he become, in other words, intimate and familiar with nature. An important result of this raised consciousness was that upper-crust outdoor organizations such as the Boone and Crockett Club, which predated the Sierra Club, drew up codes of good *sportsmanship* that were, in effect, early conservation policies. True sportsmen were not to overfish or overhunt a given area but to limit themselves in the interest of fellow and future outdoorsmen. (Human mastery and superiority over nature, however, were never doubted.) These lessons, along with vivid tales of successful hunts and fishing trips in the great outdoors, were disseminated to enthusiasts through articles in a growing list of mass-market magazines that began to appear by the 1870s, including *Field and Stream* and *Forest and Stream*. Muir's own stories of mountain climbing and glacier exploring, though directed to divergent ethical ends, may not have seemed very different to readers from this emerging genre of outdoor adventure writing.[32]

But equally important to creating an audience for Muir's appeals was the older genre of the nature essay, especially as it was written by contemporaries like John Burroughs and Mary Treat. Both were popular authors who were instrumental in encouraging "nature appreciation" as a middle-class hobby. Burroughs, later a good friend of Muir's, wrote in his first book, *Wake-Robin* (1871), that "the purpose of the author will be carried out in proportion as it awakens and stimulates the interest of the reader" in bird-watching, a pastime pursued with increasing avidity during the Gilded Age, particularly by genteel women. Women were to predominate in the membership of the newly founded Audubon Society (1886) in the first decades of its existence. (Their famous long-running campaign against the use of exotic bird feathers in ladies' hats began almost immediately.) Gardening and botany remained popular nature appreciation hobbies for genteel women, as they had been in the antebellum period. Women authors continued to conceptualize these hobbies in terms of traditional domestic caretaking, as did Catherine Beecher and Harriet Beecher Stowe in *The American Woman's Home* (1869). Yet gardening and botany might also be rewarding in themselves as pursuits for women, a point made implicitly and explicitly in books like Anna Warner's *Gardening By Myself* (1872) and Mary Treat's *Home Studies in Nature* (1885). "I sometimes think the more I limit myself to a small area," Treat wrote, indicating the confined space where many genteel middle-class women spent their days, "the more novelties and discoveries I make in natural history."[33] By the turn of the century, genteel women were to be the major grassroots constituency for defenders of wilderness and wildlife.

In addition to their reading of the outdoor adventure tale and nature essay genres, the broader genteel audience was prepared for Muir and his vision of nature by another popular artistic form as well, a genre that also reconfirmed Victorian tastes and assumptions even as it subtly transformed them: Romantic landscape painting. As early as the 1840s and 1850s artists of the Hudson River school like Thomas Cole and Frederic Church, together with the western painters Thomas Moran and Albert Bierstadt, were depicting wild nature not as an object of anxious dread or subduable utility but as a proper subject for aesthetic appreciation and nationalistic pride. What the American scene lacked in depth, antiquity, and nuance, it made up for in sheer majestic beauty, or so Cole argued along with numerous other American writers and artists (including Emerson, Thomas Jefferson, and Washington Irving) during the years of the early republic, seeking to break the nation's continuing colonial dependence on European cultural standards. And surely the "most distinctive, and perhaps the most impressive, characteristic of American scenery is its wildness," Cole declared in an 1835 Hudson River manifesto entitled "Essay on American Scenery."[34]

A sense of *scenery*, of what elements, relationships, and proportions constituted scenic beauty, was the most significant contribution of the Romantic landscape painters to the subsequent movement for wilderness preservation. A foreground with lake or river, and often an animal or human figure for scale; a background of symmetrical, cloud-swept summits bathed in golden or pearly light—these became the genre-defining features of nineteenth-century American landscape painting. Church and the Luminists made light their specialty, as their school's name suggests, depicting divine Nature as perceived by the enraptured Transcendentalist eye. Moran and Bierstadt, applying the techniques of historical painting to American nature, sometimes included a foreground wagon train or wigwam to underscore the mythic sources of national pride: the New World as Eden, as Promised Land. Viewers could find reassurance here and in the physical object of the painting itself, a wild vista enclosed and delimited within a homely, ornate frame, hanging on a familiar parlor wall or in a public museum. The meaning taken was that wild nature was beautiful and spiritual, epic and spectacular, yet comfortable all the same. The genre and its makers helped to define the aesthetic expectations of the genteel audience and, eventually, of the masses, as countless imitators and amateurs embraced and made conventional the high art of the masters. To say that a natural scene was as "pretty as a picture," that it was "*picturesque*," became a cliché of the language—it matched the idealized colors, tones, and proportions of the artist's rendition.[35] But natural scenes that failed to correspond with or live up to the high and conventionalized standards of *artifice* were often neglected if not denigrated in their worthiness for "art appreciation," or for tourism. Muir in his wilderness advocacy was to cater self-consciously to these particular tastes because he shared in them and because, as an advocate seeking to persuade the broad public to his cause, he could not afford to ignore them.

Yet painters were not the sole public arbiters of what was beautiful in the American landscape. There was also the influence of contemporary park and garden designers, preeminent among them Frederick Law Olmsted (1822–1903). Indeed, beyond his impact on genteel aesthetic values, Olmsted was a figure important in his own right to the history of the American environment. He was the chief designer of New York's Central Park and various other major urban public parks around the country; he was also a pioneer architect of suburban development, with some of his handiwork constructed near Chicago as early as the 1880s. Moreover, Olmsted was one of the earliest prominent advocates for wilderness preservation. He preceded Muir at Yosemite by several years, having been appointed commissioner in 1864 to oversee state land in the valley that just months before had been granted to California by the federal government. In this capacity Olmsted in 1865 wrote a report to the state legislature that was significant as an early plea for Yosemite's protection and as a statement of his widely influential philosophy of parks and their larger purposes, a philosophy with which Muir strongly concurred.

On one level this philosophy encompassed a social psychology of nature experience. The hustle and bustle of contemporary urban life, Olmsted argued, had left modern men and women frazzled and exhausted to the extent that "a class of disorders" had become common among genteel city dwellers, which he described as "mental and nervous excitability, moroseness, melancholy or irascibility, incapacitating the subject for the proper exercise of the intellectual and moral forces." Collectively these disorders were known as neurasthenia, an illness to which genteel men and women were especially susceptible, unlike the thick-skinned, ethnic, working-class masses. But nature could furnish a cure for neurasthenia, Olmsted believed: "It is a scientific fact that the occasional contemplation of natural scenes of an impressive character, particularly if this contemplation occurs in connection with relief from ordinary cares, change of air and change of habits, is favorable to the health and vigor of men." Natural scenery, he wrote, afforded an occasion for "the exercise of the esthetic and contemplative faculties" that were so "intimately and mysteriously associated with the moral perceptions and intuition." That which was beautiful was also *good*, in the genteel moral universe. The "emotions caused by natural scenery," by the innately human "power of appreciating natural beauty," could have a salutary and uplifting effect on the individual, according to Olmsted. The "enjoyment of scenery," he concluded, "employs the mind without fatigue and yet exercises it; tranquilizes it and yet enlivens it; and thus . . . gives the effect of refreshing rest and reinvigoration to the whole system." Olmsted was here preaching to the converted; by the 1870s and 1880s the middle-class vacation to mountains or seashore was becoming an institution of modern life.[36]

The psychological assumptions of Olmsted's park philosophy were integral to his principles of proper landscape design. For him the guiding principle was that parks, even those that were humanly made, should look as "natural" as possible. Central Park, his masterpiece, included in its initial layout a scenery of rolling hills, small lakes, wooded copses, and broad meadows. There park-goers could enjoy leisurely walks, boating, horseback riding, ice-skating, and other traditional rural recreations. Fields and tracks for ball games, racing, and other such "boisterous fun and rough sports," however, were considered to be too intrusive and inappropriate, too artificial, for the pastoral effect Olmsted hoped to achieve. Above all, Central Park was meant to provide a setting for the unencumbered and undistracted admiration of natural beauty, refining, calming, and edifying the individual spirit. Like the landscape painters, Olmsted incorporated nature into genteel culture as another elevating object of "art appreciation," a tamed, nonthreatening, and perfected nature that owed its aesthetic inspiration to the orderly aristocratic parks of the English countryside, re-created now in the midst of the polyglot American city. Yet for all of his ostensibly elitist tastes (he designed his share of private estates, including the grounds for the huge Biltmore mansion of the Vanderbilts in North Carolina), Olmsted saw his urban park plans as creatures of democratic principles. They were to be public institutions, open and accessible to all, where the disparate classes might come together in a sense of community otherwise not possible in the socially stratified workaday existence of the modern city. These parks would not be the private province for the ostentatious display of the wealthy few, nor would their scenic integrity be sacrificed to the vulgar impulses of the masses. Social harmony would be brought about by the universally civilizing influence of natural beauty.[37]

Olmsted applied these same ends and standards to his plans for the majestic naturally occurring scenery of Yosemite Valley in his 1865 report to the California legislature. But ironically, in so doing he began to draw the political battle lines within which Muir, who shared many of his assumptions, was to find himself in coming years. Olmsted recommended, for example, the restriction of "all artificial constructions" that might clash with the scenery. More to the point, he urged the legislature not to give in to the "selfishness of a few individuals" and sacrifice the "interest of uncounted millions" to frivolous and profit-hungry motives. Already in 1865 Olmsted was discovering some of the ideological consequences of preservationism, wherein the dawning "new" liberal definition of the *public interest* compellingly began to show itself. Congress had directed that "this scenery shall never be private property, but that . . . it shall be held solely for public purposes." Therefore, he argued, it was essential for legislators to enact laws "to prevent an unjust use by individuals" and for such laws to be "rigidly enforced" because "the largest interest should be first and most strenuously guarded." [38]

The California legislature chose to ignore Olmsted's policy recommendations and instead over the years showed itself much more "strenuous" in guarding the private interests of the farmers, sheepherders, innkeepers, and lumbermen who staked their claims to the scenery and resources of the valley environs. Olmsted must have seen the writing on the wall. He left California and returned to the East before the end of 1865, recognizing a bad turn for his so-far illustrious career. Later he had better luck in New York State, joining with the noted guardian of genteel culture Charles Eliot Norton in a successful campaign to create the Niagara Falls Reservation (1885). There state commissioners adhered to Olmsted's aesthetic guidelines and demolished numerous hotels, mills, and billboards along a mile stretch above the falls, restoring their scenic beauty.[39] But it was left to Muir and the passage of time to see through his proposals for Yosemite, which had to await the first galvanization of the national preservationist movement in the 1890s. As perhaps the grandest and most concrete manifestations of genteel culture, Olmsted's ideas and creations—his philosophy and practice of what a park should be, how "natural scenery" should appear—played no small role in the formation of that movement and its constituency.

YOSEMITE BECAME the first major locus of Muir's own efforts on behalf of preservation when in 1889 he was enlisted into the nascent cause (after his decade of family-rearing and gentlemanly farming) by Robert Underwood Johnson, the editor of Century magazine. Johnson was himself a nature lover and an unabashed apostle of genteel aestheticism. ("What is needed is the inculcation, by every agency, of beauty as a principle," he once wrote.) Johnson asked Muir to write a series of articles for Century on the wonders of the valley in order to build public support for the establishment of a national park there. Muir, hoping to restart his writing career, had recently been editing a volume of his essays from earlier years entitled, significantly, Picturesque California (1889). The Century articles jolted him into political action and launched him into a period of greater literary productivity. By 1891, Muir announced that he was reducing his workload at the family ranch, thanks to the sound footing on which his successful management had placed the operation and to the continuing efforts of his wife and relatives.[40] He was able to return to a life of writing and travel, culminating first in perhaps his most important book-length work, The Mountains of California (1894), which incorporated refashioned material from the Century Yosemite articles and his 1870s notebooks and magazine pieces. The book represented a summary statement of his mature thought—a body of thought permeated by the genteel sensibility.

That Muir's wilderness advocacy in The Mountains of California and later works emerged out of and responded to the genteel cultural milieu is immediately apparent in the central statement of the book: "Pursuing my lonely way down the valley," he wrote, "I turned again and again to gaze on the glorious picture, throwing up my arms to inclose it as in a frame." The domestication of wilderness, its sentimentalization, and ultimately its acceptance as a desirable object of middle-class consumption required that it be "framed" for his audience according to their own aesthetic expectations and notions of nature. In order to mobilize public opinion behind wilderness preservation, Muir had to convince the public that (in his frequently quoted words) "going to the mountains is like going home." Within his "frame" he had to draw connections in the audience's mind between particular portions of wild nature (like Yosemite Valley) and the representations and cultivations of nature (as artifice) that were more familiar and acceptable. Muir's "frame" itself, the rhetoric that he used to analogize and allude to these genteel preconceptions, was a composite voice: the comforting words of scientific authority and religious faith (fully complementary to the popular mind) outfitted in the magazine-genre styles of the travel article and adventure story.[41] By these persuasive and ingratiating means Muir attempted to elevate wilderness in the public esteem to the realm of "higher good" and "finer things," where it would be held aloft from, preserved from, the baser uses that Gilded Age Americans (with their unexamined belief in economic progress) might otherwise ordain for it.

"To artists, few portions of the High Sierra are, strictly speaking, picturesque," Muir admitted in an early chapter of *The Mountains of California*. The icy wastes of granite there did not easily lend themselves to "being made into warm, sympathetic, lovable pictures with appreciable humanity in them." [42] As a result, Muir's rhetorical goals were twofold: to convert such desolate wilderness into lovable scenery in the reader's imagination and to endow it with a value apart from its conventional status as a collection of natural resources to be conquered and developed. Here Muir was well served by his personal biocentric views and his counter-Darwinian ambivalence regarding an "inhumane" nature, for his heightened consciousness of a wild nature oblivious to human concerns made him empathetic to the bleak impression that areas like the High Sierra might make on tenderfoot tourists. Their reactions, in fact, were very similar to his own. Throughout the descriptive passages in *The Mountains of California* Muir displays the curious double consciousness of nature that appeared in his letters home from the appalling Nevada desert during the 1878 Geodetic Survey, a sensibility repelled by the harsh and the savage in natural scenes, but seeking out ways to humanize and sentimentalize them. Yet if Muir's mind had not possessed this tension, had it instead been fully enclosed within a romanticized conception of nature that lacked the check of a biocentric perspective, then the effectiveness of his rhetoric might have been undercut. It was Muir's considerable self-consciousness of the necessity of humanizing wilderness, of making it "lovable," of "framing" it—a self-consciousness born out of this inner conceptual tension—that turned *The Mountains of California* into such a successful (and "classic") work of environmental advocacy.

This self-consciousness of Muir the rhetorician is clearly portrayed in the chapter that followed the admission that the High Sierra was not altogether "picturesque" or "sympathetic." He unfolds a telling anecdote about his serving as guide for two landscape artists searching for "suitable" mountains to paint. "The general expression of the scenery—rocky and savage—seemed sadly disappointing" to them, Muir noted, reporting their response: " 'All this is huge and sublime, but we see nothing as yet at all available for effective pictures.' " He led them onward to a "typical alpine landscape"—with foregrounds, backgrounds, and peaks in proper genre proportion—which they responded to enthusiastically. Muir repeated this motif of repulsion and embrace again and again in the book. Leaving the artists to their work and walking on alone until almost nightfall, he came upon a catastrophic vista that was "one of the most desolate I ever beheld": "Somber peaks, hacked and shattered, circled half-way around the horizon, wearing a savage aspect in the gloaming, and a waterfall chanted solemnly across the lake . . . down from the foot of the glacier. The fall and the lake and the glacier were almost equally bare; while the scraggy pines anchored in the rock-fissures were . . . dwarfed and shorn by storm-winds." As was typical of him, Muir reasoned that one merely needs to view such scenes in the proper spirit to find comfort: even the "darkest scriptures of the mountains" were "illumined with bright passages of love that never fail to make themselves felt" to the traveler, for all were "terrestrial manifestations of God." Similarly, various chains of young glacial lakes, "bleak, rough bowls" surrounded by gray lifeless moraine, struck the observer "keenly" with their "cold incompleteness," causing him to be "dashed and ill at ease, as if expecting to hear a forbidding voice." But soon the "first bewildering impression begins to wear off" and "we perceive that it is not altogether terrible," Muir wrote soothingly. The "reassuring birds and flowers" scattered across the area "manifest the warm humanity that pervades the coldest and most solitary" reaches of nature.[43]

The Mountains of California and most of Muir's nature writings were couched in the first-person singular and plural, "I" and "we," or in the second-person, "you." This strategy gave his nature descriptions a sense of immediacy and provided readers not only with vicarious experience but also with Muir's own sympathetic and comforting presence as genteel wilderness guide. Once he had led his audience out of the "forbidding" High Sierra and down into the verdant valleys, his rhetorical and interpretive job became easier. The appearance of cliffs and peaks could be analogized to impressive, fantastic, or exalted (yet familiar) architectural forms (again, artifice). One row of mountains reminded him of "some gigantic castle with turret and battlement, or some Gothic cathedral more abundantly spired than Milan's." The comparison of the Yosemite Valley's rock formations to "temples" was a common one for Muir, who hoped to evoke both an aesthetic and a religious response in the reader. He also made frequent use of pastoral and parklike imagery, again as part of his effort to "frame" wilderness areas as knowable and nonthreatening. Predatory animals rarely intruded upon Muir's settings; instead, he devoted most of his attention (and the reader's) to anthropomorphized songbirds and animals like the "hilarious, exuberant" Douglas squirrel. The trees and plants of a Sierra canyon he likened to "groves" and "gardens" arranged "as if cultivated artificially." Mountain meadows, "smoothly outspread in the savage wilderness," seemed like nothing else than the "carefully tended lawns of pleasure-grounds."[44] Without a doubt, the theme uniting these analogies was the taming, perfecting, edifying, and humanizing *artifice* of genteel culture.

Muir's acceptance of the facile hierarchical cultural bias of Victorianism, which divided the world into categories of civilization versus savagery, is perhaps most blatantly revealed in the course of his infrequent allusions to Native American peoples. Unlike Thoreau or later environmental writers such as the 1930s regionalists who celebrated Native Americans' symbiotic lifestyles, Muir for the most part shared the less-than-enlightened racial views of his contemporaries. Despite his own reputation as a rough-and-ready wild man of the mountains, for example, Muir often sniffed disdainfully at the "dirtiness" of the Indians whom he encountered in the wilderness, "sadly unlike Nature's neat well-dressed animals." These "debased fellow beings" spoiled the aesthetic effect of a scene and seemed not "a whit more natural"—in the genteel sense—than "glaring tailored tourists." Muir confessed on one occasion that his reaction to a group of Indians was "desperate repulsion," much like his response to any reminder of unloveliness in nature. Only the Thlinkit tribe of Alaskan natives ever impressed him favorably with their degree of cultivation, and he paid them the ultimate compliment of the Victorian racial taxonomy, with its hierarchy of superiors and inferiors: "These so-called savages," he wrote, "seem to me to rank above most of our uneducated white laborers." [45]

Not surprisingly, given his and his genteel audience's distaste for the possible barbarizing effects of a life lived close to nature, Muir's pleas on behalf of the value of wilderness carefully played to a belief in the longstanding American myth (biblically approved) of the regenerative qualities of a *temporary* descent into the wild. Addressing himself to the same "neurasthenic" middle-class audience as had Olmsted (and as would Muir's friend the strenuous-living Theodore Roosevelt), Muir claimed that an outing up into the mountains was just the balm for modern urban dwellers' jangled nerves and pasty, degenerated bodies. The "influences of pure nature" would "kill care, save you from deadly apathy, set you free, and call forth every faculty into vigorous, enthusiastic action," he wrote. Exalting the experience still further above such bodily effects, Muir argued that the individual spirit would be rejuvenated as well, brought closer to God through intimate contact with His awesome creation, an awe inspired by natural revelation. The beauty of Sierra landscapes was "evidently predestined," Muir concluded, because "the physical structure of the rocks on which the features of the scenery depend was acquired while they lay at least a mile deep below the pre-glacial surface." Muir also reminded his churchgoing audience that an ancient, now-fallen Sequoia tree was "in its prime, swaying in the Sierra winds, when Christ walked the earth." Yet even as he "framed" the wilderness in such grand and cosmic terms, Muir was careful always to reduce his scale so that his spiritual message would remain homely and personal, nonintimidating. Borrowing (and popularizing for a more general audience) the Transcendentalist ideal of integration, he described powerfully the experience that might be had in a Sierran meadow:

> With inexpressible delight you wade out into the grassy sun-lake, feeling yourself contained in one of Nature's most sacred chambers . . . secure from yourself, free in the universal beauty. And notwithstanding the scene is so impressively spiritual, and you seem dissolved in it, yet everything about you is beating with warm, terrestrial, human love and life delightfully substantial and familiar. The resiny pines are types of health and steadfastness; the robins feeding on the sod belong to the same species you have known since childhood; and surely these daisies, larkspurs, and goldenrods are the very friend-flowers of the old home garden. Bees hum as in a harvest noon, butterflies waver above the flowers, and like them you lave in the vital sunshine. . . . You are all eye, sifted through and through with light and beauty.[46]

As this passage would seem to indicate, Muir's most fundamental beliefs about the meaning of wilderness could not entirely be contained within the bounds of the publicizing "frame" of the genteel worldview. There is a conceptual disjunction in these words—the sojourner in nature was to become integral with universal light and beauty, melding his consciousness with the divine cosmos, only to be reminded of the robins and daisies in his own backyard. Wilderness to Muir was not simply a setting for personal relaxation or invigoration, nor was its grandeur and sublimity truly reducible to the homely and sentimental scale of garden plots. His was a biocentric consciousness that could peer beyond the frame of comforting genteel presumptions, personally disturbing and transient as such widened perceptions might be. Yet he did have them, confronting a nature cold, scarred, and lifeless, before coping with the philosophical consequences as best he could: by retreating. Muir nevertheless went back for more over the years, again and again, up to the forbidding reaches of the Sierras and across barren Alaskan glaciers, perhaps because the confrontation was truly such a test for him. The experience of integration with wild nature, he believed most deeply, could be radically transformative of the individual—*redemptive*—and must be a trial. Integration with the creation ("baptism," as he called it) broke down the empty gulf between fallen humanity and a loving God. Muir's purpose in bringing people to the wilderness was in this sense fundamentally subversive, or rather, convertive.

In 1871—back in his wild-man-of-the-mountains days—Muir raged to a correspondent about the "gross heathenism of civilization," which had "generally destroyed nature, and poetry, and all that is spiritual." Modern people were "so ground and pressed by the mills of culture," he remarked, "that God cannot play a single tune upon them." Human conceit and self-centeredness—including genteel culture and the this-worldly materialism that was its foundation—must be thrown off in any genuine encounter with the pure Nature of wilderness. The consequence would be an "awakening" of the individual "from the stupefying effects of the vice of over-industry and the deadly apathy of luxury," or so Muir wrote in an 1898 essay, revealing that his spiritual agenda had changed little in the intervening years.[47] As might be expected of the son of a Campbellite, the convertive wilderness trial he set for himself was a good deal more mortifying than the one he proselytized to the uninitiated. He would climb trees in thunderstorms or stand on the shores of dead frigid lakes, while offering his public meadows and valleys suitable for framing. Biocentrism, with its dreadful message to humanity, was the cross Muir bore; natural revelation was his saving grace. Genteel wilderness advocacy, for him, became an act of natural theodicy.

This is the Muir revealed in glimpses, in conceptual disjunctions and chilling descriptions scattered throughout his writings. Casual readers did not dwell on these passages, as indeed Muir did not want them to. It would have defeated his purpose, a purpose that was increasingly defined by the scope of his own worldly engagement and responsibilities. Particularly, there was his politicization within the gathering preservationist movement. For Muir in those years public advocacy set limits to social and cultural criticism, muting most expressions of his persistently unconventional biocentric and religious views. It must also be granted that Muir was hardly a systematic or even a completely coherent thinker and that he could not fully grasp in a self-conscious manner the implications of biocentrism and Christian naturalism for genteel cultural assumptions. As will be seen, there is a social critique and a political agenda to be found in Muir's works from this period, but usually these themes were scattered and subsumed within the genteel rhetoric of wilderness promotion. As his biographers have long noted, Muir well understood that wilderness experience must remain a tourist experience for most Americans, a valued but temporary balm safely and superficially tasted from the civilized precincts of lodges, roadways, and hotels. Muir was politically sophisticated in many respects, and he knew that wilderness areas would be preserved only if they were incorporated into a mainstream lifestyle. Only then would these areas win over the influential constituency of the well-to-do necessary for their preservation. In this pragmatic sense, Muir's wilderness concept offered no subversive challenge to genteel culture. He *must* fence wilderness intellectually within the bounds of that culture.

Yet, taking a wider perspective, Muir's late-Victorian efforts to define wilderness and to encourage Americans to experience it did have their role in an important intellectual and artistic revolt against Victorianism that was being waged in the turn-of-the-century period. Muir, in effect, was "converting" his audience toward new beliefs and behaviors more profoundly than he realized. The genteel Muir could see outside the assumptions of genteel culture for the very reason that those assumptions were in the process of being displaced by a new, twentieth-century culture: modernism. The desire to bridge the gulf between the subjective self and the objective world, to achieve integration; the quest for the real, for the authentic—these were central characteristics of modernist culture. Among the harbingers of modernism were those who rejected the overcivilized, overrefined *artifice* of genteel culture as detached and delusive, and who sought instead a grounding in the realism of nature. The designers and artisans of the Arts and Crafts movement, for example, upheld *simplicity* in materials and design as the highest quality to be embodied in furniture and houses (quite in opposition to genteel ornateness). In addition, the famed architects Louis Sullivan and Frank Lloyd Wright drew their primary inspiration from the organic and the natural, even as they created some of the most "modern" buildings of their time. And Muir, for all of his conventionality, must be counted as one of this cohort of modernist innovators because of the main imperative of his advocacy. He told genteel Americans that they could not find nature in landscape paintings or in urban parks, or in the pages of his own articles and books. Their aesthetic, their culture, was not sufficient to represent or define it. Recalling an 1881 visit to Alaska, Muir proclaimed

> how fine it would be could I cut a square of the tundra sod of conventional picture size, frame it, and hang it among the paintings on my study walls at home, saying to myself, "Such a Nature painting taken at random from any part of the thousand-mile bog would make the other pictures look dim and coarse."

To appreciate nature truly, the public must go out and experience it directly themselves, in the wild. When Muir wrote "Come to the mountains and see," he helped to transform American culture.[48]

THE FINAL two and a half decades of Muir's life were devoted to ensuring that Americans would be afforded the opportunity to "come to the mountains." These were the years of preservationist activism that had been inaugurated in 1889–90 by the Yosemite National Park campaign. These were also necessarily years of "political education" for Muir, who was confronted with the difficulties of achieving preservationist goals. The phrase was his own from a 1905 letter noting in a fatigued tone the end of a long battle to wrest control of Yosemite Valley from the state of California. That battle took place because of the distinctly partial success of the earlier campaign to establish the park: the famed Yosemite Valley, the centerpiece, was not included in the park by Congress. The battle of 1905 finally brought victory, yet in the previous year Congress had returned more than 500 square miles of the original park to the public domain and private development. The issue of who would oversee and manage Yosemite remained pressing, and there was still the "everlasting Hetch-Hetchy fight" (1903–13), involving a proposed artificial reservoir in a smaller valley already within the park, which was to become a legendary lost cause of twentieth-century environmentalism.[49] For Muir and his fellow preservationists laying the foundations of the modern National Park System, every victory was to be hard-won, piecemeal, amendable, and reversible.

The constant threats to the new parks bespoke the contingency and fragility of the good amid a world governed by human sinfulness: this was the essence of Muir's political education. It was also an insight born of his Christian naturalism, which directed him, impelled him, on his personal crusade. Muir's letters and writings reflected his practical importance to the preservationist movement as advocate and lobbyist. He defined the value of wilderness, characterized the dangers to it, and proposed remedies. In many respects his rhetoric and ideas invoked themes, prescriptions, and demonologies typical of the larger contemporary mainstream reform movement known as Progressivism. But underlying his words were the imperatives of Christian naturalism, with its conception of fallen man as a willful "half animal, half angel" and with its unspoken principles of biocentric egalitarianism.[50] The tone of his post-*Mountains* preservationist writings was in general moderate, still reflective of that work's ingratiating genteel strategies. Yet on occasion—during heated junctures in the Hetch Hetchy fight, for example—the voice of Muir the thundering prophet, the "fanatic," could be heard.

The *good* at stake for Muir in the battles over the parks was twofold and synonymous: the public good and nature's good. The "public good" or the "public interest" was a central doctrine of Progressivism, its defense part of the deeper turn-of-the-century sea change in American political culture heralding the new liberalism. The conflict between individual self-interest and the public good was dramatized all too appropriately in scandals of the era that involved the country's public lands, including established or potential national parks and forest reserves. Set against the poignant backdrop of Turner's closing frontier— and the vanishing of national virtue along with it—these scandals were a discouraging spectacle of corruption, greed, bribery, exploitation, and perversion of the laws. To Muir, however, the main issue was not simply that a few individuals and companies were illegally accumulating resources at the exclusion of the rest of the public (the "little man"), as the more populist-minded would have it. Nor was his primary concern with a wasteful depletion of resources and the risk posed to the public's interest in future sustainable prosperity, as the infant utilitarian conservation movement was depicting the scandals. Rather, when Muir invoked the public good during these years of controversy, he meant it literally, in a religious sense. The good of the public, their ability to be good, to be perfected from their fallen state, hinged on their opportunity to experience God's pristine nature. Parks and forest reserves were natural instruments of revelation and, ultimately, of grace. Their exclusive ownership and despoliation by the few was consequently, in Muir's theology, one of the worst human crimes and sins imaginable.

It is no wonder then that the voice of the "fanatic" could make an appearance in Muir's writings, speaking in biblical tones on behalf of the public good. "These sacred mountain temples are the holiest ground that the heart of man has consecrated," he wrote in a 1908 letter to Theodore Roosevelt, referring to the valleys of Yosemite. "They are national properties in which every man has a right and interest." Because salvation must be open to all in the democratic setting of the parks, the "plunderers" and "tree-killers" who destroyed such places were "as unconscionable and enterprising as Satan," Muir declared; "let the government hasten to cast them out and make an end to them." Rousing himself fully to a prophetic rage, he continued:

> For it must be told again and again, and be burningly borne in mind, that just now, while protective measures are being deliberated languidly, destruction and use are speeding on faster and farther every day. The axe and saw are insanely busy, chips are flying thick as snowflakes, and every summer thousands of acres of priceless forests, with their underbrush, soil, springs, climate, scenery, and religion, are vanishing away in clouds of smoke.

The only possible path back to righteousness would require that "every acre that is left should be held together under the federal government as a basis for a general policy of administration for the public good." Muir might and did variously define that good to include the assuaging of modern urban nervousness or the improvement of physical health or the need for exposure to beauty, but fundamentally all of these elements tended to the greatest good, and highest use, that the public might find in pristine nature. Wilderness, he wrote, was for "washing off sins and cobweb cares of the devil's spinning." [51] It was for the public's redemption.

Interwoven through Muir's anthropocentric pleas there were also more subtle and radical biocentric rationales put forward for preservation, as some of his critics perceived. In his defense of nature's good Muir was accused of placing its interests before those of humankind. Mayor James D. Phelan of San Francisco, one of Muir's chief opponents in the Hetch Hetchy fight, remarked that Muir would "sacrifice his own family for the preservation of beauty." Another opponent, Congressman William Kent of California, also detected the biocentrism at the core of Muir's thinking: "[W]ith him it is me and God and the rock where God put it, and that is the end of the story." It is true that in some passages humanity fades into the background and only the landscape of God's creation is depicted, as is shown in this passage about the California redwoods, another of the natural objects that Muir championed:

> It took more than three thousand years to make some of the trees in these Western woods—trees that are still standing in perfect strength and beauty, waving and singing in the mighty forests of the Sierra. Through all the wonderful, eventful centuries since Christ's time—and long before that—God has cared for these trees, saved them from drought, disease, avalanches, and a thousand straining, leveling tempests and floods.

This depiction was a biocentric argument, an argument of intrinsic worth. The trees' value was rooted, as was Muir's whole biocentric viewpoint, in a recognition of God's immanence throughout His creation. The implications of the argument brought down on Muir the charges of fanaticism. Economic exploitation of the giant trees and other natural wonders, he proclaimed, was a sin of the highest order because in showing a "perfect contempt for Nature" the "tree-killers" also struck directly at "the God of the mountains."[52]

Despite the efforts of Muir's critics to portray him as single-mindedly biocentric and radical, uncaring of human needs, his arguments in this vein were rarely employed in isolation. The pursuit of nature's good and the public good were equivalent in Muir's mind, mutually achievable. His entire purpose in publicizing wilderness and bringing people to the parks was to secure their long-term protection. In the preface of his popular book *Our National Parks* (1901) Muir explained that he wrote about the parks "with a view to inciting the people to come and enjoy them, and get them into their hearts, that so at length their preservation and right use might be made sure." The attainment of grace through natural revelation—getting the wilderness "into their hearts"—would convert the public to act for that which was holy, the wilderness itself. For although God had cared for the redwoods and other natural places, Muir wrote in an early draft of an 1897 essay "The American Forests," God could not "save them from sawmills and fools; this is left to the American people!" In the best evangelical tradition Muir was reminding his audience that men do evil through their willfulness or complacency, but that they could do good only through positive righteous action. His deepest faith during the years of his political education was that the grace given by nature would inspire this righteousness. His deepest hope—frequently challenged over these years—was in Progress, the progress of good in the world, as he foretold in "The American Forests":

> The making of the far-famed New York Central Park was opposed . . . but straight right won its way, and now that park is appreciated. So we confidently believe it will be with our great national parks and forest reservations. There will be a period of indifference on the part of the rich, sleepy with wealth, and of the toiling millions, sleepy with poverty, most of whom never saw a forest; a period of screaming protest and objection from the plunderers. . . . But light is surely coming, and the friends of destruction will preach and bewail in vain.[53]

Muir made a significant change in "The American Forests" for publication, a revision that registered the political conflict that had erupted around forest protection by the late 1890s. Only "Uncle Sam," he now wrote, could save the forests from "fools." Muir believed that the federal government had a key role to play in enacting restrictions on forest use. Unlike Thoreau, he did not conceive of wilderness in the ideological terms of "absolute freedom," one meaning of which was a complete negative freedom beyond the reach of governments, especially the central government. Rather, the freedom that Muir found in the wilderness was a religiously defined positive freedom of personal growth and liberation from sin. Muir and the so-called Progressive generation were confronting in their time what they considered to be the consequences of too much negative individual freedom—class exploitation, concentration of wealth, urban decay, and a landscape consumed and laid waste. As Muir's friend Theodore Roosevelt said during a famous speech on conservation, "In the past we have admitted the right of the individual . . . to injure the future of all of us for his own temporary and immediate profit. The time has come for a change." To the reform-minded like Roosevelt, many of the problems that beset post-frontier America required solutions that were national in scope—corporate regulation, for example—and must be the province of the federal government. The disposition of the nation's public lands, most of which were under the oversight of federal legislation, seemed necessarily an issue that must be contended for at the national level, in the executive branch and the halls of Congress. Preservationism thus intersected with two of the major trends of the Progressive reform era that unfolded between 1890 and 1920: political centralization and modernization.[54]

Several other exigencies of national politics during this period also shaped Muir's political education, and the fate of preservationism. First and foremost, it was difficult to reverse course on public land policies that in previous decades had emphasized the free or cheap distribution of land. One statistic compiled by the Bureau of Corporations for a 1914 resource inventory report furnished evidence of the extent of the giveaway. In 1870, at the beginning of Muir's career, three-quarters of the standing timber in the country was on public land; by 1914, the year marking the end of Muir's life, four-fifths of the timber was in private hands. This sort of policy, embodied in laws like the Timber Culture Act and the Timber and Stone Act, fostered a widespread mentality that the public lands should be dispensed exclusively for private exploitation, no strings attached. Hindered by these attitudes, reform seemed all the more remote to Muir and the preservationists (and other reformers) because they had to deal with a Congress dominated by money, partisanship, local interests, and laissez-faire ideology. Muir once commented that "in Congress, a sizable chunk of gold, carefully concealed, will outtalk and outfight all the nation on a subject like forestry."[55] The two major political parties were equally suspect.

The challenge for Muir, as for others of the Progressive generation, was to find alternative means to protect the public interest, given the pervasiveness or potential of corruption among elected representatives. The storied fate of beleaguered Yosemite was a case in point. New political, legal, and institutional forms would have to be invented, designed to be insulated from the compromises and pressures of politics-as-usual. Politics would have to be purified, and in some sense nullified, in the framing of policies for parks and reserves. In their resort to these means, as in their invocation of the public interest and demand for federal activism, Muir and the preservationists were fully of their time. John Muir's political education via preservationism therefore throws light on the promise and the pitfalls of the emerging new liberal order. Still only half-created by the time of Muir's death, it was this order, this political universe, that fostered the first institutional growths and concrete achievements of preservationism, as well as some of its defeats.

PERHAPS THE MOST important political development of Muir's career occurred in 1892, with the formation of the Sierra Club. The Sierra Club was avowedly an organization devoted to outings and promotion, "to explore, enjoy, and render accessible the mountain regions of the Pacific coast; To publish authentic information concerning them." Yet it was also a single-issue pressure group much like others being formed in this period, intended to sidestep party regulars and machines and force "real issues" into the public debate, thereby focusing political energy more effectively. Such groups brought public pressure to bear on Congress, and they lobbied representatives and administrators on reform issues as diverse as consumer protection, immigration restriction, and Prohibition. The political goals of the Sierra Club were simply stated, if not so simply achieved: "To enlist the support and cooperation of the people and the government in preserving the forests and other natural features of the Sierra Nevada mountains." Muir was chosen as president of the Sierra Club at its founding, and he remained its leader and chief spokesman for the rest of his life. Its early membership was small but well-to-do and influential, including important figures like Robert Underwood Johnson, David Starr Jordan, president of Stanford University, and Warren Olney, prominent attorney and future mayor of Oakland, along with a number of Bay-area scientists, professors, businessmen, and civic leaders, all united in their enthusiasm for the Sierras.[56]

The Sierra Club was obliged to use whatever clout and connections it had almost immediately. In 1893, the first of several measures to constrict the boundaries of Yosemite National Park was submitted to Congress. The Sierra Club's response was indicative of the techniques of Progressive politics, for, rather than writing their congressmen or going hat-in-hand to party bosses, its members focused their lobbying pressure on the House Agriculture Committee, where (with the deliberations carefully followed by Johnson) the bill subsequently died.[57] These tactics were essential in the absence of a mass constituency for wilderness preservation, which did not yet exist. The advantage of pressure-group politics was that this mass support was not absolutely necessary for placing items on the government's agenda, or even for pushing them to passage. Organizationally, preservationism remained for some years confined to a comparatively small number of well-educated, well-heeled individuals, but they did have their effect on legislation and policy.

The cultivation of a constituency nonetheless became an important area of activity for the Sierra Club, just as mass education was important for any single-issue group. In a clash between competing special interests, voter pressure could be decisive. Muir's books and articles, published for a large popular audience, were a crucial dimension of the Sierra Club's mass campaign. Their famous outings, beginning in 1901, brought dozens and eventually hundreds of campers into the mountains at a time. And over the years, to an increasing extent, those campers included genteel women, who arguably comprised the broadest grassroots base of support for preservationism in the early 1900s. Women mobilized during the Progressive Era across a wide front of reform endeavor, seeking to expand the moral sphere of the feminine realm into the public sphere of politics; the regenerative promise of women's domestic influence helped to secure them the vote by 1920. As a cause of Progressive feminine politics, both resource conservation and wilderness preservation embodied the domestic ideals of clean living, moral nurture, and child care. Advocate Lydia Adams-Williams claimed that conservation was to be considered primarily as "women's work." In seeking to reclaim nature on behalf of moral, aesthetic, and religious ideals—what had been relegated by market values to the domain of feminized culture—Muir's crusade was, in a larger sense, a feminine cause. During the Hetch Hetchy fight, a newspaper cartoonist was more perceptive than he realized when he depicted Muir wearing a dress and apron and wielding a broom, "Sweeping Back the Flood." In the image, the cartoon Muir as female do-gooder is about to be swept away himself by a wall of water labeled "Hetch Hetchy Project," representing masculine control and power over nature.[58]

Beyond and supplemental to the efforts of the Sierra Club, the National Federation of Women's Clubs, an umbrella group for genteel women's groups around the nation, was instrumental in informing and mobilizing women around conservation and preservation issues. On occasion the results could be impressive. In 1904, Mrs. Lovell White of the federation presented to Congress petitions with 1.5 million signatures on behalf of saving California's Calaveras Grove of Big Trees. In 1913 the decades-long campaign by women in the federation and the Audubon Society to ban the use of exotic bird feathers in ladies' hats finally achieved success, with Congress acting to prohibit their importation. Yet overall, the success rate of mass politicking and popular pressure by the Sierra Club and these other organizations was decidedly mixed. The club's drive to add Yosemite Valley to the national park began in 1897 and did not conclude with victory until 1905, and it was a somewhat hollow victory at that; local lumbermen and stockmen with their own friends in Congress had carved away their portions from the park the year before. Moreover, the impressive outpouring of support for the Big Trees in 1904 did not immediately sway Congress. Measures were not passed to save the Calaveras Grove until 1909, and it was 1954 before all of the trees in the grove actually attained protected status.[59]

It quickly became clear to Muir and others that Congress was probably not the best guardian of either the public or nature's good. Increasingly, they looked for solutions to the president and the executive branch, to administrative and regulatory rather than purely legislative measures, again linking their movement to a larger trend of Progressive reform. In this tendency, the preservationists at least briefly joined forces with the utilitarian conservation movement led by Gifford Pinchot, who upheld a doctrine of scientific management and "wise use" of natural resources for sustainable development. Both Muir and Pinchot had been heartened by the consequences of the General Revision Act of 1891, which (perhaps unintentionally) gave the president the power to withdraw public forestlands from entry and place them in reserves. This authority—wielded on a nonpartisan basis in the national interest, according to its supporters—would prove to be essential to the establishment of the national park and forest systems over the next two decades. First President Harrison and then President Cleveland withdrew from entry almost 50 million acres of forestlands during the 1890s, saving them from—or for— development, depending on whom one asked.

Cleveland was encouraged in his actions by the National Forest Commission, a body formed in 1896 to study how existing reserves might be managed, and to what end. Muir was named an ex officio member. The commission was born after Pinchot, together with Johnson of the Sierra Club, persuaded Cleveland's secretary of the interior of its importance and got a stipend from the House Appropriations Committee chairman. The commission was funded through the National Academy of Sciences and headed by Muir's longtime friend Charles S. Sargent, a Harvard professor and the nation's top expert on botany and sylviculture. Sargent had been active in the establishment of New York State's Adirondack Park during the 1880s, a major achievement for conservation nationally that by 1907 encompassed nearly 2.1 million acres "forever kept as wild forest lands." The commission's secretary was the equally capable Gifford Pinchot, a figure who was to be as epochal as Muir in the history of American environmentalism. Trained in the latest ideas of Europe, he was one of the few foresters in America with substantial practical experience, which he obtained during the early 1890s managing the forests on Olmsted's Biltmore estate, where the Vanderbilts gave him a free hand. Joining Pinchot, Sargent, and Muir on the commission were also several renowned scientists, including Arnold Hague, an associate of John Wesley Powell.[60] The Progressive generation placed great store in these commissions of experts, for they promised everything that politics-as-usual lacked—objectivity, disinterest, scientific know-how, honesty, and integrity.

For Muir one of the main functions of the forestry commission was the exposure of corruption. The concept was known to reformers and muckrakers as "sunshine," using fact-finding procedures and exposés to bring to public scrutiny the hidden operations of private entities. The sunshine commission was intended to put teeth in the ideal of the public interest because its findings could lead to demands for regulation. Most commissions created during the Progressive decades, which looked into issues such as poverty, urban conditions, and corporate practices, were of the sunshine variety, investigatory but with no enforcement power. The National Forest Commission was no different. Yet Muir had a great optimism for its mission, the promising vision of a public aroused to action by disclosures of crime and corruption. After Congress voted in 1897 to suspend Grover Cleveland's additions to the forest reserves and restore them to the public domain, opening them again to exploitation, Muir and others were outraged. They realized that they must mobilize the public to fight the powerful lumber and livestock interests that had sponsored the measure, whose ultimate goal was to rescind all of the reserves. The conflict, Muir wrote, was between "landscape righteousness and the devil." [61] Sunshine tactics might turn the tide.

Muir was spurred to write a series of major articles for *Harper's* and the *Atlantic Monthly*, publicizing atrocities committed in existing parks and reserves along with examples of gross abuse of the land laws. "The sooner it is stirred up and debated before the people the better," he wrote of the reserves issue, "for thus the light will be let into it." And "as soon as the light comes the awakened million creates a public opinion that overcomes wrong however cunningly veiled." For, he believed, "only in darkness does vandalism flourish," and only in the consciousness of sin could the goodness in men prevail. Accordingly, Muir reported some of the findings of the Forest Commission and other bureaus investigating the state of the public lands. Readers discovered that within a reserve in the Sierras "lumbermen are allowed to spoil it at their will, and sheep in uncountable ravenous hordes to trample it and devour every green leaf within reach; while the shepherds . . . set innumerable fires, which burn not only the undergrowth . . . but countless thousands of the venerable giants." Throughout the West, deliberate theft of timber from the public domain was rampant because, Muir declared, the thieves' "consciences flinch no more in cutting timber from the wild forests than in drawing water from a lake or river." Everywhere in their wake they left "waste and confusion," lopping off huge trees with massive stumps to spare, clearing less-valuable species and leaving them to rot. In those cases where companies or individuals bothered with obtaining title to land, they often resorted to outright fraud to evade acreage limits set per claimant. Muir cited the infamous example of a lumber company that would "hire the entire crew of every vessel which might happen to touch at any port in the redwood belt," have each man file on a 160-acre plot, and "immediately deed the land to the company," whereupon the company would give "the jolly sailors fifty dollars apiece for their trouble."[62]

To protect the parks, reserves, and public lands from such depredations Muir also sought in his articles to provide some definition of their value. The issue was quite pertinent to the debate because at this time even the national parks, still recent innovations, had no special, off-limits status to prevent use of their resources. Muir is credited with helping to originate this status in essays from 1897 and later years, including "The Wild Parks and Forest Reservations of the West" and "The American Forests," subsequently collected into the *Our National Parks* volume. Urging Muir to write the articles, Charles S. Sargent told him that "no one knows so well as you the value of our forests—that their use for lumber is but a small part of the value."[63] In fact, Muir marshaled a variety of arguments on behalf of the reserves and parks, not all of them strictly preservationist.

Playing to Progressive antimonopoly sentiments, Muir defended the rights of genuine settlers to have use of the forests "for homes and bread," rights that were being denied because of the illegal expropriation and concentrated ownership of homestead lands by corporations. Muir also did not rule out lumbering as a valuable use of the reserves; as he wrote in 1895, they "must be made to yield a sure harvest of timber while at the same time all their other far-reaching uses may be maintained unimpaired" (in embryo, the eventual "multiple use" philosophy of the Forest Service in later decades). Additionally, Muir emphasized the importance of the wild forests as a watershed, the "Big Tree" (Sequoia) included. "[L]eaving all its higher uses out of the count," the Sequoia was "a tree of life, a never-failing spring, sending living water to the lowlands," Muir wrote, positing that "for every grove cut down a stream is dried up."[64]

But it was to emphasizing the "higher values" of the parks and reserves that Muir focused most of his persuasiveness and advocacy. As of the late 1890s there were only four national parks in the West: Yellowstone, Yosemite, Sequoia, and General Grant. There were thirty forest reserves, some of them among the most scenic areas in the country, including the Grand Canyon, the Black Hills, Mount Rainier, the Olympic Reserve, and the Grand Tetons. To Muir these places constituted the "wildest health and pleasure grounds accessible and available to tourists." He went out of his way to make explicit in the advocacy articles what had been more implicit in *The Mountains of California*, that for all their wildness the parks and reserves were safe and welcoming: "The snake danger is so slight it is hardly worth mentioning. Bears are a peaceable people. . . . As to Indians, most of them are dead or civilized. . . . No American wilderness I know of is so dangerous as a city home. . . . Fear nothing." The chief value of the parks and reserves for humans was scenery and recreation (and redemption). In order to build them a pool of visitors and a protective constituency, Muir pressed hard on these themes—and one other. To make them beloved places, he reiterated a phrase that came to be identified with him, the national icon, the man of the mountains: that going to wilderness was like "going home." [65]

Perhaps Muir went to such anthropocentric lengths to "frame" the wild, to make it warmly human, because he worried about lingering prejudices and fears toward it and was determined to preempt opponents claiming the areas needed taming. Yet here and there in his *National Park* essays, implicitly and explicitly, he advanced his controversial biocentric arguments on the issue of value, speaking his private thoughts frankly and undercutting to a degree the very idea of assigning human value to nature. In an essay on Yellowstone Park he noted that among visitors "the question comes up, 'What are rattlesnakes good for?' " To which Muir replied, "As if nothing that does not obviously make for the benefit of man had any right to exist; as if our ways were God's ways." Rattlesnakes, like other natural entities, he concluded, were "good for themselves, and we need not begrudge them their share of life." [66]

In any case, Muir and others in the nascent conservation movement agreed that whether valued as homestead sites, timberlands, watersheds, pleasure grounds, or creation-in-itself, the parks and forest reserves of the West demanded the oversight and management of a "permanent rational policy." For all of the land laws and revisions passed by

Congress since George Perkins Marsh's time, Muir was still forced to look overseas for models of this rational policy, just as Marsh had been. The United States in the Progressive period was only now entering a new phase of activist government. But in "The American Forests" Muir cited numerous examples of how "every other civilized nation can give us a lesson on the management and care of forests." Restrictions on lumbering and clearing, fire protection, and extensive reforestation were only a few overseas measures that appealed to Muir. The U.S. government, in sorry contrast, had a "protective policy which has never protected," he wrote, a policy that had "allowed millions of acres of the grandest forest trees to be stolen or destroyed, or sold for nothing." The Timber and Stone Act was to his mind a "dust and ashes act."[67]

One institution of the U.S. government—the U.S. Army—did attract the admiration of Muir and others, and for a tellingly Progressive reason. For several years prior to the 1897–98 forest reserves crisis, the national parks had been "efficiently managed and guarded by small troops of the United States cavalry, directed by the Secretary of the Interior," Muir wrote. "Under this care the forests are flourishing." In his view the army's efforts were quite in contrast to the "noisy, ever changing management, or mismanagement" of places like the state-controlled Yosemite Valley, with its "blundering, plundering, money-making vote-sellers who receive their places from boss politicians as purchased goods." Muir and other members of the Forest Commission, including Charles S. Sargent, believed that the army should remain at its post in the national parks and be expanded to patrol the reserves as well because it was "the only effective and reliable arm of the government free from the blight of politics." They also knew from the public land scandals that there was a considerable gulf between the intent of laws on the books in Washington and their enforcement in remote regions of the country, which the army could and did provide. A "permanent rational policy" for the parks and reserves, which protected the public good and nature's interests, would require a similar depoliticized federal entity to formulate and administer it.[68] Muir had been projecting this nonpartisan management for Yosemite since at least 1890. At the time the Forest Commission issued its report, however, there was only the army to serve as an American model of administrative efficiency and integrity.

On this issue and others more fundamental, Muir had his famous parting of the ways with Gifford Pinchot and the utilitarian conservationists in 1897. Biographers point emblematically to a hotel lobby confrontation over sheep grazing (Pinchot thought it harmless, Muir did not), when only weeks before the two men had spent a fine evening camping together on the rim of the Grand Canyon. The years 1896–98 were a time of collaboration and crisis for all of the defenders of the forests, and in the course of events the commission's proposal for scientific management of public forest reserves began to move from theory to reality—but not in the direction that Muir had desired. Pinchot gained the ascendancy in policy making with his appointment as "special forest agent" for the Interior Department in 1897 (empowered by legislation to oversee the use of the reserves) and as head of the Division of Forestry in the Department of Agriculture the following year. His utilitarian principles went with him into government. As forester of the Biltmore estate, he had several years earlier ranked the value of forests according to a rather different set of priorities than Muir's: "The first is profitable production, which will give the Forest direct utility. If this were absent, the existence of the Forest would be justified only as it lends beauty and interest to the Estate. Second, a nearly constant annual yield, which will give steady occupation to a trained force . . . and make regular operations possible." To Pinchot's mind the "trained force" necessary to managing and patrolling the reserves had to be scientifically educated, commercially oriented foresters under his direction, a system he began putting into place after his appointment to the Forestry Division, which in short order burgeoned to become the Bureau of Forestry, and by 1905, the U.S. Forest Service.[69]

Muir, outside of government, commented on these developments in a 1902 letter:

The politicians, in the interest of wealthy mine, mill, sheep, and cattle owners, of course nominate superintendents and supervisors of reservations supposed to be harmlessly blind to their stealings. Only from the Military Department, free from political spoils poison, has any real good worth mention been gained for forests, and so . . . it will be, no matter how well the Forestry Department may be organized, until the supervisors, superintendents, and rangers are brought under Civil Service Reform.

Although two years later Pinchot did incorporate his personnel under civil service regulations, Muir's suspicions ran deeper, to Pinchot's whole philosophy of the forest, which Muir was in time to denounce openly as one of "panutilization . . . shampiously" clothed as "smug-smiling philanthropy." Pointing to the surface moral utilitarian basis of Pinchot's conservationism, Muir remarked that "much is said on questions of this kind about 'the greatest good for the greatest number,' but the greatest number is too often found to be number one." Its real end was "to make everything immediately and selfishly commercial," and its consequence was despoliation. Muir was not being entirely fair to Pinchot, whose policies attempted to limit and regulate economic activity in the forest reserves (with fees and leases), and who was almost single-handedly responsible for promoting conservation into a national issue (his press releases appeared in millions of newspapers). "P. is ambitious," Muir fumed privately, "and never hesitates to sacrifice anything or anybody in his way." Nevertheless, as the new century began with Pinchot as the nation's chief forester, his philosophy became predominant in shaping official policy over the reserves. By 1909, for example, 1.5 million cattle and 7.6 million sheep (Muir's despised "hooved locusts") were grazing on reserve lands.[70]

Pinchot's ascendancy occurred because Theodore Roosevelt unexpectedly succeeded to the presidency in 1901. In Roosevelt both utilitarian conservationists and preservationists discovered that they had a friend in high places. He combined the sensibility of an avid outdoorsman with a Progressive's abhorrence of disorder and waste, and he was keen to enhance the authority of the executive branch. Pinchot was made one of his lieutenants, and conservation became a centerpiece of Square Deal reform. Stirred by recent massive forest fires and dire warnings of a future "timber famine," the public embraced conservation as an important national issue for the first time. Roosevelt employed the reserve-making power repeatedly and greatly expanded the acreage within the forest reserve system, all of which was transferred to the oversight of Pinchot's newly organized U.S. Forest Service in 1905. He created several commissions to investigate the land laws and to inventory the nation's natural resources, often with the close involvement of Pinchot. In 1908, a Governor's Conference on the Conservation of Natural Resources was convened at the White House, attended by state governors as well as national business and civic leaders. Muir and the preservationists were not invited.

While Pinchot his enemy prospered, Muir made his own appeals to the seat of power. In 1903, Roosevelt paid a visit to Yosemite, and Muir acted as his sole guide, taking the opportunity to lobby and "do some forest good," as he predicted to a correspondent before the meeting. There was an instant affinity between the two men, both larger-than-life personalities who savored the physical challenges of nature. "I fairly fell in love with him," Muir told someone after their three days of hikes and campfire conversation. He had the president's ear thereafter, yet after their visit Roosevelt in a speech reiterated his commitment to Pinchot's policies, even as he spoke phrases inspired by Muir's persuasiveness ("preservation"; "monuments in themselves"; "passed on unimpaired"). Roosevelt is credited with tripling the size of the forest system during his tenure, to 150 million acres, and with doubling the number of national parks. Most of these parks were very scenic but also of little economic value, so they were approved by Congress without much debate. Loosely applying provisions of the Antiquities Act (1906), Roosevelt designated seventeen new national monuments, including Devil's Tower and the Grand Canyon. Through Muir's personal intercession in 1906 Roosevelt established the Petrified Forest National Monument, after Muir discovered extensive pilfering and vandalism there during a stay in Arizona.[71]

Considering that a large visiting public did not yet exist for the parks and monuments, the achievements of the Roosevelt years were impressive. A good number of citizens were concerned about the "conservation" issue, and for them the contradiction between utilitarian conservation and preservation was probably not clear, just as it was not in Roosevelt's mind. For certainly economic growth could and must occur unabated, while the passing on of the nation's natural inheritance "unimpaired" to posterity was clearly possible—or so the assumption

John Muir and President Theodore Roosevelt at Yosemite Valley, 1903
(Courtesy of the Bancroft Library, University of California, Berkeley)

went.[72] This notion of "conservation" encompassed all efforts to husband nature, in reserves or in parks, and it tended to evade any hard choices. The quest for "quality of life" subsumed both the utilitarian and the moral-aesthetic agendas for nature within the optimistic glow of an expanding consumer economy. Presumably, with proper management, America's natural resources could continue to supply the unlimited growth necessary for a high standard of living based on material goods. At the same time, pristine natural areas must be available for the health and self-fulfilling leisure of every individual, theirs by birthright. The promise and the pitfalls of these conflicting demands that American consumers put on nature were to underlie much of the policy and politics of environmentalism for the rest of the twentieth century.

JOHN MUIR, entering the last battles and the final years of his life, could accept no facile answers to the dilemmas posed by wilderness preservation. As he wrote in 1910, "Nothing dollarable is safe, however guarded." This axiom was the chief lesson of his "political education," particularly as it pertained to his beloved Sierras. In the absence of broad-based popular support or awareness of strict preservationism, he relied on the help of another well-placed powerful friend, Edward Harriman, president of the Southern Pacific Railroad, to sway the California state legislature and Congress to cede Yosemite Valley to Yosemite National Park in 1905. Roosevelt signed the measure promptly, as he had promised Muir during their 1903 campout. It was Muir's last major victory for the landscape that had already come to be identified with him, with his iconic persona. His campaign to enlarge Sequoia National Park was unsuccessful during his lifetime. The battle over the dam in Hetch Hetchy Valley brought him his worst defeat. Yet in the end its loss was not surprising, for it represented the all-too-typical destiny of good in the world. "Ever since the establishment of the Yosemite National Park," he wrote in one of his last published essays, "strife has been going on around its borders and I suppose this will go on as part of the universal battle between right and wrong, however much its boundaries may be shorn, or its wild beauty destroyed." [73]

It was not that he was a "fanatic," unwilling to compromise. A farmer himself, Muir acknowledged the rights of settlers to the nonscenic public domain. In less rageful moments he agreed with the basic goals of Pinchot and the utilitarians, applied outside of the jewels of the national parks. He befriended and benefited from the friendship of railroad executives and other corporate conquerors of nature. He welcomed tourists into Yosemite and other sacred places, even in the "useful, progressive, blunt-nosed beetles" of their automobiles, as he wrote in 1912. With regard to Hetch Hetchy he had not protested vociferously in 1901 when the Interior Department granted a right of way for water conduits inside the borders of Yosemite Park, while the Sierra Club and others were preoccupied with the valley cession issue. He urged that some alternative dam site within Yosemite Park be substituted to save Hetch Hetchy in pristine condition. He found himself in alliance with the monopolistic Pacific Gas and Electric Company, which also opposed the hydroelectric dam's construction, scheming to be the main supplier of power to the city of San Francisco. "This playing at politics saps the very foundations of righteousness," Muir once wrote. Such was the substance of his political education: what amount of good in the world must be sacrificed, what compromises with evil made, so that a greater good might be achieved? It was the wisdom taught by Milton in *Paradise Lost*, one of the keystones of his moral and intellectual inheritance, carried in his knapsack on that first great venture into the wilderness, the walk to the Gulf, so long ago. "Anyhow we must be true to ourselves and the Lord," he wrote in 1912 to William Colby, director of the Sierra Club, assuming the tone of the lost cause. "But what can you expect?" he added frustratedly in another writing. "The Lord himself couldn't keep the devil out of the first reservation that was ever made." [74]

The issue clearly was wider than one lovely valley in Yosemite. The whole fragile (and ambiguous) principle of the inviolability of the national parks to economic development seemed at stake. In his famous 1912 essay on the controversy ("As well dam for water-tanks the people's cathedrals and churches"), Muir cited approvingly and took as a general principle the words in a 1903 ruling by Roosevelt's secretary of the interior, that Yosemite be preserved "for all coming time as nearly as practicable in the condition as fashioned by the hand of the Creator." But in that same late essay Muir described the "delightful and wonderful camp grounds" of Yosemite alongside the fact that the waters of the Tuolumne River in Hetch Hetchy were less pure than other streams in the park, owing to the "sewerage of camp grounds draining into it . . . occupied by hundreds of tourists and mountaineers, with their animals, for months every summer, soon to be followed by thousands from all the world"—drawn there perhaps from reading Muir's writings, and from the publicity blitz surrounding the Hetch Hetchy controversy.[75] They brought with them a desire for mass convenience at least as compelling to them, if not more so, than their yearning for pristine nature. As his contradictory account of the campgrounds reveals, Muir failed to grasp the likelihood that the inviolability of the park might be compromised as readily by visitors as by ranchers or loggers.

Muir did not live to see the day when tourist accommodations, at once the parks' salvation and their curse, were to begin seriously threatening their natural integrity, when visitors to the system would number not in the hundreds or the thousands, but in the hundreds of millions. Yet the shape of things to come was apparent soon enough after Muir's death in 1914. Stephen Mather, Muir's heir as the parks' chief defender, committed his newly founded National Park Service in 1916 to the principle of preserving the parks "unimpaired" for future generations and to building a constituency for them. He too cultivated railroad executives and took the step of organizing the National Park-to-Park Association, encouraging motorists to make the rounds each summer. Some 10,000 automobiles entered the parks in 1916. By 1919, the car count was up to 97,000 vehicles, carrying 750,000 visitors. By 1931, shortly after the end of Mather's tenure as director, 3.2 million tourists came through the gates of the park system, arriving in 897,000 automobiles.[76]

This rise in popularity of the parks—and the emergence of an ever-larger constituency for preservation—is often traced to the climactic, consciousness-raising debate over Hetch Hetchy that occurred in 1912–13. "We may lose this particular fight," Muir told Colby of the Sierra Club, referring to Hetch Hetchy, "but truth and right must prevail at last." In 1914, after the fight was lost and not long before his death, he remained philosophical: "Fortunately wrong cannot last. Soon or late it must fall back home to Hades, while some compensating good must surely follow." Muir would have been both appalled and reassured at the legacy of the Hetch Hetchy fight. The dam permit was approved in 1913 by Congress and President Wilson, who were persuaded by utilitarians like Pinchot and motivated by the more compelling Progressive issue of antimonopolistic, municipally owned water and power. Twenty years later and greatly overbudget, the dam and its conduits were completed. San Francisco had its new water supply, and PG&E obtained a concession from city fathers to sell the power to the city's residents after all. In coming years, however, "No More Hetch Hetchys" was to be the battle cry of latter-day environmentalists who continued to fight for the principle of the national parks' inviolability. In the mid-1950s, when the number of park visitors systemwide exceeded 50 million per year, the Sierra Club and affiliated groups, building a strategy on the earlier Hetch Hetchy defense, succeeded in preventing construction of a dam inside Dinosaur National Monument in Colorado, a campaign that began to galvanize the organization of the modern environmental movement proper. As part of the effort, David Brower, one of Muir's successors as president of the Sierra Club, juxtaposed "before" and "after" photographs of Hetch Hetchy to provide an object lesson. Brower subsequently used words like Muir's own ("Should we also flood the Sistine Chapel?") to halt plans for a proposed dam and reservoir within Grand Canyon National Park during the late 1960s. By then the number of visits to the national park and monument system had surpassed 100 million annually. And by then a new reservoir had inundated the remote wilderness area behind Glen Canyon Dam, which had been constructed on the Colorado River just upstream from the Grand Canyon after preservationists agreed to forgo protesting it in order to save Dinosaur National Monument.[77]

Muir's Yosemite became one of the most popular of all the national parks, which eventually numbered some four dozen, encompassing more than 40 million acres of scenic nature. At Yosemite, traffic congestion and pollution developed into major problems. The tiny Muir Woods National Monument, a 600-acre grove of redwoods near San Francisco that admirers had created to honor him in 1908, was also heavily visited. "Even the scenery habit in its most artificial forms, mixed with spectacles, silliness, and kodaks," Muir had concluded somewhat too sanguinely in 1897, "even this is encouraging, and may well be regarded as a hopeful sign of the times." To keep the parks accessible to the high demand for scenery, yet also to make it possible for Americans still to have a true wilderness experience, federal officials resorted to the elusive calculus of goods and evils that Muir had sought to balance. In the late 1950s, a funding program for highway construction and accommodations improvement was initiated by the Park Service. In 1964, Congress created the National Wilderness Preservation System, which was carefully distinguished from the overcrowded national parks and forests. The John Muir Wilderness Area, nearly 600,000 acres of rugged California mountain terrain, was established in 1984. By that year the number of park system visits was greater than 200 million. At last count, over 269 million visits were occurring annually in the park system.[78]

Legend has it that Muir was killed by the destruction of Hetch Hetchy, that the defeat "weighed heavily" on him. Colby told a mutual friend in the aftermath that Muir had been "seriously ill two or three times . . . and is now so feeble that he seldom comes to the city." The battle had persisted over the last decade of his life, and in that time Muir had pushed himself to write books based on his journals, in which he collected the stories and experiences of his many years of walks and travels in wild nature. He had published *My First Summer in the Sierra* in 1911, *The Yosemite* in 1912, and *The Story of My Boyhood and Youth* in 1913. He was working to complete *Travels in Alaska* over the hard winter of 1914 when a cold desert wind gave him pneumonia. By all accounts he died at peace with nature's God. "But let children walk with Nature, let them see the beautiful blendings and communions of death and life," he had written in the journals for the posthumous *Thousand-Mile Walk*, "and they will learn that death is stingless indeed, and as beautiful as life. . . . All is divine harmony." For "of course this destruction was creation," he believed, "progress in the march of beauty through death."[79]

> O goodness infinite, goodness immense!
> That all this good of evil shall produce,
> And evil turn to good.
> —John Milton, *Paradise Lost*,
>   book 12, lines 469–71

CHAPTER FOUR

John Wesley Powell

The revelation of science is this: Every generation is a step in progress

to a higher and fuller life; science has discovered hope.

"Darwin's Contribution to Philosophy" (1882)

John Wesley Powell
(Smithsonian Institution Photo No. 10696,
Smithsonian Institution Archives, Record Unit 95)

DURING THE presidential election of 1844 a mob burned down the private school and natural history museum of George Crookham, amateur scientist and boyhood mentor of John Wesley Powell. The incident occurred near the frontier town of Jackson in southern Ohio, where the ten-year-old Powell had settled with his parents six years earlier. The collections had taken Crookham more than five decades to amass. His library and manuscripts, also a life's work, perished in the fire. At the time young Wes was living with Crookham, seeking education as well as haven from anti-abolitionist schoolboys who had attacked him in months past. His father, Joseph, a Methodist circuit rider, was often gone for long absences; his mother, Mary, had the cares of his siblings and the family farm. His parents were close friends and associates of Crookham, sharing his unpopular abolitionist views. Wes was Crookham's favorite pupil, and he agreed to take him in; after the school burned Powell was his only student. From him Powell first learned about geology and the methods of science. He also witnessed politics, the martyrs it could make, the irrational world.[1]

In these ways and others, the antebellum midwestern frontier nurtured Powell, the boy who was to become his generation's most renowned explorer, its foremost scientist, founder of the U.S. Geological Survey, and national progenitor of conservation policy, reclamation, and regional planning. His biographers frequently marvel at Powell's rise out of the backcountry. They tell a tale of luck, hard work, and persistence. Comparisons to Lincoln are invoked. His immigrant British parents could perfectly fit the type of Tocqueville's peripatetic Americans, moving from New York state, where Powell was born, to Ohio, Wisconsin, and Illinois, where the grown Powell left them. He lived in log cabins along the way, cleared virgin stumps for planting, attended poor rural schools, and borrowed scarce books from neighbors. His father was a restless and driven man, a tailor by trade, a farmer by necessity, and a Methodist preacher by passion. More than once he uprooted the family, at last well established, simply to find new fields for soul-saving. It was he who consigned Powell to the pioneer's "life of incessant flitting," with all its deprivations and frustrations—the obstacles of his Algeresque rise, and the biographer's delight. By his thirtieth birthday,

Powell had known many challenges and disappointments, but his ambitions remained unbounded. He would be a scientist.[2]

The frontier was also formative of Powell in this more profound sense: it was here that his mind was first shaped and trained. Its very deprivations and inadequacies fostered a peculiar life of the mind, not merely the predictable eclecticism of the autodidact, but a deeply ingrained penchant for the empirical, the scientific. The family's eight years in Crookham's presence was crucial, of course. A poet neighbor or a musician might have impressed Powell differently. Instead, there was Crookham, with his roomful of specimens, his field trips, and his friendship with William Mather, the Ohio state geologist, another neighbor happy to spend time with a smart boy. Crookham was self-taught and knew the meager, ad hoc fare of rural education. He had prosperity and sons enough to give him leisure to devote to science, local history, his log lyceum, and Whig politics. He had the best library for miles around, yet still there was a paucity of books, a paucity that he turned into an opportunity. His students, Powell especially, were instructed by the countryside. He made them collectors: from leaves and twigs they learned botany, from rocks and hills, geology, from nearby Indian mounds, archaeology. For the pages of books they substituted real things, immediate, tactile, measurable facts, the evidence of the senses. As a pedagogy it had its limits—much of their work aspired no higher than classification—but it also had its richness, and its impact. When Powell himself became a country schoolteacher he too (like Thoreau) emphasized the outdoor classroom. He taught school to finance summers of lone personal excursions up and down the rivers of the still half-wild Mississippi Valley, exploring and collecting. He could not afford colleges that offered an adequate program in the sciences. Yet knowledge was to be gained out in the actual physical world, not in books but on trips: so his habits of thought were fashioned.[3]

Something about the frontier turned the minds of farmboys like Powell and John Muir, the boy inventor, to science. Certainly their time and place was determinative. In the 1840s and 1850s, natural history was all the rage among scientists, professional and amateur alike. Powell and Muir grew up in the antebellum American Midwest, a region and a culture that valued schooling and literacy. Mid-nineteenth-century civilization was transplanted there, however shallowly, and they partook of it. Life on a midwestern frontier farm must have influenced them just as strongly as New England's industrializing landscape had influenced Marsh and Thoreau. They necessarily lived a life close to nature, doing battle with it and dependent on it to the most direct degree that people may be. From a young age—Powell at twelve, on a Wisconsin homestead only sixty miles away from the Muir family's—both were put in charge of farms while their fathers concentrated on matters spiritual. They had large responsibilities and a need for practical facts regarding soil, weather, flora, and fauna. They lived in a country new to them and largely unnamed and uncategorized by the white man. They were confined to the farm, and their formal education was scattershot. They had to increase their knowledge empirically, build it bit by bit, extrapolating and interpolating well beyond what few books they had. Science was a means of knowing that was well adapted to these frontier conditions of their lives. It was "the most profound intuition of the human mind," as Powell later wrote. For Muir and Powell, two natively powerful and active intellects, science had both wonder and utility.[4]

Besides this general scientific-mindedness, many of Powell's more specific and concrete (and lifelong) scientific interests originated in the midwestern frontier landscape, as revealed by Crookham and Mather. Around Jackson there were rock outcroppings to classify, coal seams to discover, and fossil deposits to unearth. The lay and contour of the land itself were interpreted for him by Mather, read through the eyes of the surveyor and geologist. All nature seemed transparent to their categories and methods. To the mature Powell, geology and cartography remained the most fundamental of sciences, the starting point of any investigation of the world. At the same time, amateur digs in the ancient burial mounds of southern Ohio and Wisconsin sparked him toward an abiding fascination with American Indian ethnology, as did a memorable encampment of the Winnebago tribe on the Powells' Sharon farm in 1847. Years later he was to hold the directorship of the Smithsonian Institution's Bureau of Ethnology longer than any other post of his career, almost up to the time of his death.

The frontier marked Powell's worldview in profound ways other than the scientific. In the rural neighborhoods surrounding places like Jackson, Ohio; Sharon, Wisconsin; and Wheaton, Illinois, he acquired first-hand experience of the small-scale independent community life that was to play an important ideological role in his later regional planning proposals. The beneficence of Crookham was one link of such community ties. The country schoolhouse, all too familiar to Powell, was a nexus of them as well. The rough camaraderie of the wagon masters whom he met hauling grain to market, the neighbors who helped the family erect log cabins and houses—these were still other manifestations of frontier community that filled his early years. In time Crookham's and his father's Free-Soil political loyalties, debated evenings around the Powells' dinner table, elevated this mode of life to self-consciousness. Their shared Whig admiration of small town, small farm, and small factory, worked and owned by free labor, was honed to a fighting edge, a sectional edge, in the conflict over slavery. To Crookham and Joseph Powell and other Free-Soilers, the issue became stark: monied men manipulating the national government must not be allowed to impose their political economy on the remainder of the frontier; the territories to the west must be opened exclusively to the sons of toil and their kind, their ambitions. The vision stayed with Wes Powell, who carried it into war and later into government service.[5]

For this also was the nature of the frontier: there ambition could make all ties, familial or communal, tenuous, and by the 1850s Powell was an ambitious young man. Like Muir, he found in science an outlet for intellectual and psychological independence from an overbearing father. Joseph Powell intended his son for the ministry, and Muir's father would have listened sympathetically to his complaints about the boy's scientific interests. Joseph lent Powell neither moral nor financial support for his dream of a degree in science. Perhaps the needless move to Wisconsin in 1847, away from Crookham, was the beginning of the end. The development of the new farm was put into his young but capable hands, along with his brothers'. By 1850, however, Powell at age sixteen had had his fill of farm life. He tentatively began to strike out on his own over the next several years, taking up teaching as his profession, drawn homeward from time to time by pleas for help—and promises of college money—when his father moved the family not once but twice more into Illinois. The promises were almost always broken when the subject of study was discussed, but in 1858 Powell did manage one disappointing year at Oberlin, when his father at last relented on the idea of his son in the ministry. The only colleges with proper science curricula were in the East, and unattainable. Powell had to content himself with the mentorship and books of men like Crookham or Jonathan B. Turner, a former professor at Illinois College where Powell attended a year in 1855 who became Crookham's substitute; Turner's passions were agricultural improvement and the rights of farmers.[6]

In lieu of satisfying formal education, Powell took his summer excursions. At the end of the first one, in 1855, he had met his wife-to-be, first cousin Emma Dean. Their marriage was delayed six years due to Powell's lack of prospects and to his restlessness. The Mississippi Valley was scarcely large enough to contain his longings, his hunger to explore, to collect: up the Mississippi to St. Paul by boat in 1855; down the Mississippi to New Orleans and the Gulf by skiff in 1856. Then there were the tributaries: the Ohio River from Pittsburgh over to the Mississippi and down to the Gulf in 1857; then up and down the Des Moines and the Illinois in 1859, when Powell spent teaching money sufficient to marry on for a boat instead.

The prospect of war steadied him, gave his energy focus. To prepare himself for the army, he studied books on military engineering, the construction of earthworks and other defenses. After he enlisted in 1861, high-ranking officers in the western command, including General Grant, recognized his abilities. Powell was made a captain of the artillery, and he became Grant's friend. Grant gave him leave to go to Detroit and marry Emma, and he provided Emma a pass that allowed her to follow Powell wherever the army went. The next year, before the Battle of Shiloh, Powell found some Indian graves in the area and excavated them in his off-duty hours. During the battle, he lost his right arm; reportedly a ball shattered it when he raised it to order fire. Thus the famous figure of Powell the one-armed major was born. After a period of recuperation, he returned to duty in 1863. At the Vicksburg siege he and Emma passed the time by gathering a collection of fossil specimens from the Union trenches. Yet he was frustrated by his military career; he saw no real combat—what he yearned for—until he joined Sherman's forces in 1864. Powell was honorably discharged in early 1865, before the war's end. He weighed 110 pounds minus the arm; his brother Walter, a prisoner of war, was left an even emptier husk.[7]

The war was nevertheless good for Powell, weighing everything in the balance. His army rank, first of all, gave him new respect and opportunity. Illinois Wesleyan University offered him a professorship of natural science in 1865, and he accepted it. Soon thereafter he was appointed curator of the state's natural history museum, an institution and a post largely of his own creation, voted unanimously into being after he lobbied the legislature personally. The war in addition supplied Powell with influential friends and acquaintances, such as soon-to-be president Grant and General Sherman, contacts he was to use to launch his first expeditions to the Rockies in 1867 and 1868. The army life also sharpened his already considerable abilities as a manager and administrator. It made him a commander of men, a leader of organizations. Because of the war Powell became "the Major," a man capable of mounting explorations into the last unknown reaches of the West, and a man positioned to direct systematic scientific surveys of that region, to make it known.

IN 1865, the year in which Powell's professional career finally began, the course of empire resumed its westward way. After the war a whole half a continent lay awaiting the grand gesture. Such gestures came in plenty during the thirty years of the Gilded Age that encompassed Powell's career. Powell himself accomplished one, a famous one, with his boat descent of the Colorado River canyons in 1869. It was in the spirit of the times to "do things big": the consolidation of a continental empire, the building of an urban-industrial society, required it. America in the Gilded Age would have not "cattle raising," but a Cattle Kingdom, not "business leaders," but Captains of Industry, not "tribal pacification," but Custer's Last Stand, not a "bridge to Brooklyn," but the Brooklyn Bridge. Things had to happen big, and they had to happen fast. Powell perhaps encountered this zeitgeist when he first scouted the terrain of his own quest for glory. In 1867, when he and his group of amateur scientists traveled west on the initial Colorado expedition, they went by wagon—as had past generations—from Council Bluffs, Iowa, along the Platte River, joining up with a wagon train that still formed a circle for protection at night. In 1868, when Powell returned to Colorado for a second collecting trip on the Continental Divide, he and his associates traveled by rail on the new Union Pacific transcontinental line, a year away from Utah and epic completion.[8]

The first Grand Canyon descent made by Powell and his men that next year was the turning point of Powell's life and, consequently, an important event in the history of American environmentalism. The bedraggled expedition gathered little scientific data, but its leader garnered much scientific insight. After this trip and the second one of 1871–72, Powell arrived at his mature understanding of the principal geologic processes shaping the western (or any) landscape. His larger conception of nature, and the human relationship to nature, was also strongly influenced by his observations there. The Colorado River trips and the subsequent, more systematic Powell Survey of the canyonlands (1871–79) were to lead him to conclusions that would be among his most significant contributions to the tradition of American environmental advocacy: the idea of the *region*, the idea of the West as an *arid* region, and a plan for proper human adaptation and settlement in the arid West. Above all, Powell's fame from the canyon descents gave these ideas a notoriety that otherwise they would not have enjoyed. Without daring the descents, he would have been merely a very competent and unknown professor of natural history at a modest state university. But instead he and his uncredentialed notions gained entry into the highest academic circles and received subsidies from the federal government. The trips made Powell a national hero, famous much earlier and longer than Muir, the other original popularizer and institutionalizer of environmental ideals. Their elders Marsh and Thoreau had written largely in popular obscurity; the aging Marsh in 1874 even put before the Senate an appropriately obscure report on the promise and pitfalls of western irrigation. Yet it was Powell, emerging famous from the "Great Unknown," who was to attain the power and status essential to transform such an issue from a scholarly to a political concern.[9]

The 1867 and 1868 expeditions into the Rocky Mountains were his introduction to the West and its distinctive physiography. He and his men (including his broken brother, Walter, and his wife, Emma, who was not to be left behind by a traveling husband) compiled large collections of specimens that they shipped back East to sponsoring institutions. The Rockies in the 1860s were still exotic to most Americans. Indeed, on these trips Powell and his midwestern associates experienced alpine conditions for the first time in their lives. They went above the tree line and routinely crossed passes thousands of feet higher than the highest mountains in the eastern United States. During the 1867 trip Emma became the first known woman to climb Pike's Peak, more than twice as tall as any mountain she or her husband might ever have encountered, and six times higher than the Missouri Ozarks, where Powell had explored as a youth. The following year he and his group succeeded in the first ascent of Long's Peak on the Continental Divide, an elevation greater than Pike's Peak. "Glory to God!" Powell was quoted as exclaiming when they reached the summit. The sky was clear and the wind roared around them. The summit was all bare rock with a few patches of snow and no living thing but moss and lichen. From this extreme alien vantage they could see startling geographical contrasts: stretching to the west, south, and north, mountains upon mountains, with some entire ranges yet unexplored; and to the east beyond Denver, the immense flatness of the Great Plains.[10]

Not surprisingly, then, Powell concluded that one of the keys to the regional distinctiveness of the West was its dramatic geology, an observation that was to be most forcibly impressed on him the summer afterward from a boat in the depths of the Grand Canyon. If the alpine Rockies were strange to him, the "Plateau Province" encompassing the canyonlands was like an altogether different planet for eyes accustomed to the hills and woods and lazy rivers of the Midwest. It was "a whole land of naked rock, with giant forms carved in it," he described in an account of the 1869 and 1871 river expeditions: "The landscape everywhere, away from the river, is of rock—cliffs of rock, tables of rock, plateaus of rock, terraces of rock, crags of rock—ten thousand strangely carved forms; rocks everywhere, and no vegetation, no soil, no sand." Years later, in his book on the "Philosophy of Science," *Truth and Error* (1898), Powell used his and his comrades' reactions to this bizarre canyon country in the course of explaining the nature of cognition:

For many years I was engaged in an exploring expedition where all the features of the landscape were new to me and my companions. Mountains, hills, rocks, plains, valleys, streams, all were new. I was constantly discovering new plants, new animals, and strange human beings, as Indians. During all these years the fundamental doctrines of psychology often constituted the theme of my thoughts and the subject with which I beguiled the weariness of travel.

The first lines of this passage seem a more authentic and accurate memory of his river experiences than the latter sentence, yet it is not unlikely that the unnamed "newness" of the landscape around him threw his mind back on itself, as he suggests. In his earlier expedition account, Powell had written that "the Grand Canyon cannot be adequately represented in symbols of speech, nor by speech itself. . . . Language and illustration combined must fail." These were the indicators that the Plateau Province was a different kind of place, a unique region of the continent, outside the experience and knowledge of men from the East, "a scene such as the dweller in verdure-clad hills can scarcely appreciate." [11]

Yet "nothing is worthy of contemplation except the mysterious," Powell once wrote, and science had the power to decrease the area of the unknown, the "border-land" of the "zone of doubt." Powell's empirical sensibility had originally been drawn to the Plateau Province because it seemed so satisfyingly palpable and concrete an expression of the unknown: on the latest maps its landforms were blank and its rivers dotted lines. The gaps in the maps represented (or failed to represent) a "zone" 300 to 500 miles long and 100 to 200 miles wide. The "mad, raging stream" of the Colorado ran through it, dropping nearly a vertical mile from the mountains of Wyoming through the immense "canyon gorge" beginning in Utah and running to the desert flats of Arizona. "More than once have I been warned by the Indians not to enter this canyon," Powell noted in his diary at the time. "They considered it disobedience to the gods and contempt for their authority, and believed that it would surely bring upon me their wrath." But at the other end of this blank "zone" there lay knowledge, and fame.[12]

The first journey began at Green River, Wyoming, on May 24, 1869, noted precisely by biographers as a historic occasion, which it was—

the beginning of the last great undone feat of exploration in the United States. Only Powell among the crew could qualify as a professional scientist. The rest were mountain guides and war veterans hardy enough to make the voyage. Barometers, sextants, compasses, and chronometers went with them, packed into three custom-built boats with the food supplies. During the harrowing trip much of the food and many of the instruments were lost and the boats nearly so. On one occasion Powell climbed alone two miles up the walls of the Grand Canyon to harvest some boat-repairing pitch from the nearest pine trees. He was a man driven, and he drove his men. They rowed and portaged the twenty-foot boats made of heavy oak; they were roasted in the daytime and frozen at night; their food was meager and almost inedible, soaked and dried and soaked again. As one of the crew members noted in his diary, still three weeks before the end of the trip, "If Major does not do something soon, I fear the consequences, but he is contented and seems to think that biscuit made of sour and musty flour . . . is ample to sustain a laboring man. If he can only study geology he will be happy without food or shelter." They collected specimens and samples, measured altitudes, and gave names to the features they passed in the landscape, including "the most sublime spectacle in nature." Powell was the one who called it the name by which it came to be known to the world: the Grand Canyon.[13] At the end of August they emerged from it, the journey complete, once more back on the map.

After the sensation of the first trip (newspapermen from throughout the nation were waiting for Powell in Salt Lake City, where he rejoined his wife), the second river expedition was anticlimactic, but more systematic. In effect it was the beginning of the Powell Survey, because the successful first descent won him two federal subsidies from Congress, which placed his next proposed effort under the authority of the Department of the Interior. A belt fifteen miles wide on both sides of the river was to be subjected to a "Geographical and Topographical Survey." In May 1871, Powell and another group of amateurs launched themselves in three new and improved boats, again from Green River Station (in scarcely two years the place had become a veritable ghost town, after a mining boom played out).[14] This second descent was slower, more arduous, and more interrupted than the first because of low water and Powell's frequent forays from camp to see Indian villages and ruins. The slow going meant that the journey had to be delayed to pass the winter. The men were quartered in a small Mormon town, while Powell and his wife and family returned to the East.

He lobbied for more subsidies in Washington and moved his family there from Illinois in 1872. Already Powell foresaw Washington as the seat of scientific research in America, what George Perkins Marsh had dreamed of. He obtained a small office in the Smithsonian Institution's Castle, the organization that had encouraged and overseen his work since the Rockies expeditions. And as if to signify the rightness of this career move, when the second expedition resumed in July 1872, the water was high and the going fast. It was still treacherous, the Major strapped in an armchair tied amidships. Photographs of the boats and the canyons soon brought him more fame, and income: he sold the images to the public for parlor viewing in slide projectors and stereo-scopes. Meanwhile, his survey, in 1874 dubbed the "Geographical and Geological Survey of the Rocky Mountain Region," prospered. He began to attract some first-class scientific talent to his team, including G. K. Gilbert, one of the pioneers of geomorphology, and Clarence E. Dutton, who was to contribute much to the Survey's studies of the Grand Canyon and environs. Thomas Moran, the acclaimed landscape painter, was brought on board to illustrate several Survey reports, and he accom-panied Powell on some of his subsequent trips into the Rockies and canyonlands. There were to be more than two dozen trips in all during the 1870s.[15]

As Powell's survey in the Plateau Province became more systematic, so did his thinking about it. The "land of naked rock" became for him and his assistants a "rock-bound book of geology." First there was the Grand Canyon itself to explain, its structure and the processes that had formed it. This was what journal editors and congressmen and lecture audiences were most curious to know, and this too was what had most overwhelmed Powell's senses aboard a boat a mile deep in the earth. As early as 1869, soon after concluding the first descent, Powell settled on a uniformitarian explanation of the canyon's physiography. No sudden gigantic and catastrophic fissuring but an enormously long period of erosion had created it, as he later wrote in a popular version of his initial 1874 report:

> The carving of the Grand Canyon is the work of rains and rivers. The vast labyrinth of canyon by which the plateau region drained by the Colorado is dissected is also the work of waters. Every river has excavated its own gorge and every creek has excavated its gorge. When a shower comes in this land, the rills carve canyons—but a little at each storm; and though storms are far apart and the heavens above are cloudless for most of the days of the year, still, years are plenty in the ages, and an intermittent rill called to life by a shower can do much work in centuries of centuries.

The Colorado had carved out the main gorge of the Grand Canyon, while falling rains had cut the side canyons and gorges—an explanation still accepted to the present day. Faced with this evidence from the "book" of the canyonlands, *erosion* emerged in Powell's mind as one of the most awesome forces in nature: "We think of the mountains as forming clouds about their brows, but the clouds have formed the mountains. Great continental blocks are upheaved from beneath the sea by internal geologic forces. . . . Then the wandering clouds, the tempest-bearing clouds . . . with mighty power and with wonderful skill carve out valleys and canyons and fashion hills and cliffs and mountains." [16]

Other fundamental geologic processes were revealed to him by the Plateau Province landscape, and all had acted their part in forging the "sublime spectacle" of the Grand Canyon. The uplift, or "displacement," of the earth's crust had occurred there, and while the plateau's surface and strata had risen upward, the river had cut down through it, exposing older and older layers of rock. Sedimentation, too, along with erosion and uplift, had sculpted the landforms of the region. The Province of rock, "200,000 square miles in extent," over geological time had been ground into sands "and the rills have carried the sands into the creeks and the creeks have carried them into the rivers and the Colorado has carried them into the sea." Even after many years of field trips to the region, Powell could marvel at the sheer scale of the physical results, which was another of the features that distinguished the canyonlands from any other region of the country. It was truly a land on a vastly different scale, vastly unlike the eastern half of the country: "In the Grand Canyon there are thousands of gorges like that below Niagara Falls, and there are a thousand Yosemites. . . . Pluck up Mt. Washington by the roots to the level of the sea and drop it headfirst into the Grand Canyon, and the dam will not force its waters over the walls. Pluck up the Blue Ridge and hurl it into the Grand Canyon, and it will not fill it."[17]

During the 1870s and 1880s Powell's attempts to explain the structure and formation of the Grand Canyon (as well as other features of the Plateau Province, such as the Uinta Mountains) broadened and deepened his understanding of the common forces that shaped all landscapes and differentiated them in unique, *regional* ways. In 1886, Powell published what was in effect a summary of his mature geological thought in an article entitled "The Causes of Earthquakes," which was written in response to quackish explanations that had been offered in the popular press regarding the earthquake that devastated Charleston, South Carolina, earlier in the year. Ever mindful of the duty of science to correct error (as was old George Crookham), Powell carefully outlined for readers his interpretation of the latest theories. The theme that emerged most strongly was uniformitarian, applied as the general principle that it now was to the majority of geologists in the United States. For example, the sedimentation of the Great Salt Lake—the heart of the larger region that Powell called the "Great Basin"—meant that the lake was filling up "slowly, when measured in terms of human history, but rapidly, when measured in terms of earth history." In Powell's thinking virtually all geological processes were uniformitarian because all had been acting repeatedly throughout earth's immensely old history. Individual catastrophes shrank in significance when viewed from the perspective of the ages. Each catastrophe was what Powell's assistant WJ McGee called a "moderate cataclysm." Even earthquakes, the manifestations of geological displacements, were not catastrophic events in the old-school sense of the word. Rather, when rightly viewed, earthquakes were seen to be "very common," with a displacement landform such as the Sierra Nevada in California "not made in one great convulsion," but displaying a cumulative record of "thousands, or rather millions, of earthquakes."[18]

This evidence presented in "The Causes of Earthquakes" essay—

the Great Salt Lake, the Sierra Nevada—revealed the extent to which Powell's focus had widened beyond the Plateau Province by the late 1870s to include the geological characteristics of the larger western region and its subregions as a whole. The very concept of *region* was by then attaining in his mind a more strict, more scientific definition. "If we pass from one district of country to another," Powell observed, "we are likely to pass from one geologic formation to another." The "regions of the earth" were "faulted, flexed, or folded," and "some in much greater degree than others." He sketched an array of the continent's regions in a word-map for the reader: "The Appalachian region, extending from the St. Lawrence to the low wooded plains of the Gulf States, is excessively displaced; the whole Rocky Mountain region is also greatly displaced; while in the great Valley of the Mississippi displacements are much less frequent and on a much smaller scale." A regional description was necessary for "a clear conception of the nature of geologic formations and their displacements." So too regions were differentiated by and describable in terms of other geological forces. "[C]ertain regions are unloaded by rains and rivers and other regions loaded by sedimentation," Powell declared, while "certain other portions are loaded by the pouring upon them of volcanic formations." [19]

These geological definitions of American regions in "The Causes of Earthquakes" and other writings of the 1870s and 1880s reflected Powell's keen interest in compiling a comprehensive and detailed topographical map of the entire country—a massive undertaking that the Geological Survey under Powell was to begin in 1882 but that was not to be completed until a century later, in 1981. This map project was perhaps already forming itself in his mind from the earliest crude contrasts he made between eastern and western landscapes. Yet geology was not the only basis for conceptualizing and differentiating regions. There was also climate, specifically, the amount of rainfall "pouring upon them" annually. The "extreme aridity" of the Plateau Province had struck him during his expeditions there as another element of the region's strangeness ("no vegetation, no soil, no sand"). And just as he had generalized about the larger geomorphology and physiography of the western landscape from his experiences in the Province, so too was he able to draw certain inclusive conclusions about the West's climate. Defined by rainfall, the West became the "Arid Region." [20]

As a result of this conclusion, and the suggestion that the appropriations for his small Geographical and Geological Survey might thereby be made more generous, Powell in 1874 diverted his and his staff's attention somewhat away from pure science and toward a practical matter, irrigation. This sort of issue, Powell wrote, might lend itself to the start of "a general survey"—the apple of his eye—to determine the "several areas which can . . . be redeemed." [21] The question of irrigated farming in the West was also to be crucial in formulating his regional conceptualization of the continent, and ultimately it was to lead him to write his most important work, *Report on the Lands of the Arid Region* (1878).

As the title of the *Report* suggests, Powell's main focus in the work was on the West, on the disposition of its potentially irrigable and nonirrigable lands—a framing of the problem that unlocked a detailed crosssection of the region's geography. But, in addition, Powell offers in the book a larger geography, yet another set of *regional* definitions for comprehending the American landscape. Most famously there was the "Arid Region" itself, distinguishable by the onset of the eastern "limit of successful agriculture without irrigation," the "isohyetal or mean annual rainfall line of 20 inches," roughly the one hundredth meridian. Powell conceded that the West was not uniform in this regard, that there were subregions like the "Lower Columbia Region" of Washington, Oregon, and northern California that had plentiful rain. In general, however, the country could be divided further into two other major regions: the "Humid Region" of the eastern states, "where the lands receive enough moisture from the clouds for the maturing of crops," and the "Subhumid Region," which extended between the Arid and the Humid, "from the one hundredth meridian eastward to about the isohyetal line of 28 inches," where dry farming was possible but chancy. [22] Unlike the geologic regions of Powell's other writings, these climatic (or "hydrologic") regions were delineated not only by nature but also by culture, by patterns of human occupation and utilization. In the end, this definition was to have implications far beyond the merely cartographic because both the Sub-humid and the Arid regions were undergoing rapid settlement even as Powell was formulating his ideas about them in the mid-1870s. As will be seen, the *Report* was to embroil him in the debate over the nation's land laws and land-use policies, particularly after he assumed power as the director of the U.S. Geological Survey in 1881. To Powell, prosperity in the Arid Region would demand proper adaptation to, and improvements of, the basic conditions set by nature—irrigation in a land of little rain.

THE SURVEYS AND STUDIES done by Powell's parties in the West during the 1870s and 1880s—and the regional conceptualizations that came of them—could be seen as having some real application to irrigation. When pressed, Powell justified his brand of government science on precisely these grounds, and finally (in the late 1880s) he was to turn the efforts of the U.S. Geological Survey (USGS) fully toward scouting sites for irrigation works. Yet the western regions of America were also a laboratory for him, a field for pure science, and a field for study in other areas besides geomorphology or regional geography. Paleontology was one "useless" science that members of the USGS pursued under Powell's directorship, much to the outrage of appropriations committeemen. Another "wasteful" project was the Bureau of Ethnology, dearest to Powell's heart, which developed out of his longstanding interest in Native Americans that over the years grew into a passion. While awaiting spring and the launching of his first descent down the Colorado in 1869, Powell had spent the winter compiling a vocabulary of the nearby Ute tribe and recording their myths and stories. Throughout his trips in the canyonlands he took note of pueblos and cliff houses and collected crafts and artifacts. He met with the councils of many tribes in 1870 as preparation for the 1871–72 expedition, thanks to the intercession of the trusted Mormon leader Jacob Hamblin. In 1871, Powell did more ethnological research, this time on the Paiute tribe, and subsequently, in 1873, he was commissioned by the Bureau of Indian Affairs (BIA) to study the problems of the Paiutes and other tribes in Utah, Colorado, and Nevada. He enjoyed good (and informative) relations with many tribes and their leaders, and he worked on their behalf to eliminate corruption at several BIA agencies operating in the Plateau Province. The Uinkarets gave Powell a name: *Ka-pur-ats*,

John Wesley Powell conversing with a Paiute Indian on the Kaibob Plateau
near the Grand Canyon, 1873 (Photograph by John K. Hillers, courtesy of the
National Anthropological Archives, Smithsonian Institution)

"One Arm Off." [23] By the mid-1870s, there were few men in America as knowledgeable about the Indian cultures of the mountain states.

The Bureau of Ethnology, established by the same 1879 legislation that created the U.S. Geological Survey, was indicative of Powell's belief that "knowledge is a boon in itself and in its utilitarian consequences alike." The study of American Indians could provide answers to some of the most fundamental questions about the development of mankind, Powell thought: "So important are these discoveries," he wrote, "that all human history has to be rewritten" in their light, "the whole philosophy of history reconstructed." But more immediately and "practically," knowledge of Indian cultures could aid in resolving the "Indian problem" by improving white-native relations and policies. In the same way that the rapid settlement of the Sub-humid and Arid regions of the West had focused the Survey's attention on land-law revision, Powell reasoned, it made "ethnologic studies" an area of federal science that should be "pushed with the utmost vigor." The last few remaining "primitive" tribes still existed there in a remote laboratory setting. However, because of the inroads of white civilization, "all habits, customs, and opinions" of the Indians were "fading away; even languages are disappearing," Powell wrote, "and in a very few years it will be impossible to study our North American Indians in their primitive conditions."[24]

In these assertions Powell showed himself to be an intellectual precursor of twentieth-century regionalists who were to make similarly large claims about the cultural significance of Native American civilizations, and who were to voice similar worries about the survivability of indigenous peoples in the face of modernizing change. Yet those latter-day regionalists—the novelist Mary Austin, for example, and the reformer John Collier—were to be fully in sympathy with the tragedy of the Native Americans' acculturation and would, in fact, assert the superiority of Indian to white ways. To Powell, in contrast, the tribes' cultural decline and assimilation seemed inevitable and in many regards desirable. He saw them consistently as savage and inferior (albeit "interesting") peoples. It is in understanding the puzzle of Powell's fascination with Indian ethnology that many of the foundations of his thought are laid bare, especially his philosophy of history and his conception of the relationship between nature and humankind. Powell's ideas and beliefs concerning the vanishing native societies of the Arid Region reveal the intellectual wellsprings of his plans for their successor regime, the "Aryan civilization" marching westward into a future of which Powell had grandiose visions.[25] His main bequest to twentieth-century environmentalism was to lie less in his project of native cultural preservation than in the reform institutions and proposals by which he planned to encourage and to mitigate the future of white development in the West, through reclamation and conservation.

Powell's philosophy of history was based in part on the idea summed up in the phrase, "savagery is ethnic childhood." This notion encapsulated both the value he placed on Indian cultures and the Eurocentric bias from which he beheld them. Powell was certainly not alone among his scientific contemporaries in this Darwinian conceit, an early and crude application of a powerful new intellectual tool, historicism. He was a reader of Herbert Spencer, the overpraised British philosopher who seemed to Americans to confirm as universal evolutionary principle the national myth of social progress. Powell's principal ethnological influence came from the pioneer American anthropologist Lewis Henry

Morgan, author of *Ancient Society, or Researches in the Lines of Human Progress from Savagery through Barbarism to Civilization* (1877), with whom Powell corresponded for a period in the 1870s before the latter's death in 1881. As the explicit title of Morgan's work suggests, he propounded a theory of universal social evolution, claiming that all societies in their development recapitulated the stages of a human life (birth, maturity, and death—a Spencerian notion) and that the hierarchy of races was representative of these stages, ranging from childlike nonwhite savages to mature sophisticated whites. Morgan argued further that the study of present-day primitive societies could shed light on the evolution of all societies from their earliest stages and that all societies could potentially progress toward civilization at varying rates and degrees.[26]

That Powell agreed fundamentally with these doctrines is shown, for example, in his expression of admiration for the Pueblo tribes of the Southwest, who were "in a higher grade of culture than most Indian tribes of the United States"—"they had almost accomplished the ascent from savagery to barbarism when first discovered by the invading European." He added, "All the Indians of North America were in this state of transition, but the pueblo tribes had more nearly reached the higher goal." Powell's appropriation of Morgan's theory of social evolution affected his position on Indian reform—making him an assimilationist—and it led him toward an anthropological concept of *culture*. As Powell wrote, "Savagery is not inchoate civilization; it is a distinct status of society with its own institutions, customs, philosophy, and religion." But this modern concept of culture did not carry Powell's thinking further, toward an acceptance of cultural relativism. In his eyes the world would always be divided into the hierarchical evolutionary scale, and the objects of the "objective studies of mankind" that he advocated for the Bureau of Ethnology would necessarily be cultures still in a primitively "childish" yet revealingly elementary state. In Powell's late book *Truth and Error*, a paean to the scientific method, Indian beliefs about the world were usually invoked as telling examples of "error."[27]

If Powell's own belief in progressive social evolution was manifested by his great professional interest in native cultures—and concretely, by the Bureau of Ethnology that he headed—it was also apparent in the institution and projects of the Geological Survey. Both organizations were born out of his experiences in the Arid Region, and both were expressions of his deep, almost Comtean faith in science. August Comte had made science the liturgy of his "Religion of Humanity," and Powell gave up the Methodism of his parents for positivism (if, in fact, religion had ever strongly competed for his mind during his youth). Powell became the spiritual son not of Joseph Powell, the absent father, but of George Crookham, the doting teacher. To the mature Powell, science was the vanguard of human progress. As the highest embodiment of human intelligence, science was the very engine of social evolution.[28] In this truth, perhaps the most basic that Powell knew, were rooted all of his grandiose plans and visions for reclamation and conservation in the Arid Region.

Philosophically, Powell's limitless estimation of science stemmed from his understanding of the relationship between humans and their environment. It was the old question that Marsh and many before him had wrestled with: Was humanity a part of nature, or above it? Powell did think that human beings had participated in the Darwinian processes of natural evolution, such as the adaptation to environment by natural selection. He believed that "man inherited the body, instincts, and patience of the brute" and that this animal "nature thus inherited has survived in his constitution and is exhibited all along the course of history." Yet in humankind, natural evolution had also eventuated "changes in the nervous system" so that "human evolution" *diverged* from that of the "brute" and became a superior "mental evolution." To use the words of his friend Lester Ward, one of the founders of American sociology and an important influence on Powell's philosophy of science, "[I]n the development of mind, a virtually *new power* was introduced into the world . . . one of those gigantic strides which thenceforth completely revolutionised the surface of our planet." Powell thought enough of Ward's ideas to hire him on at the Geological Survey in 1881, simply to provide him with an opportunity to finish his major work *Dynamic Sociology* (1881). For Powell very strongly concurred with Ward's notions that "intellect . . . serves as a guiding power to . . . natural forces . . . directing them into channels of human advantage" and that "man, through his intelligence, has laboured successfully to resist the law of nature." Future progress in social evolution, according to Ward, would necessitate "still greater interference with the operations of natural forces, still more complete control of the laws of nature, and still more absolute supremacy of the psychic over the natural method of evolution."[29]

Writing in *Truth and Error*, Powell put the matter more succinctly, voicing a Marshian rationale for his reclamation plans in the Arid Region: "In man adaptation to environment is transmuted into the adaptation of environment to man." More pointedly, "man is not adapted to the environment of climate, but he adapts the climate to himself." Raw nature was not evolving toward perfection under the benevolent direction of a Creator, as John Muir proselytized. Instead, human activity —above all, science—perfected "brute evolution" to the degree that nature's powers became "specialized for man's purposes," and the "materials of nature" became man's "works of art." By these means, Powell wrote, man "adapts the natural environment to his wants." Given these as his guiding principles, which were fundamental to utilitarian conservation, the notion that Powell was an early prophet of symbiotic, "small is beautiful," no-growth, "green" economic doctrines (as some twentieth-century environmental writers would have it) must be qualified. His vision of development in the Arid Region was big enough:

> The capital to redeem by irrigation 100,000,000 acres of land is to be obtained, and $1,000,000,000 is necessary. . . . The great mineral deposits—the fuel of the future, the iron for the railroads, and the gold and silver for our money—must be kept ready to the hand of industry and the brain of enterprise. . . . The powers of the factories of that great land are to be created and utilized, that the hum of busy machinery may echo among the mountains—the symphonic music of industry. . . .
>
> A thousand millions of money must be used. . . . Great and many industries are to be established. . . . Millions of men are to labor.

The vision had come to him early in his travels through the Arid Region, around campfires during the first Colorado expedition in 1867. "I took the ground that ultimately agriculture and manufacturing would be developed on a large scale . . . that in a very few decades all the waters of the arid region of the United States would be used in irrigation for agricultural purposes." Over the years to come Powell's primary policy concern in this drastic adaptation of environment to human wants was for the region's resources to be profitably exploited in ways that promised to be the most successful and the most democratic. But exploited they would be—not by a powerful and wealthy few, if Powell's plans were realized, but by the "little man" in the millions. Just as he saw in the Arid Region the earth's basic geological forces laid bare, just as he perceived in its indigenous peoples elemental patterns of human life, so Powell projected an empire there, in the "developing world of America," that would be the next glorious stage in social evolution. "Human providence is more potent than flood, more potent than drought, more potent than wind," he believed. "The man of intellect wields a power that giants cannot exercise." [30]

IN 1865, Major Powell and his wife had stood in line for hours to pay their respects to the assassinated Lincoln, who was lying in state briefly in Chicago on his way to burial at Springfield. With Lincoln the dream of a free-soil empire in the West was also buried, as was much of the impulse of antebellum reform—although Powell did not then know it. The ensuing Gilded Age was not to look kindly on reformers: this Powell was to realize, in time. His plans for the lands of the Arid Region, for the men who might farm those lands, would largely come to naught. But that defeat occurred as the final act to a run of more than two decades of achievement, much of which remained intact far beyond the end of Powell's tenure in government service. His legacies were to continue to affect natural resource policy well into the twentieth century, albeit with some consequences unintended by him.

The practice of science required of Powell the practice of politics. Scientific research of the scope he projected must have substantial and regular financial and institutional support, which he surmised only the federal government, in fact, Congress alone, could supply. Powell's biographers have often remarked upon how adept he was in the ways of politics. Perhaps he gained this skillfulness during the war. A good field commander leads his men not through fear and intimidation but by knowing their limits and capabilities, what he might ask of them, and when. He must know his superiors as well, how to negotiate their orders without appearing impertinent, how to win advantages for himself and his men without seeming obsequious. The war also brought out

Powell's innate doggedness, a trait as valuable in politics as it was on the battlefield. And losing an arm and bearing witness to mass carnage must have made other, later challenges seem less daunting, whether they lay in the canyons of the Colorado or in the halls of Congress.

All of Powell's political skills, whatever their source, were necessary to achieve what he did—establishing the U.S. Geological Survey as the leading national agency for scientific research—and even what he failed to do—transforming it into an instrument of natural resource planning. To the former, successful attainment, the 1860s expeditions were essential. They inspired his projects, enhanced his reputation, and honed his political instincts. Already in those years his force and persuasiveness were evident. In 1867, for example, at Powell's urging an increased budget for the Illinois natural history museum and its curatorship was passed by the state legislature in a unanimous vote. And without being named in the original legislation that he had promoted, Powell was then unanimously appointed to the curator's position by the state board of education. He used part of the museum's budget to launch the first Rocky Mountains field trip, which was justified for the collections that it would bring.[31]

It was all neatly played, and Powell employed the same strategy of disinterest in the following decade to bring about the creation of the USGS. In 1872, he began to propose quietly to Congress the consolidation of the various surveys then at work in the West, which he considered to be overlapping and wasteful. Besides his own, there was one led by Lieutenant George M. Wheeler (under the auspices of the army), another headed by the famous Clarence King (also with the War Department as sponsor), and still another under Ferdinand V. Hayden (Department of the Interior). Each of the men behind these surveys was able and ambitious. At congressional hearings on the proposed consolidation in 1874 Powell's rivals Wheeler and Hayden made spectacles of themselves, pushing acrimoniously for consolidation only on condition that it would leave one of them in charge. Powell said nothing on his own behalf in his testimony but instead calmly outlined the reasons for unifying the surveys under civilian authority, to carry out a "general survey" for irrigation sites. The hearings concluded, and the consolidation matter remained unresolved. Yet the Powell Survey was made more institutionally secure as a result of his good showing, becoming—along with Hayden's—the "Second Division of the Survey of the Western Territories."[32]

By 1878, with the election of Rutherford B. Hayes and the appointment of the reformist Republican Carl Schurz as secretary of the interior, the political tide turned in favor of Powell's proposal. During his tenure Schurz was to become one of the first federal officials to advocate conservation of forests, recommending the creation of a commission to study foreign forestry efforts and devise revisions of the land laws. While the issue of forest conservation was never a particularly compelling one to Powell, he and Schurz were in accord that land classification in the West (which might determine which of the confusion of land laws applied to a specific parcel) needed a thorough overhaul—a goal of Powell's projected "general survey." With Schurz running interference against his competitor Hayden, Powell had a friend on the House Appropriations Committee pass a measure authorizing the National Academy of Sciences (NAS) to advise the committee on consolidation of the surveys. The head of the NAS was the eminent paleontologist and longtime Powell supporter Othniel Marsh; the committee he appointed to study the survey controversy was packed with men friendly to Powell, who had been a member of the NAS since 1875. They recommended the consolidation as expected, and the Sundry Civil Expenses Bill of 1879 contained provisions for a U.S. Geological Survey as well as (unnoticed) a Bureau of Ethnology. After the measure passed, Powell campaigned not for himself but for Clarence King to be chosen the first director. Again, he remained unimpeachable in his personal motives, even if he was using every means for his larger institutional goals. King got the nod from President Hayes, while Powell was named to head the Bureau of Ethnology. King was brilliant yet flighty, and Powell as his lieutenant at the USGS did much of the organizing of the new agency. When King resigned in 1881 to try and fail at fortune hunting, Powell was the natural choice to replace him. Once more the political winds favored him because James A. Garfield, his old friend from Illinois, was now president.[33]

Clearly, Powell knew how to maneuver in Gilded Age politics-as-usual. A contemporary said of him that he "never missed a chance to endear himself to a senator or congressman." He made them gifts of photographs of the western landscape to decorate their offices; he gave them Indian arts and crafts. He dispatched the young unmarried men of the Survey to Washington balls to dance with a senator's niece or a congressman's daughter. Powell was not above working the spoils system for menial positions, either: summer jobs with survey parties were available to the sons and nephews of the powerful. For years Powell exchanged gloves with a former Confederate member of Congress who had lost his left arm in the war, whenever one or the other bought a new pair. He hired a professional editor to prepare the publications and reports of the Survey, which proved to be good sellers with the public. Such were the means of survival in Washington, and Powell, in fact, did better than subsistence for the USGS. By 1884, its staff had grown to 200, up from 40 in 1879. Its annual budget increased almost every year, standing at the $500,000 level within half a decade of its founding, and over $800,000 in the late 1880s.[34]

If Powell was a master of politics-as-usual, he practiced the art to support programs that were scientifically innovative and valuable. The national topographic map was begun in 1882, and by the end of Powell's service in 1894 the Survey had covered 20 percent of the country, charting almost 600,000 square miles. Staff members Clarence E. Dutton and G. K. Gilbert continued their output of important studies, turning out classic works on the Grand Canyon (Dutton, 1882) and the Lake Bonneville region (Gilbert, 1890). The most prominent academic geologists in the nation, including the famous N. S. Shaler of Harvard, were hired for temporary summer research projects. Powell recruited Othniel Marsh to be staff paleontologist in 1882, and in years to come he completed pioneering excavation and classification work that defined the field. At the Bureau of Ethnology, which Powell ran out of the same office as the USGS, similar pioneering studies were issued under his directorship. The Bureau's *Annual Report*, which included independent contributions by figures such as Lewis Henry Morgan, James Mooney, and Franz Boas, was a Who's Who of American anthropology and ethnology. Powell himself oversaw the compilation of the Bureau's two-volume *Handbook of American Indians*, a basic reference on native tribes and languages for decades thereafter. He also published a first-ever map locating the homelands of all of the country's principal tribal language stocks. In recognition of the high-quality science being conducted by the USGS and the Bureau, Powell was awarded honorary degrees by Heidelberg and Harvard in 1886.[35]

Yet to make Washington a scientific center demanded more than political gamesmanship. It demanded political innovation and reform — specifically, centralization. The organic legislation establishing the Geological Survey had left ambiguous its area of operations, stating only that it would classify and examine "the national domain," which might mean the public lands only, or the nation's area as a whole, public and private. On his brief watch King had been frustrated by this vagueness, so he confined the Survey to the public lands while he worked for clarifying amendments; the project of the national map, among others, was at stake. When Powell became director, he prevailed on his Appropriations Committee connections to intervene with new wording in the 1882 Civil Expenses Bill, giving the Survey authority to "continue the preparation of a geological map of the United States"—thus extending its operations throughout the country.[36]

Powell took other steps to centralize and nationalize the Survey's (and his own) authority. He had himself named special disbursing agent for the Survey so that Congress could appropriate money to him but could not easily exercise control over how he distributed it. He curtailed or closed four regional survey offices that King had set up in the West, thereby concentrating talent and responsibilities in Washington. He laid down a uniform nomenclature of geological terms—backed by the Survey's prestige and flood of publications—in order to standardize and facilitate scientific discourse, much of which was still employed by scientists nationally and internationally well into the twentieth century. And he established a division of the Survey to oversee Yellowstone Park, with Arnold Hague in charge. (This step of Powell's was something of a coup in itself, since Yellowstone Park had earlier been founded through the efforts of Ferdinand Hayden.) Between 1884 and 1891 Hague fought a fierce battle with miners and railroad corporations to prevent them from obtaining congressional permission to build a railway through the park. With the support of big-game hunters and wilderness lovers he fought the local promoters to a standstill five times. Then, in 1891, he convinced President Harrison to use his powers under the just passed

General Revision Act to withdraw a wide protective strip around the boundaries of the park into a forest reserve, the very first to be created under the new law. By these means, Hague helped to set precedent for the principle of the inviolability of the national parks, which John Muir battled so fervently to uphold in coming years.[37]

Of course, in the Gilded Age of laissez-faire, Powell's attempts to build up the authority of his Washington-based science agency did not go unopposed. "[T]he principle of State rights is a living principle yet, and not a shadow of a shade," Senator W. W. Eaton of Connecticut avowed in the debate over the 1879 organic act. Professor James D. Dana of Yale University asserted that the Survey threatened "infringements on State rights and assumption of State responsibilities," which were best left to state-level bureaus or universities. As matters developed, there was extensive cooperation with many state surveys, but Powell's staff was excluded from studying in some states (Minnesota, Kansas, and Alabama) because of professional turf-guarding and jealousy. The closing of the USGS Denver office in 1887 aroused much local resentment, for some of its studies there had greatly aided the local mining economy. In 1884, Powell declared before a congressional investigation hearing that the Survey respected federalism (as it must for political survival), swearing his faith that "the growth of institutions is from local centers" (the history of the USGS notwithstanding). The election of the economy-minded Cleveland administration had precipitated this investigation of the prospering Survey and various other government science bureaus, which dragged on for two years. But in the end, Powell weathered this penultimate storm raised by his rivals and enemies, who could find no evidence of misspent funds or frivolous projects. As one senator conceded to him, "I have no doubt that you are doing an important work and doing it in a proper way."[38]

AS LONG AS Powell's Survey confined itself to harmless topographical mapping or paleontology, it was able to proceed with its projects year after year to a few grumblings and general acclaim. But in the late 1880s, when Powell capitalized on an opportunity to take the Survey's authority in unprecedented directions, making it in effect a national planning agency, the storm of resistance overwhelmed and finally unseated him. Powell's mastery of politics-as-usual had preserved and extended his agency's mandate in preceding years, but this attempt to move beyond Gilded Age political culture, toward the new liberalism and regional planning of the twentieth century, was too far a reach politically and ideologically.

The issue was irrigation in the Arid Region. The surrounding controversy evolved complexly as it unfolded between 1888 and 1891. It all started as an effort to employ federal hydrographic surveying to encourage cession of federal lands to the states for private investment in irrigation works or, potentially, (in the words of one official) a "system of irrigation to be carried on by the general government" — federal reclamation. The legislation was sponsored by senators William M. Stewart of Nevada and Henry M. Teller of Colorado, who launched the bill as Powell's strong supporters but eventually became his worst enemies. Powell had drafted the original part of the measure establishing the Irrigation Survey under the USGS "for the purpose of investigating . . . the segregation of the irrigable lands in such arid region, and for the selection of sites for reservoirs and other hydraulic works."[39] He left unspoken the determination of what entities, public or private, were to finance and construct these works, and in whom the rights and access to them would reside.

An amendment attached to the 1888 bill changed its intent drastically from what Stewart and Teller had wanted and inadvertently handed Powell and the USGS far more power than they had ever before enjoyed. The amendment's sponsors were responding to local outrage over land speculation and water monopoly, yet they knew not what they did. The rider stipulated that "all the lands . . . selected by such United States surveys . . . are from this time henceforth reserved from sale as property of the United States, and shall not be subject . . . to entry, occupation, or settlement." The USGS Irrigation Survey and the General Land Office now had the authority to invalidate the land claims of thousands of individuals and companies in the West, and theoretically they could (in the words of one aghast congressman) "stop emigration to the West . . . stop progress, stop the settling up of the country." An attorney general's ruling in 1889 brought about this unthinkable turn of events, invalidating almost 140,000 filings on 9 million acres — every parcel entered since the passage of the 1888 legislation.[40] Westerners and their representatives went into an uproar.

Powell had not sought this authority. "I have not done it. I never advocated it. That reservation was put into the law independently of me," he complained to Senator Stewart, who in his wrath attacked Powell as "drunk on power" at hearings convened the following year. Yet Powell brought this scapegoating on himself because he would not repudiate the consequences of the attorney general's ruling: he believed that the invalidation of the claims, wiping the arid landscape clean of the arbitrary land-law grid, was "wise." In fact, Powell had protested too much at the hearings, for his actions showed that he anticipated the possibility of survey planning in the region. His men were directed to chart the best sites of "hydraulic works" regardless of current claims or construction, regardless even of territorial, state, or county lines. Although much of the Irrigation Survey's initial mapping had been done in Colorado and Nevada (to please Stewart and Teller), Powell's surveyors looked past all man-made boundaries (and the powerful interests they represented) for "a unit of country well defined in nature," the "hydrographic basin."[41] Unfortunately, throughout the few trying years of the Irrigation Survey's existence, Powell did not play the political game with his usual skill. His ideals, his plans for the Arid Region, got in the way, and they ultimately brought his career to an end.

What those plans were Powell had first articulated back in 1878 with his *Report on the Lands of the Arid Region*, and they "had not been materially modified by developments of the last ten years," he observed in 1888. They were of a character to alienate virtually everyone concerned with western irrigation and settlement—small individual settlers already filed, large land companies, advocates of federal reclamation, and boosters of state and private water development. Powell called his plans the "district or colony system," which would redraw the land grid to "conform to topographic features" in the Arid Region and encompass the "interdependent and unified interests and values" of the farmers who would live there. "Such a district of country is a commonwealth by itself," made so by "nature herself," Powell wrote.[42] This vision of the "hydrographic basin" district culminated his decades of interest in the *region* concept. Geological substructure, topography, stream courses, climate, and vegetation, as well as human culture, the "wants" and institutions of men—all were synthesized by Powell in the idea of the hydrographic basin. He had first begun to define the concept in the 1878 *Report*, and he grasped it more holistically by 1890, advocating and defending it in the very midst of the 1888–91 Irrigation Survey crisis, especially in a *Century* essay entitled "Institutions for the Arid Region," one of the most important writings of his career.

The basin, Powell began, was a "unit of country" that was "bounded above and on each side by heights of land that rise as crests to part the waters," which fed and flowed into neighboring basins "segregated" from one another because of these natural barriers. In the *Report* he had differentiated the types of lands within each basin, proposing the land division best suited to each zone of climate and vegetation. First, at the lowest elevation, on the plains and mesas of the river valleys, there were the "irrigable lands," which Powell thought could be developed into farms as small as 40 to 80 acres in extent (rather than the customary 160 acres), profitable because of the intense cultivation possible with irrigation. More radically, Powell proposed that ultimate ownership of water resources should be public, "in the hands of the people," and that on irrigated farms "the right of the water should inhere in the land where it is used." All irrigation works would be overseen by members of an "irrigation district" seated in the hydrographic basin. These riparian reforms would guarantee each settler irrigation, quite in contrast to the practice of "prior appropriation" (or control of water through separate private claims, independent of abutting land) that now determined water rights in many areas of the West. This democratic "user right" would require a distribution of land that must "conform" to stream beds or canals and provide access to "the greatest possible number of water fronts," obviating the "present arbitrary system of dividing the lands into rectangular tracts." The whole pattern of settlement would necessarily be affected in this systemic adaptation to the Arid Region, and Powell foresaw that "residences should be grouped" rather than scattered so that settlers could have "the benefits of the local social organizations of civilization—schools, churches, etc." [43]

Above the irrigable lands, at the middle elevations, there lay (in Powell's basin concept) the "pasturage hills," and at the highest altitudes, the "timber lands." According to Powell, "the grasses of the pasturage lands are scant, and the lands are of value only in large quantities," which he set at 2,560 acres—yet another adaptation of the property grid to the landscape. Each projected pasturage farm would have a small, irrigated twenty-acre plot on a waterfront, and each would in its larger expanse be unfenced, allowing herds to "roam in common" under the "communal regulations" of a "pasturage district." As for the timberlands above, in the original 1878 Report Powell recommended that they be retained for use by "lumbermen and woodmen" because the uplands were "too far from the agricultural lands to be owned and utilized directly by those who carry on farming by irrigation." But in 1890 he revealed a change in his thinking, which was related to his firmer holistic grasp of the interconnected natural systems of the hydrographic basin. "The men who control the farming below must also control the upper regions where the waters are gathered from the heavens and stored in reservoirs," he wrote. "Every farm and garden in the valley below is dependent upon each fountain above," and so "every man is interested in the conservation and management of the water supply" originating in the mountain forests. In Powell's vision, "nature herself" dictated that the people of a hydrographic basin must constitute "a body of interdependent and unified interests," a "commonwealth within itself." [44]

Powell found in the hydrographic basin a natural setting for the Jeffersonian neorepublican values that had long ago been inculcated in him by the Free-Soil sentiments of his father and George Crookham, and by a youth lived in frontier communities. He believed he saw them practiced in the Mormon settlements of Utah, which were so successful in their irrigation arrangements. His idyll was a small-scale, agrarian, petty-commercial, localistic, cooperative mode of life. As he wrote in "Institutions for the Arid Region," "I love the cradle more than the bank counter. The cottage home is more beautiful to me than the palace. I believe that the school-house is primal, the university secondary; and I believe that the justice's court in the hamlet is the only permanent foundation for the Supreme Court at the capital. Such are the interests which I advocate." To spread and preserve these interests was the purpose of his reforms: that "the entire arid region be organized into natural hydrographic districts," with the end to "establish local self-government by hydrographic basins" across the West. His very faith in republican ideals made the plan seem reasonable, and realizable, for "the people in such a district have common interests, common rights, and common duties, and must necessarily work together for common purposes." Every man of them was "a freeman king with power to rule himself, and they may be trusted to their own interests."[45] Virtue and independence would make the plan both feasible and imperative.

Powell's political beliefs were widely misunderstood in his own time and have remained so to subsequent generations. His contemporary critics did not recognize their own past political traditions, neither Powell's new restatement of republicanism, nor even the much vaster renaissance of the ideology that was occurring all around them in the Populist movement, which peaked nationally in the same years that marked the Irrigation Survey's brief existence. Powell sought to establish an agrarian-republican society in the Arid Region; the Populists sought to make one viable in the Plains and Southern states of the Subhumid and Humid Regions. Their opponents called them wild-eyed radicals. Powell's proposals were labeled variously "un-American" and "Utopian," "Russian" and "medieval."[46] They were rejected not once but twice, when they were published in 1878 and when Powell proposed them during the years of the Irrigation Survey crisis.

The cause of this hostile and incomprehending reaction to Powell's plans lay in their apparent threat to private property and states' rights. Justice in the Arid Region, Powell wrote, demanded that "all the waters" be considered "common property" until "distributed among the people." Moreover, the "cooperative labor or capital" of the little men he envisioned settling there would be necessary to utilize those waters. "[E]ach such community should possess its own irrigation works" and control them by "communal regulations," just as each community would regulate the pasturage areas and timberlands. Yet the irrigable land itself would be held privately and individually, "in severalty." Through this modified riparian framework Powell hoped to foster the wide distribution of wealth on which republican society flourished, but his goal was also to prevent monopoly power from taking hold of the one resource that created the greatest agricultural value in the Arid Region. Yet to adherents of the absolute rights of property, especially the already existing rights of local holders (who were pressuring Congress), such ideas made Powell a "revolutionist," a characterization that was only confirmed by the threat of the Irrigation Survey to current titles and claims. That he wanted to impose this "un-American" system on the West through measures of the federal government—measures that would nullify present ownership of land and water rights by individuals and companies—threw more fuel on the ideological fire. The suspicions that the director of the "new-fangled" USGS was not regular in his loyalty to states' rights and localism were renewed and reinforced. And, in fact, Powell's projected hydrographic basins, each a "commonwealth within itself," would have rendered many state borders obsolete, which was his intention.[47] Otherwise, Powell believed, the West faced the prospect of endless legal disputes among the states over water courses that ignored their geometrical boundaries.

To many of his critics, Powell's plans raised the specter of "paternalism," a powerful central government intimately involved in the lives and economy of the Arid Region. "We are centralizing until we are now looking after the health of the people by taking charge of their food," one congressman railed. Later scholars would consider Powell at the very least the father of federally sponsored reclamation.[48] Both characterizations of Powell and his conception of the role of federal authority in his proposed system are inaccurate, yet the confusion over his plan stemmed from the delicateness of the ideological balancing act he was attempting—so delicate that many could not even imagine its possibility, and they therefore mistook his words. This balancing act was to make Powell less a precursor of new liberalism (a bastard child of his, at most) than a founder of utopian regionalism, which offered modern America an alternative to a centralized government and economy.

It is true that Powell had worked hard to build a federal scientific establishment in Washington and that, when the occasion arose, he grasped the opportunity to exercise planning and regulatory authority from this national seat. To Powell's mind, however—and here he occupied a common ground with the new liberals—such a concentration of power was essential to protect a broader democratic ideal, the public interest. And science was the means to ascertain that interest, Powell and others believed; only by science could policies be objective and disinterested; only science could determine the greatest good for the greatest number. Powell shared the confidence of his colleague Lester Ward that because of science "a large body of truth has been accumulated by which to be guided" in the solution to social problems, and that this knowledge implied a "truly positive philosophy, i.e., a philosophy of action" that must challenge the dogma of laissez-faire. Washington as the national capital was the natural site of scientific research in the public interest, Powell argued further. Many projects were simply beyond the means of the private sector: "A hundred millionaires could not do the work in scientific research now done by the General Government" — nor should they, monopolizing the information to themselves. "Knowledge is for the welfare of all the people," he affirmed. The government "should do the work and pay for it from the public treasury," and "all that results from the expenditure should be given back to the people at large." Similarly, Powell wrote, the "general government must bear its part in the establishment of institutions for the arid region," classifying lands and distributing them to the people, holding some areas "in trust," dividing water resources fairly among all parties, and adjudicating disputes. In principle, Powell was even willing to go as far as supporting federal regulation of corporations — "the adjustment of the relations of the corporations to the public and to each other" — one of the key justifications for federal activism and centralization put forward by the dawning Progressive generation.[49]

Yet sharply contrary to this positivist faith in public-interest governance, Powell (like George Perkins Marsh) had the evidence of his own career in corrupt Washington politics to question the wisdom of federal involvement in the Arid Region or anywhere else. This aversion to politics-as-usual lay behind his famous forewarning in "Institutions for the Arid Region," "I say to the government: Hands off! Furnish the people with institutions of justice, and let them do the work for themselves. The solution to be propounded, then, is one of institutions to be organized for the establishment of justice, not of appropriations to be made and offices created by the government." Powell, in short, was not the father of federal reclamation for the simple reason that he opposed federal money or construction efforts in Arid Region water projects. As a former frontiersman himself, he was convinced that the men of the irrigation districts could build the needed reservoirs and canals "to some extent by cooperative labor," just as he had seen the Mormons accomplish. Where their own work was insufficient, "ultimately and gradually great capital must be employed in each district"—procured not from the federal government but from local revenues and private lenders. "Let them obtain this capital by their own enterprise as a community," Powell wrote. "Constituting a body corporate, they can tax themselves and they can borrow moneys." The corruptible federal government must have no more involvement than simply facilitating this local collective economic development through Powell's proposed decentralized framework, his "institutions of justice." To allow any greater national role would be tantamount, he feared, to "nationalizing the agricultural institutions of the arid country." [50]

The deeper sources of Powell's aversion to federal power were rooted in his republican sympathies. He truly wanted to believe that "the growth of institutions in America is from local centers." Even in the midst of his own institution building in Washington, Powell had (in his words) "done all within his power to build up State geological surveys." As someone who upheld federalism, he also found a substantial role for state governments in his plan for the Arid Region, which would provide courts of appeal from the irrigation districts, set up an inspection system, and draft general water rights regulations, among other legal functions. As a further bulwark for decentralization there were the hydrographic basin districts themselves, the purpose of each "to establish local self-government" and serve as "a commonwealth within itself." Writing of the republican citizens who were to people his districts, Powell stated his allegiance to localism in no uncertain terms: "The interests are theirs, the rights are theirs, the duties are theirs; let them control their own actions." [51]

So ran the axes of Powell's delicate ideological balance: a grassroots agrarian political economy for the Arid Region that was dedicated to cooperative private enterprise but would be federally planned, implemented, and enforced. It was the product of his unlikely twin faiths, science and republicanism, both running deep within him to the long ago days of George Crookham's backwoods natural history museum. Powell's was not the only such plan being floated in the late nineteenth century that looked to national regulation, high technology, and other thoroughly modern means to resuscitate the old localist community life of independent producers. His was part of a shared vision of an elusive ideological country known to a generation as the Cooperative Commonwealth. Ebenezer Howard's Garden City concept lay there, as did Charles Macune's Subtreasury Plan; Edward Bellamy's Nationalist Boston was situated within it, as was Henry George's Single Tax utopia and Terrence Powderly's Knights of Labor platform. Like Powell, they could describe the commonwealth in some compelling detail—the flaws disguised in a golden haze—but they could not realistically say how to get there, nor convince the mass of Americans to join them. Their plans, like Powell's, were to provoke close observers to endless hypotheticals: Would farmers in the irrigation districts "necessarily" have "common interests" and "common purposes," or know how to determine them? How could these small farmers raise the "great capital" required for their water works, especially when few if any commercial lenders would in these same years do business with the cooperatives of the Populists? How could land and water monopolies be prevented should district farmers choose to sell out to a single wealthy buyer? How would pre-Survey lands already privately owned be irrigated if Powell's irrigable lands were only those still to be distributed to settlers? How could elected representatives displace one land system with another and have any hope of surviving politically? And so the questions might continue, an exercise for the imagination, yet not even there could the fragile harmony of the plan—power, human nature, idyll—be maintained.[52]

No sooner had Powell's Irrigation Survey begun to map the Cooperative Commonwealth in the Arid Region, one of its ideal locations, when it disappeared like a desert mirage. As George Crookham had fifty years before, so Powell discovered to his dismay that the people did not care to be "enlightened." Economic self-interest, states' rights, and localism certainly played their roles in dooming Powell's plans and the Irrigation Survey itself. For someone who claimed to value local self-government, Powell should not have been surprised that the "little men" of the West looked on a Washington bureaucrat (and academic) with suspicion, or that they wished to preserve the existence and prerogatives of their county and state governments. Yet this ideological opposition was only part of a maelstrom of political forces that engulfed Powell by 1890. Like a true utopian, he with his vision had sidestepped certain crucial issues of power, which now were visited on him with a vengeance. He learned, for example, that the concept of "the region" might foster not cooperation but division and animosity. Plains states congressional representatives, whose constituents were stricken by severe drought after 1889, had little sympathy for a project to promote extensive irrigation and settlement in the West. They pushed instead for the creation of a rival Artesian Well Survey to aid farmers in their own section of the country. The Artesian Survey competed for funding with Powell's own enterprise, and it was set up in the Department of Agriculture, beyond the influence of Powell's operations in the Interior Department. He fought his Artesian competitors, whose findings could potentially make his planned irrigation works obsolete, by (mistakenly) criticizing their scientific assumptions, but to no avail. Meanwhile, the Democrats won control of Congress in the 1890 elections, and they had little use for a controversial spendthrift Republican appointee like Powell.[53]

Perhaps most painful to Powell during these years of the Irrigation Survey crisis were the attacks that were launched against him by fellow scientists. In early 1890, paleontologist E. D. Cope led the charge when he very publicly questioned Powell's scientific competency and depicted him as a dispenser of patronage comparable to a machine precinct boss. Cope was an old enemy who took the opportunity to kick Powell when he was down. But Powell's feud with members of the rising national forestry movement was more damaging. The work of his Irrigation Survey was hindering proposals to establish federal forest reserves. His projected basin districts would place such forests under the control of private farmers rather than public officials, the latter course advocated by the American Forestry Association. Powell opposed the idea of a national forestry commission to study the problem of deforestation; he did not want yet another scientific bureau to compete with the USGS. Powell also questioned the necessity or benefit of maintaining extensive forest cover in watershed uplands. Removing the trees might very well increase water flow for irrigation, he speculated. For these views Powell soon found himself on the receiving end of criticism by the august director of Harvard's Arnold Arboretum, Charles S. Sargent, a social and scientific aristocrat who implicitly reminded Powell that he was, after all, a frontier autodidact with no earned degree. Powell's pseudoscientific conclusions regarding forest cover represented "eccentric deviations from the teachings of experience in all times and countries," Sargent editorialized in his influential magazine, Garden and Forest. Powell had even failed to compose a "sustained and coherent argument," Sargent added. These words must have stung deeply.[54]

In mid-1890, Congress undid the work Powell had done. Opponents canceled the Irrigation Survey, repealed the measure closing entry to homesteads on lands not yet classified, and restored all of the rights and holdings earlier invalidated by the attorney general. Then they began to tear apart the Geological Survey as a whole. Its appropriation was cut in half; the staff of the paleontology division was cut from twenty-eight to six; plum positions for top geologists were reduced from five to two; and a budget was drawn up with salaries and number of employees specified. By 1893, the Bureau of Ethnology had also been seriously undermined. Looking over the wreckage, perhaps Powell echoed his boyhood mentor after the burning of the country lyceum: "It will take more years than I have left to build . . . over again."[55] He resigned from the USGS in 1894, though he hung on as director at the Bureau of Ethnology, a post largely honorary in his last years.

POWELL LIVED OUT the rest of his life a man injured, which surely his reputation was. After decades of correcting the misconceptions of his countrymen, this ultimate rebuke to his self-taught expertise must have pained him. In his forced retirement he wrote Truth and Error, publishing it in 1898. The book was a labored attempt to demonstrate his learnedness. Hegel, Kant, Emerson, Spencer—all were dispensed with in short order, and "philosophy" made a pejorative word, a species of self-delusion. In contrast, "the history of science is the history of the discovery of the simple and the true," Powell wrote; "in its progress fallacies are dispelled and certitudes remain." So Powell liked to believe, but in fact truth is complex, fallacies persist, and certitudes change. "All philosophy," Powell might say, yet the consequences of his own substantial legacy to twentieth-century environmentalism were evidence enough for a world riddled with irony and irrationality, science included.[56]

The several directions in which Powell's institutional and intellectual legacy unfolded after 1900 was one hallmark of the untenableness of his delicately balanced, technocratic, neorepublican political vision, of its unstable equilibrium. Powell retired in 1894 and died in 1902, so in examining his legacy it becomes necessary to speak of Powell's men, the personnel of the Survey and the Bureau whose careers were shaped by him. They and their careers weave prominently through the early history of conservation and reclamation in America, thanks in part to Director Powell and the standard-setting quality of USGS science. Yet these men by and large also were his wayward heirs, carrying fragments of his overarching vision in directions he did not desire or intend.

Detached from Powell's devotion to the ideals of republican independence and agrarian localism, the centralizing tendencies of federal science and scientific planning took their natural course in the hands of these less ideologically complicated men. There was, for example, the role of Arnold Hague and the Survey in the creation of the national forest reserve system. Hague's efforts did not end with his successful move to protect Yellowstone's boundaries in 1891. In 1896, he was appointed to the Forest Commission, in which Gifford Pinchot and John Muir were also members, and which was instrumental in the establishment of an administrative framework for the still infant system. The Major did not like Pinchot's proposals for centralized administration and a corps of trained foresters (an "army of aliens," Powell called them), but Hague worked closely with Pinchot on the divided commission and sided with him for utilitarian federal management of the forests to conserve water and timber supplies. In the following year, Congress assigned the USGS the task of surveying the new reserves laid down by President Cleveland and ordered the agency to make plans "to regulate their occupancy and use and to preserve the forests therein from destruction." To fulfill these new responsibilities, Hague and C. D. Walcott, who was Powell's handpicked successor as director of the Survey, arranged to have Pinchot appointed as a forestry consultant in the Department of Interior. It was Pinchot's first position in the federal government and a post from which he launched his campaign to establish the U.S. Forest Service—and eventually, he hoped, a unified policy-making authority over all natural resources in the public domain.[57]

Two other men from Powell's Survey, Frederick G. Newell and WJ McGee, were also allies in Pinchot's federal conservationist cause. In 1901, on the accession of the activist and nationalist Theodore Roosevelt to the presidency, Newell and Pinchot drafted a speech for him on forest and water policy. In the address, Roosevelt publicly advocated the consolidation of forest system oversight into Pinchot's newly formed Bureau of Forestry, and he proposed that "irrigation works should be built by the National Government." Over Powell's dead body the landmark Newlands Act of 1902 set such a program into motion, though with a few provisions that would have dismayed New Nationalists as much as they would have heartened Powell: construction was to be self-financing, with the cost of irrigation works repaid by farmers over a fixed period of years; in addition, the states would have a say in how one-half of these revenues were spent within their borders. State water rights and laws, however, were left intact, creating a legal tangle as unchallengeable by his successors as for Powell himself; current right-holders were no more willing to be subjected to national regulation than they had been to local "communal regulation." With these modest legislative beginnings, the first small projects in the West got under way, all administered by a new division of the Geological Survey, the Reclamation Service, which was headed by Newell, the chief hydrographer. By 1907, the Reclamation Service had outgrown the Survey and was made a separate agency of the Department of the Interior, with Frederick Newell as its director. In 1910, Congress asserted its power of the purse against this executive branch aggrandizement and began financing water projects on its own porcine initiative, with results much as Powell had feared: many technically questionable projects were constructed at the behest of locals and their congressmen or by Reclamation Service and Army Corps technocrats eager for work. In due course the repayment schedule for farmers was made so favorable that their irrigation became, in effect, subsidized, and farmers entered a dependent and antirepublican but (in good years) a very profitable relationship with the national government.[58]

Some echoes of Powell's ideals could be heard in the words of his friend WJ McGee, another self-taught boy of the frontier who had been with the Major since 1882 and who ran the Bureau of Ethnology for him during his final years. (A stipulation in each man's will instructed that after death their preserved brains be compared for size; Powell won.) After 1900, McGee also associated himself with the dynamic Pinchot, who called him "the scientific brains of the Conservation movement." In 1907, McGee was appointed secretary to the Inland Waterways Commission, a quintessentially Progressive panel of experts formed to study and inventory water resources. The panel included Pinchot, Newell, and representatives of the Army Corps of Engineers. The next year McGee became a member of the National Conservation Commission, a larger undertaking that was to inventory national resources in toto. "This is an age of science and ours is a nation of science," McGee optimistically opened "Water as a Resource," an essay he published in 1909. "Now is the time of conquest over nature in a practical sense. . . . The conquest will not be complete until these waters are brought under complete control." In a later essay, published not long before his death in 1911, McGee framed the conservationist political struggle in terms Powell would have approved of: "Ample resources indeed remain," he wrote, "but the question also remains whether these shall be held and used by the People . . . or whether they shall go chiefly into the hands of the self-chosen and self-anointed few." It must always be remembered, he declared, that "each holder of the sources of life is but a trustee . . . and is responsible to all men and for all time for making the best use of them in the common interest . . . in which each will feel that he lives not for himself alone but as part of a common life for a common world and for the common good." Pinchot capitalized on antimonopoly, national unity-craving rhetoric like McGee's, which could be an effective spur to public opinion during the Progressive Era. But, in fact, he and the young U.S. Forest Service enjoyed relatively good relations with lumber companies, stockmen, and other big-time users of the public domain. Congress nonetheless abolished the National Conservation Commission and its program in 1909 by refusing to fund it, signaling their displeasure with executive and Pinchotesque oversight of resource policy.[59] Pinchot found Congress and the interest groups and local powers-that-be it represented as difficult to overcome as had Powell, albeit on behalf of a centralizing agenda opposed to much that Powell's vision stood for.

What, then, was left of that vision in the twentieth century? The Geological Survey in the post-Powell decades dwindled somewhat in stature. According to one critic it became a "department of practical geology" that methodically pursued the national topographic map project and aided the oil and mining industries in resource discovery but comparatively neglected the research into pure science that had made the nineteenth-century USGS under Powell the scientific "center of the world." In the tradition of Arnold Hague at Yellowstone, the Survey did play a significant part in the organization of the National Park Service under Stephen Mather in 1916. Although Powell had not been especially sympathetic to the cause of wilderness preservation, it was yet another important impact on the history of American environmentalism traceable only unintentionally to him, through the influential men he trained and the capable institution he created.[60]

It was the regionalists of the twentieth century who were Powell's most faithful descendants, attempting again in their own time his utopian synthesis of agrarian-republicanism, high technology, and scientific planning. Benton MacKaye, one of the intellectual leaders of the regional planning movement of the 1920s and 1930s, began his career during the 1910s in the Planning Division of Pinchot's Forest Service, proposing in one report that Alaska be settled according to a colony-community plan inspired by Powell's projections for the Arid Region. (Within a few years MacKaye left the Forest Service, no more at home there than Powell would have been.) The regionalist historian Lewis Mumford, a close collaborator with MacKaye, placed Powell among their direct intellectual progenitors, whom he traced back in America to George Perkins Marsh. Powell's Bureau of Ethnology also helped to instigate an intellectual sea change in scholarly and artistic appreciation of Native Americans, which in the work of regionalists like Edgar Hewett, Mary Austin, and John Collier reached more pluralistic conclusions than his own. Yet the regionalists of MacKaye's and Mumford's generation were no more successful in implementing their updated versions of Powell's vision than he had been. Property lines still got in the way, as did greed, individualism, power politics, prejudice, and the weight of history.[61]

When the federal government became a full-fledged welfare state during the depression of the 1930s and a war state in the 1940s, the Arid Region greatly benefited, and so did the Bureau of Reclamation and the Army Corps of Engineers. Enormous federally financed dams and water projects provided jobs for the jobless, morale for the nation, and, ultimately, electricity for war production. Hoover, Shasta, Grand Coulee, and Bonneville—at the time the four largest concrete dams in the world —were constructed between 1930 and 1945, and dozens of other smaller works were completed in the period as well. Even after the national emergency passed, the dam-building continued, servicing Cold War defense industries and suburban sprawl across the West, while vast networks of federally subsidized irrigation channels made the desert bloom. So the government men pushed development forward, planless and heedless.[62]

"The Bureau of Reclamation engineers are like beavers. They can't stand the sight of running water," said David Brower of the Sierra Club, one of their chief critics in the years following World War II. The modern postwar environmental movement got its start by organizing to oppose various elements of the Upper Colorado River Storage Project, which included much of Powell's original area of exploration in the Plateau Province. Environmentalists may have succeeded in stopping a dam at Echo Park on the Green River and another proposed for the Grand Canyon, but they failed to halt the dam at Glen Canyon, fifteen miles upstream on the Colorado. This dam created Lake Powell, one of the largest man-made reservoirs in the world, backing up 200 miles through the canyonlands of southern Utah. It was dedicated in 1969, on the one hundredth anniversary of the arrival of the men and boats of the first Powell expedition at Glen Canyon, which was named by them. At the ceremony one booster exclaimed, "Major Powell would have approved of this lake. May it ever be brimmin' full."[63]

Lake Powell symbolized how its namesake's paradoxical yet compelling vision of the Arid Region was a most ambiguous legacy. The fervent promoters of large-scale federal reclamation called Powell one of their own, yet so did the dam-builders' most radical environmental-ist opponents. Lake Powell was christened "supposedly to honor but actually to dishonor the memory, spirit and vision of Major John Wesley Powell," wrote Edward Abbey in his raging indictment of the modern urban-technological West *Desert Solitaire*. The heroic descent of Powell's bare-bones expedition into the most wild of all American wildernesses endeared him to radicals like Abbey, who placed Powell even before Muir and Thoreau in his pantheon of men of the wilderness. Need-less to say, Powell's advocacy of democratic and communitarian values also put him high in the radicals' esteem. Yet their comprehension of Powell's vision was as incomplete as that of the reclamationists. Powell was praised by Abbey—not quite accurately—for being one of those rare explorers of the wilderness who "found in it something more than merely raw material for pecuniary exploitation." [64] But in one sense, per-haps, the radicals and their activities in the late twentieth century did express the legacy of John Wesley Powell. Increasingly, they resorted to "monkeywrenching," the sabotage and booby-trapping of equipment and resources slated for development, to resist the environmental con-sequences of science and technology divorced from utopian impulse and ethical constraint—the very plight of Powell's splayed intellectual bequest. If the gouged, flooded, nuclear-tested, and denuded landscape of the West was what human intelligence had wrought, they reasoned, then better that these things did not exist at all.

Glen Canyon Dam, with Lake Powell behind it, was their most hated and desired target. In 1981, a group of Earth First! protesters unfurled a 300-foot black plastic banner in the shape of giant crack down the dam's concave surface. "The loveliest explosion ever seen by man," Abbey dreamed, would be the charge "reducing the great dam to a heap of rubble in the path of the river," draining Lake Powell and returning the Colorado to the "mad, raging stream" that Powell and his men had once floated upon. [65]

Epilogue

Every new fact, illustrative of the action and reaction between humanity and the material world around it, is another step toward the determination of the great question, whether man is of nature or above her.

George Perkins Marsh, Man and Nature

THE CONFLICTING meanings given by radicals and boosters to Glen Canyon Dam are emblematic of the divided mind that has characterized the relationship of twentieth-century Americans to nature. The modern environmental movement, inspired by the words of Marsh, Thoreau, Muir, and Powell, reflected this disjunction. On the one hand, by the 1960s and 1970s tens of millions of Americans would have agreed with Edward Abbey about the value of wilderness and the necessity of its preservation, even though they might reject his extremist means. Yet, on the other hand, those same Americans would also demand the ever-higher standard of living and economic growth that hydroelectric plants like Glen Canyon Dam made possible, courtesy of federal reclamation and utilitarian conservation. This unexamined fissure in American attitudes toward nature, which caused it to be cherished as well as devoured, stemmed out of widely held values central to modern consumer culture, visible already by the time of Muir and Powell. Modern Americans pursued happiness through leisure and recreation in nature and through a gadget-laden, automobile-dependent, materialistic lifestyle. To make their fellow citizens see how these behaviors were problematic from an ecological point of view was one of the central challenges facing environmentalists in the late twentieth century.

What do Marsh, Thoreau, Muir, and Powell still have to say to an America about to enter a new millennium? Certainly George Perkins

Marsh's "great question" remains vital to our age, as are many of the answers that he and his nineteenth-century counterparts provided. The noted environmental historian William Cronon has suggested in a recent essay that to attempt to discuss the human-nature relationship in terms of the worldviews of dam-boosters and monkeywrenchers creates a "dangerous dualism" in our thinking that "sets humanity and nature at opposite poles." Particularly, Cronon and others implicate both Thoreau and Muir in the definition of wilderness that falsely supposes it to be an untouched, pristine, and sacred place that exists today much as it did in times primeval, empty of all human influence. In fact, argues Cronon, pointing to the blind sides of this notion, America's "wild" areas were inhabited and shaped for thousands of years by indigenous peoples, and modern-day wilderness parks are very much artificial institutions. It is extremely difficult to distinguish between the human and the natural, Cronon and the attendees at a 1994 symposium on the subject concluded; human constructions *of* and *in* nature tie us inextricably to the material world. The symposium called for a "reinvented" concept of nature, one that might recognize the "full continuum of a natural landscape that is also cultural, in which the city, the suburb, the pastoral, and the wild each has its proper place," as Cronon put it.[1] Within this continuum the ideological extremes represented by monkeywrenchers and corporate developers might possibly be reconciled.

Whatever their role in fostering the incoherence of contemporary environmental thought, Thoreau and Muir offer fresh sources of ideas for the project of "reinventing nature," as do Marsh and Powell. This "past," one might say, is still quite "usable." After all, it was John Muir who helped to convince Americans that "going to the mountains is like going home," thereby making wilderness part of the "continuum" of environments that tens of millions of people have experienced in subsequent decades. This integration of wild nature into everyday life, whether on weekend outings or summer vacations, was the very essence of its institutionalization—offering not an "escape from history" but the addition of wilderness to the personal histories of countless individuals.[2] If Muir's religious rhetoric encouraged the widespread misconception that the scenery in national parks was humanly unviolated, fresh from the hands of the Creator, it is also true that a popular sense of their "sacredness" has protected the parks in the political arena over several generations. The continued survival of the national park and wilderness preservation systems in the increasingly crowded world of the twenty-first century may require that environmentalists take a new look at Muir's old-time religion. To counter conservative charges that environmental measures curb freedom and put the welfare of nature before that of human beings, some reminders that human beings are sinful and nature is God's handiwork could turn the tide among a national polity that has been drifting politically to the right.

Thoreau, for his part, is no doubt open to criticism that his depiction of wilderness as a sphere of "absolute freedom" led latter-day readers to some unrealistic expectations regarding it. But we should recall from Thoreau his idyll of a "partially cultivated country" as the best setting in which to live. In his eyes, "wooded towns" like Concord, humanly scaled and sculpted into "parks and groves, gardens, arbors, paths, vistas," with the "primitive swamps scattered here and there in their midst," represented the "perfection of . . . landscapes." To dismiss this vision as anti-urban pastoralism is to forget that Concord was a bustling, cosmopolitan place (with the likes of Emerson, Hawthorne, and Fuller strolling around) and that Thoreau needed this "urbane" richness just as much as he desired wilderness solitude. A mixed landscape that holistically incorporated the cultivated and the wild would present to each individual the diversity of environments necessary for a rounded human life. Thoreau meant to contribute toward this mixture with his most concrete proposal for wilderness preservation, one that would protect not some far-flung immense tract, untrammeled and forbidding, but rather a "primitive forest, of five hundred or a thousand acres" on the outskirts of town.[3] If we were to adapt this vision (as we already have on a small scale, in "nature centers," farmland preservation programs, "growth boundaries," and suburban "green corridors"), wild nature could be a constant presence and relief for the quietly desperate residents of megalopolis. Indeed, megalopolis would undergo a rather different kind of "urban renewal."

To achieve and maintain such a balance between wild and cultivated landforms would require humankind to become, in Marsh's famous words, a "co-worker with nature." What he meant was that economic development should mimic and cooperate with natural processes, not dominate them. Marsh had his own idea for a wilderness park, which he (supposedly a "utilitarian conservationist") justified on both anthropocentric and biocentric grounds: "[S]ome large and easily accessible region of American soil should remain as far as possible in its primitive condition, . . . a garden for the recreation of the lovers of nature, and an asylum where indigenous trees . . . plants . . . beasts may dwell and perpetuate their kind." Marsh's central message to us, however, is that to rectify the disturbing impact of human beings on nature's harmonies demands much more than setting aside such an "asylum" for wildlife. We must tend to the landscapes where we live and work. The critical issues are the manner in which a landscape will be utilized, and by whom—which is why the debate between monkeywrenchers and developers has an air of unreality about it. Marsh urges us to remember that virtually anywhere we go on the planet we will find evidence that humankind "made the earth," the results of the "assiduous husbandry of hundreds of generations" involved in "reciprocal action and reaction" with nature. Environmentalists today are still coming to grips with this revelation (discovering that their beloved primitive forests were actually logged a century ago, for example). But the extent to which humans have "lived in" nature, leaving few areas absolutely pristine, does not justify any and all present economic exploitation, as some defenders of development have claimed, taking liberties with a question of recent theoretical interest: If humans are "part of nature," is not everything humanly wrought also "natural"? Marsh speaks to this debate with his ethic of the "co-worker." Whether our use of nature is construction or recreation, we must make natural forces our "best auxiliaries" and proceed with "foresight and wisely guided industry."[4]

John Wesley Powell attempted this feat in the Arid Region, and both his attempt and his failure are instructive to us. Economic development should "conform" to its natural setting, Powell proposed. Where possible, we should seek out the "unit of country well defined in nature," such as a river course and its watershed—his "hydrographic basin"—or more generally, a "region." For the purposes of charting and directing present and future growth, Powell asserted, each region should be defined by the "interdependent and unified interests and values" of its inhabitants—a projection that we may take as more normative than realistic. If the citizens of a regional development were collectively to take responsibility for its cultivation as a balanced, sustainable landscape, then their interests and values might become "interdependent and unified." Their region, their community and its environs, would be a "commonwealth within itself." Powell's ideas refer us to place, the sense of place: its importance to living well with nature (and with tradition and history), its role in awakening people to the "duties" they have to enhancing their local environment.[5]

Powell also reminds us that sensitivity to place does not merely "happen" but requires planning in some strong or weak form. Recently, an experiment in this sort of symbiotic planning occurred at—of all places—Glen Canyon Dam. Over the past several years conservation biologists and others involved in park and wildlife management have of necessity been obliged to find practical ways of reconciling the "dangerous dualism" dividing humanity from nature. For them, the needs and demands of environmentalists, developers, tourists, and urban consumers must all be mediated within real-world policies governing fragile landscapes. One important opportunity to do so arose in 1996 at the Glen Canyon facility, where the mandate to use water primarily for electrical power generation was broadened (at least temporarily) to include ecosystem management of the downstream Grand Canyon. In the experiment (overseen in part by the U.S. Geological Survey), the waters of Lake Powell were released to create an artificial flood that emulated the natural rhythm of the Colorado River, long interrupted by the presence of the dam. A preprogrammed "mad, raging" torrent swept through the canyon, and a survey of the results was encouraging: new beaches, sandbars, and backwater pools were created, restoring and expanding habitats for fish and wildlife. Yet, although more symbiotic flow-rate guidelines were approved for Glen Canyon Dam in 1996, it remained to be seen whether other hydroelectric dams in the West would also adopt similar procedures, or even whether the revised regulations at Glen Canyon could survive political assault by those interested in keeping power generation its paramount mission.[6]

Powell's hope had been that the political mechanisms for planning could be democratic and communal. But the experiment at Glen

Canyon, and the earlier fate of Powell's own evocative plans for the Arid Region, have significant lessons for us: we should not delude ourselves that environmental planning can occur without some compromise or coercion, without "politics," in other words; and we should not underestimate the ideological and institutional obstacles in America that must be accommodated or overcome for a landscape plan to be implemented. As metroplexes, subdivisions, golf courses, and mega-malls continue to sprawl and consume the countryside helter-skelter into the next century, Powell's vision remains a compelling alternative, if only for consciousness-raising purposes. Contemplating this vision, residents of a locality must ask themselves: Who is making the development decisions affecting this place we call home? Powell's environmental populism could strike a chord in a citizenry that is becoming more aware of the growing disparities of wealth and power both nationally and globally.

Such talk of planned environments and anciently humanized landscapes is usually off-putting to radical preservationists, who wonder what room is left in the world for their spiritualized ideal of true wilderness. The dreams of Edward Abbey and the Earth First! partisans for restoring the Colorado River to its former raging glory embody a yearning to save nature from human evisceration. Thoreau confronted a similar despair as he observed the wilds of Maine falling under the axe. His solution—that we may perceive the wild wherever nature is—should offer some solace to lovers of the wilderness. Thoreau could find the wild in a seed or a thawing bank of sand. "It is in vain to dream of a wildness distant from ourselves," he declared. In our age of chaos science and stochastic ecology, Thoreau's belief in a "constant *new* creation" happening throughout the physical world is much less of a conceptual leap.[7]

Yet if wild nature signified boundless novelty and personal freedom to Thoreau, it also demanded individual humility, both psychological and intellectual—a quaint notion for us in our postmodern era of pervasive narcissism, self-esteem mongering, and celebrity worship. To understand what he meant, we might want to follow Muir's imperative and "come to the mountains and see." As an example we might consider the philosopher George Santayana, who traveled through Muir's Sierras a number of years ago and came away from them appropriately humbled.

During an address that concludes with one of the great passages in the English language, Santayana told his audience of the fate of all things human within the "wild, indifferent, noncensorious infinity of nature":

> When you transform nature to your uses . . . you cannot feel that nature was made by you or for you. . . . Much less can you feel it when she destroys your labour of years in a momentary spasm. You must feel, rather, that you are an offshoot of her life; one brave little force among her immense forces. When you escape, as you love to do, to your forests and your sierras, I am sure again that you do not feel you made them, or that they were made for you. . . . It is no transcendental logic that they teach. . . . It is rather the vanity and superficiality of all logic, the needlessness of argument, the relativity of morals, the strength of time, the fertility of matter, the variety, the unspeakable variety, of possible life. . . . Everywhere is beauty and nowhere permanence. . . . You are admonished that what you can do avails little materially, and in the end nothing.

But the "society of nature" did offer some compensation to individual human beings, Santayana emphasized, unwilling to finish on such a bleak note. For, ultimately, through the "wonder and pleasure" experienced in the "presence of a virgin and prodigious world," he proclaimed, "you are taught speculation."[8]

Notes

PREFACE

1. For discussion of the terminology and chronology of environmental history, see Bryan Norton, *Toward Unity*, especially pp. 3–38, 74–98; Koppes, "Efficiency/Equity/Aesthetics"; Meine, "Utility of Preservation," pp. 131–72; Nash, ed., *American Environmentalism*, pp. 6–7; Callicott, "Whither Conservation Ethics?," pp. 15–17; and Hays, *Beauty, Health, and Permanence*, pp. 13–39.

CHAPTER ONE

1. Lowenthal, *Vermonter*, p. xi. Much of the biographical information for this chapter is taken from this indispensable book.

2. Ibid., p. ix.

3. Strong, *Dreamers*, p. 27; Lowenthal, *Vermonter*, p. 327.

4. On Marsh in this period, see Lowenthal, *Vermonter*, pp. 21–48. Regarding New England distinctiveness, see Nissenbaum in Ayers et al., *All Over the Map*, pp. 39–40, 51–52. For the larger post-Revolutionary context, see Wood, *Radicalism of the American Revolution*; Shalhope, *Roots of Democracy*; Wiebe, *Opening of American Society*; and Sellers, *Market Revolution*.

5. An excellent study of New England waterways is Steinberg, *Nature Incorporated*, pp. 57–59, 65, 79. For statistics on railroads, see McPherson, *Battle Cry*, p. 12.

6. On antebellum growth and development in general, see McPherson, *Battle Cry*, pp. 6–46.

7. *Man and Nature*, p. 280; Steinberg, *Nature Incorporated*, p. 53.

8. Cooper, *Rural Hours*, pp. 130–32, 95, 160, 152, 290–91; see Taylor, *William Cooper's Town*, for an account of the early years of Cooperstown and the Otsego Lake region.

9. MacCleery, *American Forests*, pp. 19, 11; Michael Williams, *Americans and Their Forests*, p. 118.

10. On early Woodstock development, see Lowenthal, *Vermonter*, pp. 11–15. For a discussion of New England deforestation, see McKibben, "An Explosion of Green," p. 63. On Concord, see Richardson, *Henry Thoreau*, pp. 15–16, and Whitney and Davis, "From Primitive Woods to Cultivated Woodlots."

11. Lowenthal, *Vermonter*, pp. 16, 30, 174, 160–62.

12. Ibid., pp. 8–9. On the Federalists, see Wood, *Radicalism of the American Revolution*, and Banner, *Hartford Convention*.

13. Lowenthal, *Vermonter*, p. 69. The standard work on the Whigs is Howe, *Political Culture of the American Whigs*. See also Wiebe, *Opening of American Society*, pp. 234–52, and Faragher, *Sugar Creek*, pp. 146–50, 190–96.

14. Howe, *Political Culture of the American Whigs*, p. 36; "Rutland County," pp. 3, 24, 20, 5.

15. *Goths*, p. 37; "Rutland County," p. 20; Howe, *Political Culture of the American Whigs*, p. 143; Hollinger and Capper, eds. *American Intellectual Tradition*, 1:269, 266–67.

16. On women and the environment in the era of industrial-capitalist transformation, see Merchant, *Ecological Revolutions* and *Earthcare*. See also Norwood, *Made from This Earth*.

17. Cooper, *Rural Hours*, pp. 104, 107–9, 152–53.

18. Norwood, *Made from This Earth*, pp. 16–17, 20–21.

19. Cooper, *Rural Hours*, pp. 153–54.

20. Lowenthal, *Vermonter*, p. 69.

21. Ibid., pp. 107–8, 75; "Rutland County," p. 23; *Goths*, p. 39.

22. Lowenthal, *Vermonter*, p. 175.

23. *Man and Nature*, p. 280.

24. Ibid., pp. 3, v–vi.

25. Lowenthal, *Vermonter*, p. 58; *Goths*, p. 38.

26. Lowenthal, *Vermonter*, pp. 175, 30; Curtis, Curtis, and Lieberman, *World of George Perkins Marsh*, p. 25. On notions of political pathology, see Howe, *Political Culture of the American Whigs*, pp. 74–75, and Wood, *Creation of the American Republic*, pp. 35–36.

27. "Rutland County," pp. 3, 6.

28. Ibid., pp. 6, 17–18; "Artificial Propagation of Fish," pp. 10–11. On the issue of fisheries depletion and early conservation ideas in New England, see Cumbler, "Fish, Fisheries Commissions and the Connecticut River," pp. 73–91.

29. "Rutland County," p. 6; *Man and Nature*, pp. 281, 158.

30. Lowenthal, *Vermonter*, p. 141; *Man and Nature*, p. 42.

31. *Man and Nature*, p. 53. On the emergence of ecology and the "new geography," see Worster, *Nature's Economy*, pp. 133–37, 194–96, and Bowler, *Environmental Sciences*, pp. 204–8.

32. Lowenthal, *Vermonter*, pp. 270, 248; *Man and Nature*, p. 13.

33. Lowenthal, *Vermonter*, p. 272; *Man and Nature*, p. 29.

34. *Man and Nature*, pp. 32, 36, 42. On conceptions of nature, see Worster, *Nature's Economy*; Bowler, *Environmental Sciences*; and Botkin, *Discordant Harmonies*.

35. *Man and Nature*, pp. 38, 37, 41, 36.

36. Lowenthal, *Vermonter*, p. 326. On Romanticism and nature, see Frye, *English Romanticism*; Nash, *Wilderness*; and Oelschlaeger, *Idea of Wilderness*.

37. *Man and Nature*, pp. 465, 43, 41, 4.

38. Ibid., pp. 28, 273, 35, 19.

39. Lowenthal, *Vermonter*, p. 250; *Man and Nature*, p. 186; Richardson, *Henry Thoreau*, p. 16.

40. *Man and Nature*, pp. 92, 96.

41. Ibid., pp. 34, 42.

42. Ibid., pp. 465, 9, 7.

43. Ibid., pp. 7, 9, 48, 46, 43.

44. Ibid., pp. 43, 46.

45. *Man and Nature*, pp. 233, 257, 279, 280, 44. On Marsh as progenitor of private forestry, see Cox, "Stewardship of Private Forests," pp. 188, 190.

46. *Man and Nature*, pp. 43–44, 112, 250.

47. Ibid., pp. 259, xix; "Oration," p. 75; Zaslowsky, *These American Lands*, p. 68; Lester, ed., *Environmental Politics*, p. 23; Ise, *United States Forest Policy*, p. 24; Clepper, *Professional Forestry*, p. 6. On early European forestry, see Fernow, *Brief History*, pp. 101, 38, 208, 98–100.

48. "Oration," p. 89.

49. *Man and Nature*, pp. 259, 193; R. V. Marsh to GPM, November 27, 1858, Marsh Collection, University of Vermont Archives, Burlington.

50. *Man and Nature*, pp. 52, 51. For evidence of Marsh's leanings toward Radical Republicanism, see his 1865 essay entitled "Were the States Ever Sovereign?."

51. "Rutland County," p. 5; *Man and Nature*, p. 258.

52. "Irrigation," p. 16; *Man and Nature*, pp. 250, 259.

53. Lowenthal, *Vermonter*, p. 268.

54. Michael Williams, *Americans and Their Forests*, pp. 144–45; Nash, *Wilderness*, pp. 96–97; Merchant, *Ecological Revolutions*, pp. 227–28.

55. Lowenthal, *Vermonter*, pp. 268, 246, 274; *Man and Nature*, p. ix; Strong, *Dreamers*, p. 37.

56. *Man and Nature*, p. 249; Lowenthal, *Vermonter*, p. 329.

CHAPTER TWO

1. Richardson, *Henry Thoreau*, p. 389; Harding, ed., *Contemporaries*, p. 25; *Walden*, pp. 135, 397; *A Week . . . Cape Cod*, p. 331; Marsh, *Man and Nature*, p. 249.

2. Harding, ed., *Contemporaries*, pp. 166–67.

3. The biographical material for this chapter is taken from several notable studies, including the excellent Richardson, *Henry Thoreau*; Harding, *Days of Thoreau*; Bridgman, *Dark Thoreau*; and Lebeaux, *Young Man Thoreau*. For a briefer portrait, see Strong, *Dreamers*.

4. Harding, ed., *Contemporaries*, p. 218; Thoreau, *Natural History*, p. 93. On the role of Thoreau's journal in his intellectual life, see Rossi, "The Journal," pp. 137–55.

5. *Natural History*, p. 130.

6. Letter from Thoreau to Daniel Ricketson, February 12, 1859, in Harding and Bode, eds., *Correspondence*, p. 546; Harding, *Days of Thoreau*, p. 9.

7. Harding, *Days of Thoreau*, p. 31; *Walden*, p. 378; Shepard, ed., *Heart of Thoreau's Journals*, p. 48.

8. *Walden*, p. 53. On the Panic of 1837 and Thoreau's crisis of vocation, see Milder, *Reimagining Thoreau*, p. 3.

9. Harding, ed., *Contemporaries*, p. 45. On the disestablishment of the Congregational Church, see Rose, *Transcendentalism*, pp. 7, 10, 15. Rose's work is an excellent study of the origins and social thought of the Transcendentalists.

10. *Journal of Henry D. Thoreau*, 1:282 (hereafter cited as *Journal* with appropriate volume number); Shepard, ed., *Heart of Thoreau's Journals*, p. 209; *Journal*, 10:190–91.

11. Rose, *Transcendentalism*, p. 68. The literature on Romanticism is vast, but some standard works include Frye, *English Romanticism*; Abrams, *Mirror and the Lamp*; Barzun, *Classic, Romantic, and Modern*; Bloom, ed., *Romanticism and Consciousness*; and Raymond Williams, *Culture and Society*. See also Chai, *Romantic Foundations*, and Dahlstrand, "Science, Religion, and the Transcendentalist Response."

12. Hegel quoted in Toews, *Hegelianism*, p. 4.

13. Shepard, ed., *Heart of Thoreau's Journals*, p. 88; *Journal*, 1:133.

14. Richardson, *Henry Thoreau*, p. 73; Rose, *Transcendentalism*, p. 67; Shepard, ed., *Heart of Thoreau's Journals*, p. 40.

15. Richardson, *Henry Thoreau*, p. 73; Rose, *Transcendentalism*, p. 68; Emerson, *Essays and Lectures*, p. 69. On the Scottish Common Sense school in America, see Howe, *Political Culture of the American Whigs*, pp. 27–32.

16. Rose, *Transcendentalism*, p. 69; Richardson, *Henry Thoreau*, p. 204; *Journal*, 4:410, 12:389; *Walden*, p. 379; *Journal*, 6:294. On the Rousseauean origins of the "nature" solution, see LaFreniere, "Rousseau and the European Roots of Environmentalism," pp. 41–72. For Thoreau's list of important works of Eastern philosophy, see letter from Thoreau to B. B. Wiley, December 12, 1856, in Harding and Bode, eds., *Correspondence*, p. 447.

17. Harding, ed., *Contemporaries*, pp. 111, 66; Shepard, ed., *Heart of Thoreau's Journals*, p. 108.

18. *Journal*, 4:163; Shepard, ed., *Heart of Thoreau's Journals*, p. 27; *A Week . . . Cape Cod*, pp. 23, 30; *Maine Woods*, p. 109; Shepard, ed., *Heart of Thoreau's Journals*, pp. 170, 185–86; *Journal*, 9:337.

19. Nash, *Rights of Nature*, p. 37; Shepard, ed., *Heart of Thoreau's Journals*, p. 174.

20. *Journal*, 5:135; *Maine Woods*, pp. 247–48.

21. *Maine Woods*, pp. 161–65, 248.

22. *Journal*, 4:163. On the environmental transformation of New England, see Merchant, *Ecological Revolutions*, and Cronon, *Changes in the Land*.

23. *Journal*, 9:335–36. On Thoreau's sexuality, see Harding, "Thoreau's Sexuality," pp. 23–44. On the pre-industrial cosmos of the Earth (or Corn) Mother, see Merchant, *Earthcare*, pp. 92–108.

24. Shepard, ed., *Heart of Thoreau's Journals*, p. 193; *Journal*, 10:118; *Maine Woods*, pp. 247–48.

25. *The Week . . . Cape Cod*, pp. 9, 194, 197; *Journal*, 9:310; *Walden*, p. 99.

26. *Maine Woods*, pp. 16–17; *Walden*, p. 92.

27. *Maine Woods*, pp. 107, 110–11, 108, 88; *Journal*, 4:445; *Natural History*, p. 116.

28. Adams, *Novels*, p. 982; Harding, ed., *Contemporaries*, pp. 103, 149; Richardson, *Henry Thoreau*, p. 113.

29. *Maine Woods*, pp. 85, 94–95. On the Ktaadn experience, see Garber, *Thoreau's Redemptive Imagination*, especially pp. 98–99.

30. *Maine Woods*, pp. 86, 210; *Walden*, p. 366; Richardson, *Henry Thoreau*, pp. 114–15; *A Week . . . Cape Cod*, pp. 979–80, 935–36. For a discussion of Thoreau's reaction to the ocean, see Paul, "From Walden Out," pp. 74–81.

31. Shepard, ed., *Heart of Thoreau's Journals*, p. 124.

32. *Journal*, 2:406; Shepard, ed., *Heart of Thoreau's Journals*, p. 191; *Journal*, 6:4; *Faith in a Seed*, p. 8; Richardson, *Henry Thoreau*, p. 384.

33. *Walden*, pp. 353–55, 357. On the recurrence of the leaf or foliate form in Thoreau's writings, see Machann, "Foliate Pattern," pp. 37–56.

34. *Walden*, pp. 356–57, 380. See commentary on a circular letter that Thoreau received from the Association for the Advancement of Science in *Correspondence*, edited by Harding and Bode, p. 310.

35. *Faith in a Seed*, pp. 101, 151, 160. On the influence of Humboldt, see Walls, *Seeing New Worlds*. For a discussion of Thoreau as a botanist, see Angelo, "Thoreau as Botanist," pp. 15–29. On Thoreau and the Concord forests, see Whitney and Davis, "From Primitive Woods to Cultivated Woodlots," pp. 70–81. On forest succession in general, see Perry, *Forest Ecosystems*, and Pianka, *Evolutionary Ecology*.

36. Shepard, ed., *Heart of Thoreau's Journals*, p. 191; Richardson, *Henry Thoreau*, pp. 383, 380; *Natural History*, pp. 130, 128.

37. *Journal*, 1:129, 4:445.

38. Ibid., 1:241; *Walden*, pp. 99, 114; Shepard, ed., *Heart of Thoreau's Journals*, pp. 172–73.

39. Shepard, ed., *Heart of Thoreau's Journals*, p. 29.

40. *Walden*, pp. 385, 397, 392 (this volume includes "Civil Disobedience"); Herr, "A More Perfect State," pp. 474–75. In addition to Herr's insightful essay on Thoreau's politics and social thought, see Stoehr, *Nay-Saying in Concord*; Neufeldt, *Economist*; and Simon, "Thoreau and Anarchism."

41. *Walden*, pp. 387, 396; Harding, ed., *Contemporaries*, p. 212.

42. *Walden*, pp. 403–4.

43. *Maine Woods*, p. 210; *Natural History*, pp. 93, 113–14; *Journal*, 4:446.

44. *Maine Woods*, p. 323; *Natural History*, pp. 105–6, 112.

45. *Walden*, p. 366; *Natural History*, p. 112.

46. *Journal*, 9:43; *Natural History*, pp. 100, 114–15; *Walden*, p. 135.

47. *Journal*, 5:135, 8:221–22; *Maine Woods*, p. 208.

48. *Journal*, 3:381–82.

49. Bridgman, *Dark Thoreau*, p. 45; Shepard, ed., *Heart of Thoreau's Journals*, p. 148.

50. *Maine Woods*, p. 163.

51. Ibid., p. 244; *Journal*, 10:51, 14:307.

52. Journal, 14:307, 5:45–46. On the Anglo-American commons tradition, see Thompson, *Whigs and Hunters*, pp. 29–32, 104, 120–22, 134, 240; Faragher, *Sugar Creek*, pp. 132–33; and Hahn, *Roots of Southern Populism*, pp. 59–60, 243, 252–53.

53. *Natural History*, p. 100; *Walden*, p. 386.

54. *Walden*, p. 366; *Journal*, 14:305.

55. Herr, "A More Perfect State," p. 475; *Journal*, 12:387; *Maine Woods*, pp. 212–13. There were some earlier proposals than Thoreau's for nature preserves, such as the "nation's Park" suggested by artist George Catlin for the Great Plains region. See Nash, ed., *American Environmentalism*, pp. 31–35.

56. *Walden*, p. 297; *Maine Woods*, p. 213.

57. Shugart, *Hot Springs of Arkansas*, pp. 3–4, 32; Bedinger, *Valley of the Vapors*, p. 25; Brown, "Henry M. Rector Claim," p. 291; Yard, *National Parks Portfolio*, p. 218; Jansma and Jansma, "Engelmann in Arkansas Territory," p. 236; Van Cleef, *Hot Springs of Arkansas*, pp. 7–8, 19–20; Shofner and Rogers, eds., "Hot Springs in the Seventies," p. 40n; U.S. Congress, Senate Committee Report, *Modifying the Boundary*, p. 4. Interestingly, Hot Springs National Park, so designated in 1921, was for many years the most visited of all the units in the system, despite its overdevelopment and tiny size. See Foresta, *America's National Parks*, pp. 11–12.

58. Richardson, *Henry Thoreau*, p. 106.

59. *Journal*, 12:387; *Faith in a Seed*, pp. 170, 173; *Walden*, p. 386.

60. *Walden*, p. 409.

61. *Reform Papers*, pp. 132, 125, 115, 137, 183.

62. *A Week . . . Cape Cod*, p. 587.

63. *Walden*, p. 407.

64. Richardson, *Henry Thoreau*, pp. 316–17; Flader and Callicott, eds., *River of the Mother of God*, p. xiv.

65. *Natural History*, p. 100; Nash, *Rights of Nature*, pp. 166–67; Manes, *Green Rage*, pp. 165–74.

66. *Maine Woods*, pp. 210–11. For radical commentary on Thoreau, see Abbey, *Best of Edward Abbey*, especially pp. 277, 281, 285.

67. *Maine Woods*, pp. 211–12; Shepard, ed., *Heart of Thoreau's Journals*, p. 31. On MacKaye, see Thomas, "Lewis Mumford, Benton MacKaye, and the Regional Vision."

68. Letter from Thoreau to H. G. O. Blake, May 21, 1856, in *Letters to Various Persons*, p. 138; Richardson, *Henry Thoreau*, pp. 383, 380; *A Week . . . Cape Cod*, p. 249; *Natural History*, p. 105; *Walden*, p. 369.

CHAPTER THREE

1. Badè, *Life and Letters*, 1:158, 152, 155 (hereafter cited as *Life and Letters* with appropriate volume number); *Thousand-Mile Walk*, pp. 1–2; *Story of My Boyhood and Youth*, p. 160.

2. See Darrah, *Powell*, pp. 73–143.

3. For a contextualized discussion of the 1862 land laws, see McPherson, *Battle Cry*, pp. 450–52; see also Zaslowsky, *These American Lands*, pp. 118–19.

4. Turner, *Frontier in American History*, p. 38; Stegner, *Beyond the Hundredth Meridian*, p. 308.

5. Stegner, *Beyond the Hundredth Meridian*, p. 307.

6. The biographical details for this chapter were taken from several very able studies, including Turner, *Rediscovering America*; Fox, *John Muir and His Legacy*; Michael P. Cohen, *Pathless Way*; and Badè, *Life and Letters*.

7. The classic essay indicting Christianity for environmental ills is Lynn White Jr., "Historical Roots of Our Ecologic Crisis." For a recent expression of the same idea in the context of Muir's life, see Bryan Norton, *Toward Unity*, pp. 7, 19–20. Counterarguments in support of a doctrine of Christian stewardship have been offered by figures such as Wendell Berry; see his book, *The Gift of Good Land*, pp. 267–81. For an overview of the debate over religion and attempts in the last twenty years to formulate a "green" Christianity, see Nash, *Rights of Nature*, pp. 87–120, and Christopher Vecsey, "American Indian Religion," pp. 171–76. Regarding Muir's Christian influences, see Turner, *Rediscovering America*, pp. 66–71; Callicott, "Whither Conservation Ethics?," p. 17; Stoll, "God and John Muir," in Sally Miller, ed., *John Muir*, pp. 64–81; and Williams, "John Muir, Christian Mysticism, and the Spiritual Value of Nature," in the same volume, pp. 82–99.

8. *Life and Letters*, 1:23, 91, 95, 141; Burns, *Selected Poems*, p. 12.

9. *Life and Letters*, 1:216, 147; *Thousand-Mile Walk*, p. 172.

10. *Story of My Boyhood and Youth*, pp. 35–36; *Life and Letters*, 1:72–73. On the tradition of natural theology and its widespread influence, see Weiner, *Beak of the Finch*, pp. 49–51; see also the classic text, Paley, *Natural Theology*.

11. *Story of My Boyhood and Youth*, p. 157; *Life and Letters*, 1:376.

12. *Life and Letters*, 1:253, 268, 312; *Thousand-Mile Walk*, p. 212.

13. *Life and Letters*, 1:332–33, 378; Wolfe, ed., *John of the Mountains*, pp. 153–54; *Life and Letters*, 2:355, 216; *Thousand-Mile Walk*, pp. 173, 39.

14. *Life and Letters*, 1:378, 209; Wolfe, ed., *John of the Mountains*, p. 118; *Thousand-Mile Walk*, pp. 210–11.

15. Wolfe, ed., *John of the Mountains*, pp. 435–36; Burns, *Selected Poems*, pp. 123, 67; *Thousand-Mile Walk*, pp. 98–99.

16. *Thousand-Mile Walk*, pp. 141–42, 136, 138, 157. On Muir's departure from Christianity, see Turner, *Rediscovering America*, pp. 144–47.

17. *Thousand-Mile Walk*, pp. 138–39, 157, 173. On biocentric equality, see Devall and Sessions, *Deep Ecology*, pp. 67–69.

18. *Thousand-Mile Walk*, p. 140; Fox, *John Muir and His Legacy*, p. 6.

19. Wolfe, ed., *John of the Mountains*, p. 317.

20. Worster, *Nature's Economy*, p. 180; *Thousand-Mile Walk*, pp. 139, 164; Oelschlaeger, *Idea of Wilderness*, pp. 191, 178.

21. *Thousand-Mile Walk*, p. 195; *Life and Letters*, 1:289, 294, 297; *First Summer*, p. 128. See Dean, "Muir and Geology," in Sally Miller, ed., *John Muir*, pp. 168–93.

22. Appleman, ed., *Darwin*, pp. 83, 85; Weiner, *Beak of the Finch*, p. 58.

23. Michael P. Cohen, *Pathless Way*, p. 53; Wolfe, ed., *John of the Mountains*, p. 118; *Story of My Boyhood and Youth*, p. 1; *Mountains of California*, pp. 174, 176–77, 249; *Our National Parks*, p. 177; *First Summer*, pp. 242–43.

24. Adams, *Novels*, pp. 926, 1132; Fox, *John Muir and His Legacy*, p. 82.

25. Michael P. Cohen, *Pathless Way*, p. 101; *Life and Letters*, 1:328–29; *Steep Trails*, pp. 54, 56–57. For a discussion of Muir and Thoreau on mountaintops, see Castellini, "On the Tops of Mountains," in Sally Miller, ed., *John Muir*, pp. 152–66.

26. Powell, *Exploration*, pp. 28, 32; *Life and Letters*, 2:97, 104–5, 108.

27. *Life and Letters*, 2:211; Thoreau, *Walden*, p. 365. Muir's wife actually encouraged him to return to writing and traveling—see excerpts from letters in Wolfe, ed., *John of the Mountains*, p. 282.

28. On the Gilded Age and early-twentieth-century context, see Cashman, *America in the Gilded Age*; Mary Beth Norton et al., *A People and a Nation*, vol. 2; Jackson, *Crabgrass Frontier*; Kasson, *Amusing the Million*; and Hays, *Response to Industrialism*.

29. On mass production, see Hounshell, *American System*. On consumer values, work, and leisure, see Kasson, *Amusing the Million*, and Rodgers, *Work Ethic*.

30. For analysis of genteel culture and cultural hierarchy, see Shi, *Simple Life*, pp. 154–214; Orvell, *Real Thing*; Schlereth, *Victorian America*; and Levine, *Highbrow/Lowbrow*.

31. On competition and the desire for order, see Chandler, *Visible Hand*, and Wiebe, *Search for Order*.

32. For discussion of the frontier myth, see Slotkin, *Fatal Environment*. On the place of hunting, fishing, and outdoor recreation in early conservation consciousness, see Reiger, *American Sportsmen*; Dunlap, "Sport Hunting"; and Shi, *Simple Life*, pp. 201–12.

33. Burroughs, *Deep Woods*, p. xiii; Norwood, *Made from This Earth*, pp. 19–22, 99–101; Bonta, *American Women Afield*, p. 23.

34. Nash, *Wilderness*, p. 81. On noted landscape painters, see Minks, *Hudson River School*. For a discussion of the nationalist meanings of American scenery, see also Garber, *Thoreau's Redemptive Imagination*, pp. 53–54.

35. On the relation between historical and landscape painting, see Novak, *Nature and Culture*. For a definition of the picturesque, see Heffernan, *Re-creation of Landscape*, especially pp. 4–5.

36. Nash, ed., *American Environmentalism*, pp. 46–50. On vacationing, see Schlereth, *Victorian America*, pp. 213–17, and Huth, *Nature and the American*, pp. 105–28.

37. Kasson, *Amusing the Million*, p. 13. On Olmsted's design philosophy, see William Wilson, *City Beautiful*, pp. 9–34, and Dana White, "Frederick Law Olmsted, the Placemaker," pp. 91–101.

38. Nash, ed., *American Environmentalism*, pp. 50–51, 45.

39. On Olmsted and the Niagara Falls campaign, see Runte, "Beyond the Spectacular," especially pp. 32–33, 42–43, 48–49.

40. Nash, ed., *American Environmentalism*, p. 93.

41. *Mountains of California*, pp. 35, 42. On Muir's voice and persona, see Oravec, "John Muir, Yosemite, and the Sublime Response." For an insightful discussion of the "genteel wilderness," see Michael P. Cohen, *Pathless Way*, pp. 236–73.

42. *Mountains of California*, pp. 34–35.

43. Ibid., pp. 35–36, 40, 86–87, 59.

44. Ibid., pp. 46, 132, 62, 88.

45. *First Summer*, pp. 58–59, 219; *Travels in Alaska*, p. 115.

46. *Mountains of California*, pp. 91, 56, 12, 130, 90.

47. Sally Miller, ed., *John Muir*, p. 91; Shi, *Simple Life*, p. 197.

48. *National Parks*, p. 7; *Mountains of California*, p. 149. For discussion of modernism, see Singal, "Towards a Definition of American Modernism"; Orvell, *Real Thing*; Shi, *Simple Life*; O'Gorman, *Three American Architects*; and Schwartz, *Matrix of Modernism*.

49. *Life and Letters*, 2:356, 384; Runte, *National Parks*, p. 63.

50. *Our National Parks*, p. 3.

51. *Life and Letters*, 2:419; *Our National Parks*, pp. 270–72, 1.

52. Michael P. Cohen, *History of the Sierra Club*, pp. 21, 28; *Our National Parks*, p. 272; *Yosemite*, p. 197.

53. *Our National Parks*, pp. xvii, 271; Wolfe, ed., *John of the Mountains*, p. 431.

54. *Our National Parks*, p. 272; Nash, ed., *American Environmentalism*, p. 89. On Progressive politics and reform, see Wiebe, *Search for Order*; McGraw, *Prophets*; and Link and McCormick, *Progressivism*.

55. Michael Williams, *Americans and Their Forests*, p. 426; *Our National Parks*, p. 270.

56. On the early Sierra Club, see Michael P. Cohen, *History of the Sierra Club*, especially p. 9.

57. Turner, *Rediscovering America*, p. 292.

58. On women and conservation during the Progressive period, see Merchant, *Earthcare*, pp. 109–36; for quote, see p. 119. For the Muir cartoon, see Jones, *Muir and the Sierra Club*, p. 183.

59. Merchant, *Earthcare*, pp. 112–13.

60. On the creation of Adirondack Park, see Terrie, *Forever Wild*, pp. 96–97, 102, 104; Turner, *Rediscovering America*, p. 301; and Michael Williams, *Americans and Their Forests*, p. 414.

61. *Life and Letters*, 2:400. On the concept of the sunshine commission, see McGraw, *Prophets*.

62. *Life and Letters*, 2:401; *Our National Parks*, pp. 25, 257, 266, 260.

63. *Life and Letters*, 2:402.

64. *Our National Parks*, pp. 271, 247; Michael Williams, *Americans and Their Forests*, p. 413.

65. *Our National Parks*, pp. 10, 9, 21, 43, 74.

66. Ibid., p. 43.

67. Ibid., pp. 258–59, 254–56.

68. Ibid., pp. 30, 263.

69. Strong, *Dreamers*, pp. 64, 67. Strong provides a good basic portrait of Pinchot. See also Char Miller, *Gifford Pinchot*.

70. *Life and Letters*, 2:344; Fox, *John Muir and His Legacy*, pp. 113, 130; *Yosemite*, p. 193; Rowley, *U.S. Forest Service Grazing and Rangelands*, pp. 46, 83; Wolfe, ed., *John of the Moun-*

tains, p. 348. For an excellent analysis of Pinchot's policies, see Hays, *Conservation and the Gospel of Efficiency.*

71. *Life and Letters,* 2:412–13; Strong, *Dreamers,* p. 140; Turner, *Rediscovering America,* p. 334n. See Runte, *National Parks,* for his argument regarding the relation of low economic value and the creation of parks. On the Antiquities Act and the early national monuments, see Rothman, "Second-Class Sites," pp. 45–51.

72. *Life and Letters,* 2:412–13.

73. Runte, *National Parks,* p. 48; *Yosemite,* p. 193. For an account of the Hetch Hetchy controversy, see Nash, *Wilderness,* pp. 161–81, and Turner, *Rediscovering America,* pp. 336–43.

74. *Life and Letters,* 2:378, 389; Strong, *Dreamers,* pp. 106–7; Fox, *John Muir and His Legacy,* p. 141; Turner, *Rediscovering America,* pp. 339, 341.

75. Runte, *National Parks,* p. 79; Turner, *Rediscovering America,* p. 339; *Yosemite,* pp. 197, 194, 196.

76. Strong, *Dreamers,* p. 127; Swain, *Federal Conservation,* p. 131.

77. Zaslowsky, *These American Lands,* pp. 24, 34; Nash, *Wilderness,* pp. 316, 231, 215; *Life and Letters,* 2:389; Strong, *Dreamers,* p. 110; Lowitt, *New Deal,* pp. 192–93; Michael Williams, *Americans and Their Forests,* p. 459; Reisner, *Cadillac Desert,* p. 295; Michael P. Cohen, *History of the Sierra Club,* pp. 167, 178.

78. Nash, *Wilderness,* p. 172; *Our National Parks,* p. 2; *Albuquerque Journal,* May 26, 1996. Figures include monuments, recreation areas, and other units of the system.

79. Fox, *John Muir and His Legacy,* p. 145; *Thousand-Mile Walk,* pp. 70–71; *Our National Parks,* p. 47.

CHAPTER FOUR

1. An account of this episode is given in Darrah, *Powell,* p. 14. Other biographies used for this chapter include Stegner's classic *Beyond the Hundredth Meridian;* Terrell, *Man Who Rediscovered America;* and the portait of Powell in Strong, *Dreamers,* pp. 39–59.

2. Marsh, *Man and Nature,* p. 280. On Powell's early life, see Darrah, *Powell,* pp. 3–29; Stegner, *Beyond the Hundredth Meridian,* pp. 8–16; and Terrell, *Man Who Rediscovered America,* pp. 24–55.

3. For discussion of Powell's relationship with Crookham, see Darrah, *Powell,* pp. 3–16, and Stegner, *Beyond the Hundredth Meridian,* pp. 13–15.

4. *Truth and Error,* p. 394. Stegner, in *Beyond the Hundredth Meridian* (p. 15), is suggestive on this theme of frontier science and empiricism for Powell and Muir.

5. On Free-Soil ideology, see Foner, *Free Soil, Free Labor.*

6. On Powell's young adult years, see Darrah, *Powell,* p. 30–46.

7. For an account of Powell's war service, see Darrah, *Powell,* pp. 47–72, and Strong, *Dreamers,* pp. 40–41.

8. For the general history of the West in this period, see Richard White, "It's Your Misfortune," and Limerick, *Legacy of Conquest.* On the issues of land and water, see Pisani, *To Reclaim a Divided West;* Reisner, *Cadillac Desert;* and McMath, *American Populism,* especially pp. 19–49.

9. *Exploration,* p. 247.

10. Darrah, *Powell*, pp. 100–101.

11. *Exploration*, pp. 206, 394, 125; *Truth and Error*, p. 281.

12. *Truth and Error*, p. 8; "Causes of Earthquakes," p. 390; Powell and Porter, *Down the Colorado*, p. 2.

13. Terrell, *Man Who Rediscovered America*, p. 88; *Exploration*, p. 394. For an account of the canyon trip, see Stegner's brilliant rendition in *Beyond the Hundredth Meridian*, pp. 54–111. See also Darrah, *Powell*, pp. 120–43, and Terrell, *Man Who Rediscovered America*, pp. 56–102.

14. Darrah, *Powell*, pp. 153, 162.

15. *Ibid.*, p. 213; Manning, *Government in Science*, pp. 24–26; Dupree, *Science*, p. 201; Terrell, *Man Who Rediscovered America*, p. 162. Manning and Dupree are both indispensable sources on the scientific establishment of this period.

16. "Causes of Earthquakes," p. 385; *Exploration*, pp. 390, 393; Darrah, *Powell*, pp. 147, 149–50; Manning, *Government in Science*, pp. 23–26.

17. Darrah, *Powell*, pp. 216–17; *Exploration*, pp. 393, 390.

18. "Causes of Earthquakes," pp. 370, 381–82; Manning, *Government in Science*, p. 87. On acceptance of uniformitarianism, see Bruce, *Launching*, pp. 30, 127.

19. "Causes of Earthquakes," pp. 372–73, 375, 379–80.

20. Darrah, *Powell*, p. 216; *Exploration*, p. 206; *Report on the Lands of the Arid Region*, p. 13.

21. Manning, *Government in Science*, p. 27; Darrah, *Powell*, p. 202.

22. *Report on the Lands of the Arid Region*, pp. 11–13.

23. Terrell, *Man Who Rediscovered America*, p. 116.

24. Manning, *Government in Science*, p. 137; Darrah, *Powell*, pp. 269, 254–55.

25. Webb, *Great Plains*, p. ii. On the 1930s Indian regionalists, see Robert L. Dorman, *Revolt of the Provinces*, pp. 55–80.

26. Darrah, *Powell*, p. 256. On Morgan's ideas, see Bieder, *Science Encounters the Indian*, especially pp. 234–36.

27. *Exploration*, pp. 111, 113; Darrah, *Powell*, pp. 256, 261; *Truth and Error*, pp. 1–3, 328–30, 341.

28. On positivism and scientific culture in this period, see Dale, *In Pursuit of a Scientific Culture*; Ross, *Origins of American Social Science*; and Bruce, *Launching*.

29. Terrell, *Man Who Rediscovered America*, p. 268; *Truth and Error*, p. 201; R. Jackson Wilson, ed., *Darwinism*, pp. 127, 130, 132.

30. *Truth and Error*, pp. 201–3; Terrell, *Man Who Rediscovered America*, p. 269; "Institutions," pp. 66, 72; Pisani, *To Reclaim a Divided West*, p. 144.

31. Darrah, *Powell*, pp. 80–81.

32. *Ibid.*, pp. 181, 211.

33. Terrell, *Man Who Rediscovered America*, pp. 204–10. On Carl Schurz, see Nash, ed., *American Environmentalism*, pp. 59–62.

34. Terrell, *Man Who Rediscovered America*, pp. 232–34; Manning, *Government in Science*, pp. 122, 204.

35. Dupree, *Science*, pp. 212–13; Manning, *Government in Science*, pp. 74–83; Terrell, *Man Who Rediscovered America*, pp. 226–27; Darrah, *Powell*, p. 267.

36. Manning, *Government in Science*, p. 125.

37. Darrah, *Powell*, pp. 286, 276; Manning, *Government in Science*, pp. 151–67.

38. Manning, *Government in Science*, pp. 68, 66, 119–20, 108, 125. On the political culture of Gilded Age America at the state and federal level, see Keller, *Affairs of State*.

39. Pisani, *To Reclaim a Divided West*, pp. 152–53, 143; Manning, *Government in Science*, pp. 169–70.

40. Manning, *Government in Science*, pp. 174–75; Pisani, *To Reclaim a Divided West*, p. 150.

41. Terrell, *Man Who Rediscovered America*, p. 264; "Institutions," p. 67.

42. Pisani, *To Reclaim a Divided West*, p. 145; *Report on the Lands of the Arid Region*, pp. 34, 41; "Institutions," pp. 67–68.

43. Terrell, *Man Who Rediscovered America*, p. 250; *Report on the Lands of the Arid Region*, pp. 55, 34, 51; "Institutions," p. 68. On riparian doctrine versus prior appropriation, see Pisani, *To Reclaim a Divided West*, pp. 11–12, 31, 34–37, 46; see also Webb, *Great Plains*, pp. 431–37, 450–51.

44. "Institutions," pp. 67–68; *Report on the Lands of the Arid Region*, pp. 34–36, 46. Donald Worster offers a perceptive treatment of Powell's ideas in *Unsettled Country*, pp. 1–30.

45. "Institutions," pp. 71, 68, 70.

46. Manning, *Government in Science*, p. 199.

47. "Institutions," pp. 67–69; *Report on the Lands of the Arid Region*, pp. 35–36; Pisani, *To Reclaim a Divided West*, pp. 46, 144–45; Darrah, *Powell*, p. 249.

48. Manning, *Government in Science*, p. 199; Terrell, *Man Who Rediscovered America*, p. 261; Pisani, *To Reclaim a Divided West*, p. 145.

49. Darrah, *Powell*, p. 132; Terrell, *Man Who Rediscovered America*, pp. 240–41, 229; "Institutions," p. 69.

50. "Institutions," pp. 66, 68–69; Manning, *Government in Science*, p. 182.

51. Manning, *Government in Science*, p. 125; "Institutions," p. 68.

52. On the garden city idea, see Buder, *Visionaries and Planners*. The Populists and the Knights of Labor are examined in Goodwyn, *Democratic Promise*, and in Dubofsky, *Labor Leaders*. On the Single Tax and the adversary tradition as a whole, see Thomas, *Alternative America*. Some of my "hypotheticals" were suggested by Pisani's analysis in *To Reclaim a Divided West*, pp. 143–68.

53. Pisani, *To Reclaim a Divided West*, pp. 153–59. See also Stegner, *Beyond the Hundredth Meridian*, pp. 330–31, 338–42.

54. Pisani, *To Reclaim a Divided West*, pp. 160–63.

55. Ibid., p. 164; Manning, *Government in Science*, pp. 204–11; Terrell, *Man Who Rediscovered America*, pp. 265–66; Darrah, *Powell*, p. 14.

56. Terrell, *Man Who Rediscovered America*, p. 266; *Truth and Error*, p. 8.

57. "Institutions," p. 67; Dupree, *Science*, pp. 242–43.

58. Dupree, *Science*, p. 248. On the Newlands Act, see Pisani, *To Reclaim a Divided West*, especially pp. 322–25; see also Reisner, *Cadillac Desert*, especially pp. 115–24.

59. Dupree, *Science*, pp. 400, 250; McGee, "Water," pp. 37, 39; Nash, ed., *American Environmentalism*, pp. 81–83. On the early Forest Service, see Clary, *Timber and the*

Forest Service, pp. 3–66. On the struggle over control of conservation policy, see the classic account in Hays, *Conservation and the Gospel of Efficiency*, pp. 39–46, 57–58, 66, 122–240.

60. Manning, *Government in Science*, p. 224; Dupree, *Science*, p. 248.

61. Mumford, *Culture of Cities*, p. 302. On MacKaye and Powell, see Thomas, "Lewis Mumford, Benton MacKaye, and the Regional Vision." For an account of the demise of the regionalists, see Robert L. Dorman, *Revolt of the Provinces*, pp. 249–306.

62. See Reisner, *Cadillac Desert*, pp. 151–75.

63. McPhee, *Encounters with the Archdruid*, pp. 165–66, 163, 196.

64. Abbey, *Desert Solitaire*, pp. 173, 191.

65. Manes, *Green Rage*, p. 6; Abbey, *Desert Solitaire*, p. 165; Powell and Porter, *Down the Colorado*, p. 2.

EPILOGUE

1. Cronon, ed., *Uncommon Ground*, pp. 81, 89. See also Richard White, *Organic Machine*, p. xi.

2. *Mountains of California*, p. 42; Cronon, ed., *Uncommon Ground*, p. 80.

3. *Maine Woods*, p. 211; *Journal*, 12:387.

4. *Man and Nature*, pp. 35, 53; Huth, *Nature and the American*, p. 169; Lowenthal, *Vermonter*, pp. 248, 141. For a discussion of the preservationist reaction to historically humanized nature, see Pollan, *Second Nature*. The theme of the human and natural intertwined in human creations recurs throughout Richard White's *Organic Machine*, as the title implies.

5. "Institutions," pp. 67–68; *Report on the Lands of the Arid Region*, p. 33. For an excellent discussion of "place" and contemporary regional landscape planning, see Hiss, *Experience of Place*.

6. On conceptions of landscape planning becoming prevalent among ecologists and conservation biologists, see Callicott, "Whither Conservation Ethics?," especially pp. 18–20; Perry, *Forest Ecosystems*, pp. 536–41, 557–71; and Agee and Johnson, eds., *Ecosystem Management*, pp. 7–13, 78–81, 87–94, 154–55, 175, 186, 194, 218, 226–32. On the Glen Canyon Dam experiment, see *High Country News*, July 22, November 11, and December 23, 1996.

7. Richardson, *Henry Thoreau*, p. 383; *Journal*, 9:43.

8. *Mountains of California*, p. 149; Santayana, "The Genteel Tradition in American Philosophy," in Hollinger and Capper, eds., *American Intellectual Tradition*, 2:108–9. On Santayana's visit to California, see McCormick, *George Santayana*, pp. 193–211. For an analysis of Santayana's views of nature, see Sarah Ellen Dorman, "Connoisseur of Chaos."

Bibliography

Abbey, Edward. *The Best of Edward Abbey*. San Francisco, 1988.

———. *Desert Solitaire*. New York, 1968.

Abrams, M. H. *The Mirror and the Lamp: Romantic Theory and the Critical Tradition*. New York, 1971.

Adams, Henry. *Novels, Mont St. Michel, The Education*. New York, 1983.

Agee, James K., and Darryll R. Johnson, eds. *Ecosystem Management for Parks and Wilderness*. Seattle, 1988.

Angelo, Ray. "Thoreau as Botanist." *Thoreau Quarterly* 15 (1983): 15–29.

Appleman, Philip, ed. *Darwin*. New York, 1979.

Ayers, Edward L., et al. *All Over the Map: Rethinking American Regions*. Baltimore, 1996.

Badè, William Frederic, ed. *The Life and Letters of John Muir*. 2 vols. Boston, 1924.

Banner, James M., Jr. *To the Hartford Convention*. New York, 1970.

Barzun, Jacques. *Classic, Romantic, and Modern*. Chicago, 1975.

Bedinger, M. S. *Valley of the Vapors: Hot Springs National Park*. Philadelphia, 1991.

Berry, Wendell. *The Gift of Good Land*. San Francisco, 1981.

Bieder, Robert E. *Science Encounters the Indian, 1820–1880*. Norman, Okla., 1989.

Bloom, Harold, ed. *Romanticism and Consciousness*. New York, 1970.

Bonta, Marcia Myers, ed. *American Women Afield: Writings by Pioneering Women Naturalists*. College Station, Tex., 1995.

Botkin, Daniel B. *Discordant Harmonies: A New Ecology for the Twenty-First Century*. New York, 1990.

Bowler, Peter J. *The Environmental Sciences*. New York, 1993.

Bridgman, Richard. *Dark Thoreau*. Lincoln, Nebr., 1982.

Brown, Walter L. "The Henry M. Rector Claim to the Hot Springs of Arkansas." *Arkansas Historical Quarterly* 15, no. 4 (Winter 1956): 281–92.

Bruce, Robert V. *The Launching of Modern American Science*. New York, 1987.

Buder, Stanley. *Visionaries and Planners: The Garden City Movement and the Modern Community*. New York, 1990.

Buenker, John D., John C. Burnham, and Robert M. Crunden. *Progressivism*. Rochester, Vt., 1977.

Burns, Robert. *Selected Poems*. New York, 1993.

Burroughs, John. *Deep Woods*. Salt Lake City, 1990.

Callicott, J. Baird. *Earth's Insights*. Berkeley, 1994.

———. "Whither Conservation Ethics?." *Conservation Biology* 4, no. 1 (March 1990): 15–20.

Cashman, Sean Dennis. *America in the Gilded Age*. New York, 1984.

Chai, Leon. *The Romantic Foundations of the American Renaissance*. Ithaca, N.Y., 1987.

Chandler, Alfred D., Jr. *The Visible Hand: The Managerial Revolution in American Business*. Cambridge, Mass., 1982.

Clary, David A. *Timber and the Forest Service*. Lawrence, Kans., 1986.

Clepper, Henry. *Professional Forestry in the United States*. Baltimore, 1971.

Cohen, I. Bernard. *Revolution in Science*. Cambridge, Mass., 1985.

Cohen, Michael P. *The History of the Sierra Club*. San Francisco, 1988.

———. *The Pathless Way: John Muir and American Wilderness*. Madison, Wisc., 1984.

Cooper, John Milton, Jr. *Pivotal Decades*. New York, 1990.

Cooper, Susan Fenimore. *Rural Hours*. Syracuse, 1995.

Cox, Thomas R. "The Stewardship of Private Forests," *Journal of Forest History* 25, no. 4 (October 1981): 188, 190.

Cronon, William. *Changes in the Land: Indians, Colonists, and the Ecology of New England*. New York, 1983.

———, ed. *Uncommon Ground: Toward Reinventing Nature*. New York, 1995.

Cumbler, John T. "The Early Making of an Environmental Consciousness: Fish, Fisheries Commissions and the Connecticut River." *Environmental History Review* 15, no. 4 (Winter 1991): 73–91.

Curtis, Jane, Will Curtis, and Frank Lieberman. *The World of George Perkins Marsh*. Woodstock, Vt., 1982.

Dahlstrand, Frederick C. "Science, Religion, and the Transcendentalist Response to a Changing America." In *Studies in the American Renaissance: 1988*, edited by Joel Myerson. Charlottesville, Va., 1988.

Dale, Peter Allan. *In Pursuit of a Scientific Culture: Science, Art and Society in the Victorian Age*. Madison, Wisc., 1989.

Darrah, William Culp. *Powell of the Colorado*. Princeton, 1952.

Devall, Bill, and George Sessions. *Deep Ecology*. Salt Lake City, 1985.

Dorman, Robert L. *Revolt of the Provinces: The Regionalist Movement in America, 1920–1945*. Chapel Hill, 1993.

Dorman, Sarah Ellen. "Connoisseur of Chaos: George Santayana's Fluid Conservatism, 1918–1952." Ph.D. dissertation, Brown University, 1995.

Dubofsky, Melvyn, ed. *Labor Leaders in America*. Urbana, Ill., 1986.

Dunlap, Thomas R. *Saving America's Wildlife: Ecology and the American Mind, 1850–1990*. Princeton, 1988.

———. "Sport Hunting and Conservation." *Environmental Review* 12, no. 1 (Spring 1988): 51–60.

Dupree, A. Hunter. *Science in the Federal Government: A History of Policies and Activities to 1940*. Cambridge, Mass., 1957.

Emerson, Ralph Waldo. *Essays and Lectures*. New York, 1983.

Faragher, John Mack. *Sugar Creek: Life on the Illinois Prairie*. New Haven, 1986.

Fernow, Bernhard E. *A Brief History of Forestry*. Toronto, 1911.

Flader, Susan L., and J. Baird Callicott, eds. *The River of the Mother of God and Other Essays*. Madison, Wisc., 1991.

Foner, Eric. *Free Soil, Free Labor, Free Men*. New York, 1970.

Foresta, Ronald A. *America's National Parks and Their Keepers*. Washington, D.C., 1984.

Foulds, H. Eliot, Katherin Lacy, and Lauren G. Meier. *Land Use History for Marsh-Billings National Historical Park*. Boston, 1994.

Fox, Stephen. *John Muir and His Legacy: The American Conservation Movement*. Boston, 1981.

Frye, Northrup. *A Study of English Romanticism*. Chicago, 1968.

Garber, Frederick. *Thoreau's Redemptive Imagination*. New York, 1977.

Glacken, Clarence. *Traces on the Rhodian Shore*. Berkeley, 1967.

Goodwyn, Lawrence. *Democratic Promise: The Populist Moment in America*. New York, 1976.

Hahn, Steven. *The Roots of Southern Populism*. New York, 1983.

Harding, Walter. *The Days of Henry Thoreau*. Princeton, 1982.

———, ed. *Thoreau as Seen by His Contemporaries*. New York, 1989.

———. "Thoreau's Sexuality." *Journal of Homosexuality* 21 (1991): 23–44.

Harding, Walter, and Carl Bode, eds. *The Correspondence of Henry David Thoreau*. New York, 1958.

Hays, Samuel P. *Beauty, Health, and Permanence: Environmental Politics in the United States, 1955–1985*. Cambridge, Mass., 1987.

———. *Conservation and the Gospel of Efficiency: The Progressive Conservation Movement, 1890–1920*. Cambridge, Mass., 1959.

———. *The Response to Industrialism, 1885–1914*. Chicago, 1957.

Heffernan, James A. W. *The Re-Creation of Landscape: A Study of Wordsworth, Coleridge, Constable, and Turner*. Hanover, N.H., 1984.

Herr, William A. "A More Perfect State: Thoreau's Concept of Civil Government." *Massachusetts Review* (Summer 1975): 470–87.

Hiss, Tony. *The Experience of Place*. New York, 1990.

Hollinger, David A., and Charles Capper, eds. *The American Intellectual Tradition*. 2 vols. New York, 1993.

Hounshell, David A. *From the American System to Mass Production, 1800–1932*. Baltimore, 1991.

Howe, Daniel Walker. *The Political Culture of the American Whigs*. Chicago, 1979.

Huth, Hans. *Nature and the American: Three Centuries of Changing Attitudes*. Lincoln, Nebr., 1972.

Ise, John. *The United States Forest Policy*. New Haven, 1920.

Jackson, Kenneth T. *Crabgrass Frontier: The Suburbanization of the United States*. New York, 1985.

Jansma, Jerome, and Harriet H. Jansma. "George Engelmann in Arkansas Territory." *Arkansas Historical Quarterly* 50, no. 3 (Autumn 1991): 225–48.

Jones, Holway R. *Muir and the Sierra Club: The Battle for Yosemite*. San Francisco, 1965.

Kasson, John F. *Amusing the Million*. New York, 1978.

Keller, Morton. *Affairs of State*. New York, 1977.

Koppes, Clayton R. "Efficiency/Equity/Aesthetics: Toward a Reinterpretation of American Conservation." *Environmental Review* 11, no. 2 (Summer 1987): 127–46.

LaFreniere, Gilbert F. "Rousseau and the European Roots of Environmentalism." *Environmental History Review* 14, no. 4 (Winter 1990): 41–72.

Lebeaux, Richard. *Young Man Thoreau*. Amherst, Mass., 1977.

Leopold, Aldo. *A Sand County Almanac*. New York, 1984.

Lester, James P., ed. *Environmental Politics and Policy*. Durham, 1995.

Levine, Lawrence W. *Highbrow/Lowbrow: The Emergence of Cultural Hierarchy in America*. Cambridge, Mass., 1988.

Limerick, Patricia. *The Legacy of Conquest*. New York, 1987.

Link, Arthur S., and Richard McCormick. *Progressivism*. Arlington Heights, Ill., 1983.

Lowenthal, David. *George Perkins Marsh: Versatile Vermonter*. New York, 1958.

Lowitt, Richard. *The New Deal and the West*. Norman, Okla., 1984.

MacCleery, Douglas W. *American Forests: A History of Resiliency and Recovery*. Durham, 1994.

McCormick, John. *George Santayana*. New York, 1987.

McGee, WJ. "Water As a Resource." *Annals of the American Academy of Political and Social Science* (May 1909): 37–50.

McGraw, Thomas K. *Prophets of Regulation*. Cambridge, Mass., 1984.

Machann, Clinton. "The Foliate Pattern: Evidence of Natural Process in Thoreau." *Thoreau Journal Quarterly* 13, nos. 1 and 2 (January and April 1981): 37–56.

McKibben, Bill. "An Explosion of Green." *Atlantic Monthly* (April 1995): 61–83.

McLoughlin, William G. *Revivals, Awakenings, and Reform*. Chicago, 1978.

McMath, Robert C., Jr. *American Populism*. New York, 1993.

McPhee, John. *Encounters with the Archdruid*. New York, 1985.

McPherson, James. *Battle Cry of Freedom: The Civil War Era*. New York, 1988.

Manes, Christopher. *Green Rage: Radical Environmentalism and the Unmaking of Civilization*. New York, 1990.

Manning, Thomas G. *Government in Science; the U.S. Geological Survey, 1864–1894*. Lexington, Ky., 1967.

Marsh, George Perkins. "Address Delivered Before the Agricultural Society of Rutland County." Rutland, Vt., 1848. University of Vermont Archives, Burlington.

———. "Annual Report of the Railroad Commissioner." Burlington, 1858–59. University of Vermont Archives, Burlington.

———. *The Goths in New-England*. Middlebury, Vt., 1843. University of Vermont Archives, Burlington.

———. "Irrigation: Its Evils, the Remedies, and the Compensations." U.S. Senate, 43rd Congress. Washington, D.C., 1874.

———. *Man and Nature*. Cambridge, Mass., 1965.

———. "Oration." New Hampshire State Agricultural Society Transactions, Concord, 1857. University of Vermont Archives, Burlington.

———. "Report . . . on the Artificial Propagation of Fish." Burlington, 1857. University of Vermont Archives, Burlington.

————. "Were the States Ever Sovereign?" *The Nation* (July 6, 1865): 5–8.

Marx, Leo. *The Machine in the Garden: Technology and the Pastoral Ideal in America.* New York, 1967.

Meine, Curt. *Aldo Leopold.* Madison, Wisc., 1988.

————. "The Utility of Preservation and the Preservation of Utility: Leopold's Fine Line." In *The Wilderness Condition,* edited by Max Oelschlaeger. Washington, D.C., 1992.

Merchant, Carolyn. *Earthcare: Women and the Environment.* New York, 1996.

————. *Ecological Revolutions: Nature, Gender, and Science in New England.* Chapel Hill, 1989.

Milder, Robert. *Reimagining Thoreau.* Cambridge, Mass., 1995.

Miller, Char. *Gifford Pinchot.* Milford, Pa., 1992.

Miller, Sally M., ed. *John Muir: Life and Work.* Albuquerque, 1993.

Milton, John. *Paradise Lost.* Edited by Merritt Y. Hughes. Indianapolis, 1962.

Minks, Louise. *The Hudson River School.* New York, 1989.

Muir, John. *The Mountains of California.* New York, 1985.

————. *My First Summer in the Sierra.* New York, 1987.

————. *Our National Parks.* San Francisco, 1991.

————. *Steep Trails.* San Francisco, 1994.

————. *The Story of My Boyhood and Youth.* San Francisco, 1988.

————. *A Thousand-Mile Walk to the Gulf.* Boston, 1981.

————. *Travels in Alaska.* San Francisco, 1988.

————. *The Yosemite.* San Francisco, 1988.

Mumford, Lewis. *The Cultures of Cities.* New York, 1938.

Nash, Roderick. *The Rights of Nature: A History of Environmental Ethics.* Madison, Wisc., 1989.

————. *Wilderness and the American Mind.* New Haven, 1982.

————, ed. *American Environmentalism: Readings in Conservation History.* New York, 1990.

Neufeldt, Leonard N. *The Economist: Henry Thoreau and Enterprise.* New York, 1989.

Norton, Bryan G. *Toward Unity Among Environmentalists.* New York, 1991.

Norton, Mary Beth, et al. *A People and a Nation.* Vols. 1 and 2. Boston, 1995.

Norwood, Vera. *Made from This Earth: American Women and Nature.* Chapel Hill, 1993.

Novak, Barbara. *Nature and Culture.* New York, 1980.

Oelschlaeger, Max. *The Idea of Wilderness.* New Haven, 1991.

O'Gorman, James F. *Three American Architects: Richardson, Sullivan, and Wright, 1865–1915.* Chicago, 1991.

Oravec, Christine. "John Muir, Yosemite, and the Sublime Response: A Study in the Rhetoric of Preservationism." *Quarterly Journal of Speech* 67 (August 1981): 245–58.

Orvell, Miles. *The Real Thing: Imitation and Authenticity in American Culture, 1880–1940.* Chapel Hill, 1989.

Paley, William. *Natural Theology: or, Evidences of the Existence and Attributes of the Deity, Collected from the Appearances of Nature.* Boston, 1836.

Paul, Sherman. "From Walden Out." *Thoreau Quarterly* 16, nos. 1 and 2 (Winter/Spring 1984): 74–81.

Perry, David A. *Forest Ecosystems*. Baltimore, 1994.

Pianka, Eric R. *Evolutionary Ecology*. New York, 1994.

Pisani, Donald J. *To Reclaim a Divided West: Water, Law, and Public Policy, 1848–1902*. Albuquerque, 1992.

Pollan, Michael. *Second Nature: A Gardener's Education*. New York, 1991.

Powell, John Wesley. "The Causes of Earthquakes." *The Forum* 2 (December 1886): 370–91.

————. *The Exploration of the Colorado River and Its Canyons*. New York, 1961.

————. "Institutions for the Arid Lands." In *American Environmentalism*, edited by Donald Worster. New York, 1973.

————. *Report on the Lands of the Arid Region of the United States*. Cambridge, Mass., 1962.

————. *Truth and Error*. Chicago, 1898.

Powell, John Wesley, and Eliot Porter. *Down the Colorado*. New York, 1988.

Reiger, John F. *American Sportsmen and the Origins of Conservation*. Norman, Okla., 1986.

Reisner, Marc. *Cadillac Desert: The American West and Its Disappearing Water*. New York, 1986.

Richardson, Robert D., Jr. *Henry Thoreau: A Life of the Mind*. Berkeley, 1986.

Rodgers, Daniel T. *The Work Ethic in Industrial America, 1850–1920*. Princeton, 1980.

Rose, Anne C. *Transcendentalism as a Social Movement, 1830–1850*. New Haven, 1981.

Ross, Dorothy. *The Origins of American Social Science*. Cambridge, Mass., 1991.

Rossi, William. "The Journal, Self-Culture, and the Genesis of Walking." *Thoreau Quarterly* 16, no. 3 (Summer/Fall 1984): 137–55.

Rothman, Hal. "Second-Class Sites: National Monuments and the Growth of the National Park System." *Environmental Review* 10, no. 1 (Spring 1986): 45–56.

Rowley, William D. *U.S. Forest Service Grazing and Rangelands*. College Station, Tex., 1985.

Runte, Alfred. "Beyond the Spectacular: The Niagara Falls Preservation Campaign." *New York Historical Society Quarterly* 57, no. 1 (January 1973): 30–50.

————. *National Parks: The American Experience*. Lincoln, Nebr., 1987.

Schlereth, Thomas J. *Victorian America: Transformations in Everyday Life, 1876–1915*. New York, 1991.

Schwartz, Sanford. *The Matrix of Modernism: Pound, Eliot, and Early 20th-Century Thought*. Princeton, 1985.

Sellers, Charles. *The Market Revolution: Jacksonian America, 1815–1846*. New York, 1991.

Shalhope, Robert E. *The Roots of Democracy: American Thought and Culture, 1760–1800*. Boston, 1990.

Shepard, Odell, ed. *The Heart of Thoreau's Journals*. New York, 1961.

Shi, David E. *The Simple Life: Plain Living and High Thinking in American Culture*. New York, 1985.

Shofner, Jerrell H., and William Warren Rogers, eds. "Hot Springs in the Seventies." *Arkansas Historical Quarterly* 22 (Spring–Winter 1963): 24–48.

Shugart, Sharon. *The Hot Springs of Arkansas Through the Years 1803–1996*. Hot Springs, Ark., 1996.

Simon, Myron. "Thoreau and Anarchism." *Michigan Quarterly Review* 23, no. 3 (Summer 1984): 360–84.

Singal, Daniel Joseph. "Towards a Definition of American Modernism." *American Quarterly* 39 (1987): 7–26.

Slotkin, Richard. *The Fatal Environment: The Myth of the Frontier in the Age of Industrialization, 1800–1890*. Middletown, Conn., 1986.

Stegner, Wallace. *Beyond the Hundredth Meridian: John Wesley Powell and the Second Opening of the American West*. Lincoln, Nebr., 1982.

Steinberg, Theodore. *Nature Incorporated: Industrialization and the Waters of New England*. Amherst, Mass., 1994.

Stoehr, Taylor. *Nay-Saying in Concord: Emerson, Alcott, and Thoreau*. Hamden, Conn., 1979.

Strong, Douglas H. *Dreamers and Defenders: American Conservationists*. Lincoln, Nebr., 1990.

Sutton, S. B. *Charles Sprague Sargent and the Arnold Arboretum*. Cambridge, Mass., 1970.

Swain, Donald C. *Federal Conservation Policy, 1921–1933*. Berkeley, 1963.

Taylor, Alan. *William Cooper's Town*. New York, 1995.

Terrell, John Upton. *The Man Who Rediscovered America: A Biography of John Wesley Powell*. New York, 1969.

Terrie, Philip G. *Forever Wild*. Philadelphia, 1985.

Thomas, John L. *Alternative America: Henry George, Edward Bellamy, Henry Demarest Lloyd, and the Adversary Tradition*. Cambridge, Mass., 1983.

———. "Lewis Mumford, Benton MacKaye, and the Regional Vision." In *Lewis Mumford: Public Intellectual*, edited by Thomas P. and Agatha C. Hughes. New York, 1990.

Thompson, E. P. *Whigs and Hunters: The Origin of the Black Act*. New York, 1975.

Thoreau, Henry David. *Faith in a Seed*. Washington, D.C., 1993.

———. *The Journal of Henry D. Thoreau*. 14 vols. Edited by Bradford Torrey and Francis H. Allen. Boston, 1949.

———. *Letters to Various Persons*. Edited by Ralph Waldo Emerson. Boston, 1865.

———. *The Maine Woods*. New York, 1987.

———. *Natural History Essays*. Salt Lake City, 1988.

———. *Reform Papers*. Edited by Wendell Glick. Princeton, 1973.

———. *Walden and Civil Disobedience*. New York, 1986.

———. *A Week, Walden, The Maine Woods, Cape Cod*. New York, 1985.

Toews, John Edward. *Hegelianism: The Path Toward Dialectical Humanism, 1805–1841*. Cambridge, Mass., 1985.

Trachtenberg, Alan. *The Incorporation of America*. New York, 1982.

Turner, Frederick. *Rediscovering America: John Muir in His Time and Ours*. New York, 1985.

Turner, Frederick Jackson. *The Frontier in American History*. Tucson, 1986.

U.S. Congress. Senate Committee on Energy and Natural Resources. *Modifying* the Boundary of Hot Springs National Park. 103rd Congress, 1st sess., July 16, 1993. S. Rept. 103-97.

Van Cleef, A. The Hot Springs of Arkansas. Edited by William R. Jones. Silverthorne, Colo., 1995.

Vecsey, Christopher. "American Indian Religion, Christianity, and the Environment." Environmental Review 9, no. 2 (Summer 1985): 171–76.

Walls, Laura Dassow. Seeing New Worlds: Henry David Thoreau and Nineteenth-Century Natural Science. Madison, Wisc., 1995.

Webb, Walter Prescott. The Great Plains. New York, 1931.

Weiner, Jonathan. The Beak of the Finch: A Story of Evolution in Our Time. New York, 1994.

White, Dana F. "Frederick Law Olmsted, the Placemaker." In Two Centuries of American Planning, edited by Daniel Schaffer. Baltimore, 1988.

White, Lynn, Jr. "The Historical Roots of Our Ecologic Crisis." Science 155 (March 10, 1967): 1203–7.

White, Richard. "It's Your Misfortune and None of My Own": A New History of the American West. Norman, Okla., 1991.

———. The Organic Machine: The Remaking of the Columbia River. New York, 1995.

Whitney, Gordon G., and William C. Davis. "From Primitive Woods to Cultivated Woodlots: Thoreau and the Forest History of Concord, Massachusetts." Journal of Forest History 30, no. 2 (April 1986): 70–81.

Wiebe, Robert H. The Opening of American Society: From the Adoption of the Constitution to the Eve of Disunion. New York, 1985.

———. The Search for Order, 1877–1920. New York, 1967.

Williams, Michael. Americans and Their Forests: A Historical Geography. Cambridge, Mass., 1992.

Williams, Raymond. Culture and Society, 1780–1950. New York, 1983.

Wilson, R. Jackson, ed. Darwinism and the American Intellectual. Chicago, 1989.

Wilson, William H. The City Beautiful Movement. Baltimore, 1989.

Wolfe, Linnie Marsh, ed. John of the Mountains. Madison, Wisc., 1966.

Wood, Gordon S. The Creation of the American Republic, 1776–1787. New York, 1970.

———. The Radicalism of the American Revolution. New York, 1992.

Worster, Donald. Nature's Economy: A History of Ecological Ideas. Cambridge, Mass., 1977.

———. An Unsettled Country: Changing Landscapes of the American West. Albuquerque, 1994.

Yard, Robert Sterling. The National Parks Portfolio. Washington, D.C., 1931.

Zaslowsky, Dyan. These American Lands: Parks, Wilderness, and the Public Lands. New York, 1986.

Index

34–35; influence on Thoreau, 52, 67–68, 72, 83; as popular architectural style, 133

Clavé, Jules, 38

Cleveland, Grover, 158, 159, 201

Colby, William, 168, 169, 171

Cole, Thomas: and Hudson River school, 136; and cultural nationalism through scenery, 137

Collier, John, 192, 216

Comte, August, 194

Conservation, xiv, 37, 219; defined, xiii; policy dilemmas of, 39, 165–67; and new liberalism, 109–10, 153–55; public interest arguments for, 110, 150–51, 160–61; and land-law scandals, 150; as feminine cause, 156; forest fires and timber famine set stage for, 164

Consumerism: and need for resource conservation, 131, 165–66, 219; and wilderness preservation, 131, 165–66, 168, 219; advent of, 131–32

Cooper, Susan Fenimore, xii, 21, 43, 66, 67; *Rural Hours*, 10–11, 17, 18, 67; on deforestation, 17, 18

Cope, E. D., 211

Cronon, William, 220

Crookham, George, 175–76, 187, 194, 209, 210, 212

Dana, James D., 201

Darwin, Charles, 43, 74, 122–23, 125

Darwinism, 28, 120; in popular mind, 127, 133–34

Desert Land Act (1877), 108

Dick, Thomas, 115

Dickinson, Emily, 55

Dinosaur National Monument, 170, 217

Dutton, Clarence E., 185, 199

Earth First!, 218, 224

Eaton, W. W., 201

Ecology: Marsh's geographical method of, 27, 32–34, 76; Thoreau's study of Concord area, 74–77, 100; stochastic, 224

Emerson, Ralph Waldo, 18, 121, 212, 221; as Thoreau's mentor, 50, 54, 55, 61–62, 72; spiritual crisis of, 54, 59, 60; on epistemology, 58–59; *The American Scholar*, 60; *Nature*, 60; and Romantic integration, 61; wants Muir as disciple, 116; and cultural nationalism, 137

Enlightenment: concepts of natural order, 28, 56, 58–59, 116, 122

Environmentalism, 181, 192, 216; defined, xiv, 227 (n. 1); as major force in post–World War II politics, 44, 97–98; tensions and dilemmas of, 168–71, 218, 219–20, 222–24; emergence of modern movement, 169–70, 217

Exceptionalism: Marsh links to conservation, 21–22, 34–35; and Thoreau's wilderness ethic, 82–83; Muir plays to fears over, 130, 150; Powell's plans embody, 196

Forest reserves: and origins of the National Forest System, 158–65. *See also* General Revision Act; U.S. Forest Service

Forestry: early history in Europe and America, 38. *See also* Marsh, George Perkins; Pinchot, Gifford

Free-Soil Party: views of, 178, 205

Frontier: in antebellum period, 6–7, 19, 34–35, 69, 131; in Gilded Age period, 42, 180–81, 183. *See also* Turner, Frederick Jackson

Fuller, Margaret, 55, 221

Gandhi, Mohandas, 97

Gender: women and environment, xii, 16–18, 65–67; antebellum strictures on, 16; masculine dominion over nature, 16, 66–67, 135, 196; feminine nature appreciation, 18, 136; paternal responsibility for nature, 19, 36–37, 135; feminized representations of nature, 30, 67, 126, 156–57, 225; masculine and feminine recreation in nature, 135–36; Gilded Age strictures on, 136; genteel women as environmental constituency, 136, 156–57

141, 149, 153, 155, 158–59, 168; taps
into genteel sensibility, 141–48; views
on Native Americans, 144–45; transcends genteel, 146–49; favors modern tourism, 148, 167, 168, 170; and
modernist culture, 148–49; Christian
naturalism and wilderness advocacy
of, 150–53; *Our National Parks*, 152,
160–61; "The American Forests,"
153, 160, 162; on National Forest
Commission, 158–63; as muckraker,
159–60; supports multiple-use doctrine, 160, 167; praises foreign models of forest management, 162;
breaks with Pinchot, 163–65; criti-
cizes utilitarian conservation, 164;
Travels in Alaska, 171; *The Yosemite*, 171.
See also Biocentrism; Preservationism; Progressivism; Transcendentalism; Victorianism
Muir Woods National Monument,
170
Mumford, Lewis, 44, 216

National Academy of Sciences: funds
National Forest Commission, 158;
aids in creation of U.S. Geological
Survey, 198
National Conservation Commission,
215
National Federation of Women's Clubs,
157
National Forest Commission, 158–63,
211, 213
National Forest System. *See* Forest
reserves
National Park Service, 169, 170, 216
National Park System: early years,
160–61; and principle of inviolability,
168–69; number of visits to, 169–71
National Wilderness Preservation Sys-
tem, 170
Native Americans: relationship to
nature, 65–67. *See also* Powell, John

Wesley; Regionalism; Thoreau,
Henry David
Newell, Frederick G., 214
Newlands Act (1902): passage and con-
sequences of, 214
Niagara Falls Reservation, 140
Norton, Charles Eliot, 140

Olmsted, Frederick Law, 91; social psychology of park design, 138–39; and
genteel nature appreciation, 138–41;
park design philosophy, 139–40;
helps to protect Niagara Falls, 140;
proposals for Yosemite Valley, 140; as
designer of Biltmore estate grounds,
158
Outdoor recreation: role in fostering
conservation, 135

Pacific Railroad Act (1862), 108
Paley, William, 115, 122
Petrified Forest National Monument,
165
Pfeil, Friedrich, 38
Phelan, James D., 152
Phelps, Almira: and women's scientific
nature appreciation, 18
Pinchot, Gifford, xii, 44; as leader of
utilitarian conservationists, 37, 157,
215–16; experience as forester, 158;
as secretary of National Forest Commission, 158, 163, 213; defines uses
of forests, 163; as head of U.S. Forest
Service, 163, 164, 215; ascendancy of,
163–65, 213–14
Populists, 206, 210
Powderly, Terrence, 210
Powell, John Wesley, xii, xiii, xv, xvi,
128, 158; first expeditions to Rockies,
105, 106, 181–82; shaped by frontier,
105, 175–79; as promoter, 106, 184–
85, 196–99; as institution builder,
106–7, 175, 185, 191, 197–200; at
Grand Canyon, 106–7, 182–85; politi-

Stewart, William M., 202, 203
Stowe, Harriet Beecher, 55, 136
Sullivan, Louis, 148

Teller, Henry M., 202, 203
Thoreau, Henry David, xii, xiii, xv, xvi,
5, 18, 45, 106, 111, 121, 123, 125, 127,
129, 130, 176, 177, 181, 218; at Walden
Pond, xi, 6, 50, 51, 53, 66, 69, 78, 81,
85; "Walking, or The Wild," 1, 47,
51–52, 70, 77, 82–83, 84–85, 117;
boyhood influences on, 7, 11, 52–53;
A Week on the Concord and Merrimack
Rivers, 8, 50, 68, 100; witnesses environmental destruction, 32, 64,
85–89; estrangement from bourgeois
values, 49, 53–54, 66–67, 78, 82;
interest in Native Americans, 49, 55,
65, 67, 100; asceticism of, 49, 78;
concept of nature, 49–50, 62–63,
70–73, 75–77; obsession with
nature, 49–50, 100–101; Walden, 50,
51, 53, 61, 68, 72, 75, 80–81, 96, 98,
100; interest in natural history, 50,
62, 73–77, 99–100; The Maine Woods,
50, 69, 87–88, 99; wilderness ethic
of, 50, 69–70, 81–87, 98–99; career
of, 50, 74, 100; protest of Mexican
War, 50, 79; antislavery views of, 50,
79, 80–81, 82, 95–96; "Resistance to
Civil Government," 50, 80–81, 82,
89–90, 95, 97; confused sexuality of,
51, 66; personality of, 51–54; crisis of
vocation and identity, 53, 59, 100–
101; religious sensibility of, 54, 74;
and Eastern religions, 60–61; idea of
the "Wild," 62, 69–70, 73, 77–78,
81–82, 84–85, 86, 95–96, 98, 100–
101; on organicism, 63–64, 75, 78,
100; ambivalence toward science,
64–65, 73–77, 100; "highest use"
concept, 64–65, 84, 87–88, 92; agrarian-republicanism of, 65, 67–69, 73;
fascination with indigenous folk cultures, 65–69, 94; use of frontier values and mythology, 69, 82–84, 85;
impact of brother's death, 70–72; Mt.
Ktaadn (Katahdin) and biocentrism,
71–72, 74, 98, 121, 127, 128; enthusiasm for Darwinism, 72, 75–77, 81;
Cape Cod, 72–73; "The Succession of
Forest Trees," 76; "The Dispersion of
Seeds," 76, 94–95, 100; ideal of freedom, 77–79, 81–82, 90, 95–96, 101,
153; apolitical tendencies, 79, 92, 93,
95; political philosophy of, 79–81,
88–90, 95–96; on commoner's
rights, 88–89, 91–92; on nature's
rights, 90–91; failures as an activist,
92, 93, 95–96; late thoughts on
forestry, 94–95; legacies of, 96–99,
219–20, 221, 224; utopian vision of,
99, 221. See also Biocentrism; Preservationism; Romanticism; Transcendentalism
Timber and Stone Act (1878), 154, 162
Timber Culture Act (1873), 108, 154
Transcendentalism, 50, 54, 62, 65,
73, 86, 111, 114, 119, 137; and self-
creation, 53, 58, 84; as offshoot of
Romanticism, 55–61; and notions
of divinity, 60–61, 65; doctrine of
higher law, 65, 76, 79, 80, 87, 93;
Muir's partial acceptance of, 116–17,
121, 146
Treat, Mary, xii; and nature essay genre,
136
Turner, Frederick Jackson, 108–9, 110,
130, 150. See also Frontier
Turner, Jonathan B., 179

Udall, Stewart, 44
U.S. Forest Service, 43, 216; creation
of, 163, 165, 214. See also Pinchot,
Gifford
U.S. Geological Survey, 175, 190, 193,
194, 197, 201, 212, 213–14, 216; and
national topographical map, 188,

199, 200; creation of, 197–98, 200;
  Powell as director of, 198, 199,
  200–201, 211; scientific research of,
  199–200, 223

Victorianism: and genteel culture,
  defined, 112, 132–34; and nature
  appreciation, 135–41
Virgil, 67–68

Walcott, C. D., 213
Wallace, Alfred Russel, 127
Ward, Lester, 194, 208
Warner, Anna, 136
Webster, Daniel, 15
Wheeler, George M., 197

Whig Party: political culture of, 12–16,
  19–20, 21, 25, 28, 30, 31, 40–41,
  108
White, Mrs. Lovell: and Calaveras Grove
  campaign, 157
Wilderness: traditional notions of, 29,
  69–70, 83; producerist views of,
  131–32; falsely pristine view of, 220;
  and stochastic ecology, 224
Wilderness Society, 97
Wright, Frank Lloyd, 148

Yellowstone National Park, 160, 161,
  200–201, 216
Yosemite National Park, xi, 170; creation of, 149, 156, 157, 167